WOMEN IN DRAMATIC PLACE AND TIME

Contemporary female characters on stage

Geraldine Cousin

ROUTLEDGE

London and New York

First published 1996
by Routledge
11 New Fetter Lane, London EC4P 4EE
29 West 35th Street, New York, NY 10001

Routledge is an International Thomson Publishing company

© 1996 Geraldine Cousin

Typeset in Garamond by
Poole Typesetting (Wessex) Ltd, Bournemouth

Printed and bound in Great Britain by
TJ Press (Padstow) Ltd, Padstow, Cornwall

British Library Cataloguing in Publication Data
A catalogue record for this book is available from the British
Library

Library of Congress Cataloging in Publication Data
A catalog record for this book has been requested

ISBN 0–415–06733–2 (hbk)
0–415–06734–0 (pbk)

CONTENTS

ACKNOWLEDGEMENTS

I owe a huge debt of gratitude to all the dramatists whose work is discussed in this book for the excellence of their plays. I am additionally grateful to Caryl Churchill and Timberlake Wertenbaker for answering my queries about, respectively, *The Skriker* and *The Grace of Mary Traverse*. Anna Furse kindly helped me to obtain a copy of *Augustine (Big Hysteria)* while this was still unpublished. Members of Scarlet Theatre and Foursight Theatre likewise provided me with a copy of, in the first instance, *Vows*, and, in the second, *Frankenstein's Mothers*. Gráinne Byrne of Scarlet Theatre, and Jill Dowse, Kate Hale and Sue Pendlebury of Foursight Theatre also gave generously of their time and energy. My thanks to Suzanne Lynch for finding and sending me a copy of *Bondagers*, and to Richard Dyer for his constant encouragement. Kate Brennan was endlessly patient in her preparation of the manuscript. As a small expression of my gratitude, the book is dedicated to her along with my two sisters. Last, but emphatically not least, I would like to express my thanks to all the students on my *Women and Theatre* course whose comments over the years have enriched my understanding of the plays I discuss.

Ley Lines

Whose is the voice
that cries upon the endless wastes,
diminishes,
then lifts again?
Who calls through time?
Tell me your name.

Whose steps are these
imprinted in the sand –
erased,
remade,
lost,
yet found again?

Whose are the tracks
in which my feet now fit?
Whose breath breaks through my mouth
to claim,
'They are mine, my sister'?

PROLOGUE

My prologue begins with a room – the four walls and a door within which so many women have been confined. To be more exact, my starting point is the leaving of that room, and the slamming of a door. Furthermore, the four walls are really only three (and these not substantial), for they construct a play, not a real world, and the departing woman – Ibsen's Nora – has only a fictive existence. Even her exit through the outer door that leads to the street has to be taken on trust. As readers and audiences, we hear but do not see it. Nora goes into the outside world but what remains on view is the interior of the doll's house.

But, though it occurs only in offstage space, Nora's departure from the doll's house has acted as an inspirational model, both for actual women and for the fictional characters who create my subject matter. With Nora, at the commencement of her journey, are, potentially, many other women, and, though the terrain of Nora's future remains unknown, she is the prototype of later travellers. Their search for strategies of survival, for maps with which to orientate themselves in previously unexplored land-scapes, is predicated upon Nora's self-chosen exit from the physical and ideological spaces to which she had been as-signed.

The world beyond the doll's house has proved a bewildering as well as an exhilarating place to those travellers, for the old signposts that signified 'woman' no longer act as reliable guides. Maps clarify the form and destination of journeys, however, and, in Charlotte Keatley's words, 'the text of a play' is 'a map. I see a territory', she continues, 'and spend years trying to explore it. The play I finally write is the map I produce in order to enable

1

the audience to explore that territory as well' (Keatley 1990a: 139). Theatre is ideally suited to the mapping of potential worlds, for, within the defined parameters of performance time and place – its focus on now and here – a multiplicity of timescales and places mesh together. Theatre gives form to, and foregrounds, Otherness. It is a place of transformation, a *tabula rasa* that returns always to a state of blankness, yet is forever haunted by possibility.

Through its highlighting of transformability, and of the making anew that follows each act of erasure, theatre is also an apposite medium within which women can give free expression to tongues that have repeatedly been silenced, and explore their current and future possibilities. The main body of this book focuses on selected late-twentieth-century plays by women dramatists. It is concerned with female characters' quests for clear and distinctive voices with which to tell their stories to date, and determine their future narratives, and with their attempts to leave, or alternatively to refashion, the environments in which they find themselves. The room from which Nora exits is my first and also my paradigmatic setting, just as the story of her departure is retold with many variations.

In her role as prologue, Nora is assisted by three characters, whose stories are discussed next, and who are taken from two early-twentieth-century plays by women. Mary and Janet are from Githa Sowerby's 1912 play, *Rutherford and Son*, which Sheila Stowell has valuably analysed in *A Stage of Their Own* as in part a retelling of *A Doll's House*. Though they eventually make opposite decisions in relation to the domestic room that, as in *A Doll's House*, forms the play's setting, one decision echoes and the other reworks Nora's own. Judith in Clemence Dane's *Granite* (1926) I see also as Nora-linked, but, in her case, this is because she is a kind of shadow self of Nora, in that she is forcibly prevented from escaping from a room, and from the power of a man. These four women, the rooms that seek to contain and diminish them, and their plays' imagined offstage worlds together create brief introductory scenes to the main action of the book. Though only occasionally referred to directly in that action, the women's stories inform the choices available to, and the decisions reached by their later dramatic counterparts.

2

THE ROOM AND THE WILDERNESS:
RUTHERFORD AND SON AND *GRANITE*

The setting for *Rutherford and Son* is the living room of John Rutherford's house on the edge of a stretch of moorland close to the River Tyne. It is 'a big square room furnished in solid mahogany and papered in red, as if to mitigate the bleakness of a climate that includes five months of winter in every year' (Sowerby 1991: 141). Though far enough from the village to establish its superior status, the house is still close enough to allow Rutherford to reach the glass manufacturing Works he owns in only a few minutes. In Rutherford's house – for it is unquestionably his – live his sister, Ann; his children: Janet, Richard (a clergyman) and John; plus John's wife, Mary. There are also the unseen characters of the servant, Susan, and John's and Mary's baby son. Rutherford lives entirely for the Works, which, at the time of the play's action, are in poor straits financially. He has brought up his children without affection, setting them rigid codes of behaviour to which they had to adhere. The plot revolves around John's and Janet's attempts to free themselves from their father's control. John, who three months prior to the start of the play has returned home because he was unable, or unwilling, to support his wife and son, has discovered a cheap means of producing a vital element in the Rutherford manufacturing process. When John insists on selling, rather than giving, the formula to his father, Rutherford persuades his foreman, Martin, who has helped John with his experiments, to divulge the formula's contents. John responds by first stealing money for his journey from his father's desk, and then leaving the house for good. It is therefore the husband in *Rutherford and Son* who, as Sheila Stowell writes in *A Stage of Their Own*, 'In a reversal of the sexes . . . like Ibsen's Nora, walks out of the family home to the sound of a closing door' (Stowell 1992: 147). Mary and the baby remain behind, and, though John talks of sending for them when he is settled, it is clear that this will not happen.

While John's final exit from the room contains echoes of Nora's, Mary's actions at the end of the play radically rewrite the final moments of *A Doll's House*. *Rutherford and Son* concludes with a round-the-table confrontation that, in Stowell's words, 'has its roots in Ibsen's play' (ibid.: 149). In *Rutherford and Son* the man and woman who face each other across a table are not husband and wife, however, as in *A Doll's House*, but father-in-law and daughter-in-law, and, whereas Nora anatomised the failure of a marriage and announced her decision to leave in order to find a sense of self in the outside world, Mary employs skills she has acquired outside the home in order to define the terms on which she will remain there. She has earned her own living, and, though it was a poor one – insufficient, if she returns to the workplace, to support her child along with herself – it has taught her how to strike a bargain. After John's departure, Rutherford has no son who can inherit the Works when he dies, and Mary therefore offers him a deal. She and her son will remain in his house, materially cared for by Rutherford. For ten years the child will be entirely hers. Rutherford must never interfere in his upbringing. After ten years it will be Rutherford's turn, and he will then be free to train the boy up for the Works. When Rutherford expresses surprise that Mary is willing to trust the child to him, after the, in her view, disastrous way he has brought up his own children, she replies that in ten years' time he will be an old man, no longer able to make people afraid of him. The play ends with the sound of the child waking up. Mary goes to him, while 'Rutherford sits sunk in his chair, thinking' (Sowerby 1991: 189). As in *A Doll's House* therefore, the final moments focus on a man alone within the domestic setting he has controlled throughout the play's action. Whereas Torvald, however, finds Nora's actions difficult to comprehend, Rutherford ponders Mary's words, and there is at least the possibility that they will beneficially affect his future course of action.

Prior to their final confrontation, Mary has little contact with Rutherford, who largely ignores her until this point in the play. Janet, by contrast, is in rebellion against her father from the beginning, though initially this rebellion is hidden and furtive. She has been conducting a clandestine affair with Martin, and, when he discovers this, Rutherford sacks Martin and orders Janet to leave his house. Janet's original response to her father's rejection of her is a belief that she and Martin will now be able to build a life together, but it transpires that, though Martin desired her, he never loved her. He offers to marry Janet in order to 'right' her in Rutherford's eyes, but she refuses to go with him on these terms and leaves alone. Though initially enforced by her father's command, the nature of her exit is therefore self-

determined. Its active, self-purposed quality is further strengthened by the fact that Janet succeeds in articulating her anger at
the father, who has previously forbidden her any means of
expression beyond the life he has dictated for her, before she
goes out into the surrounding countryside that she has earlier
referred to as 'the blank o' the moors' (ibid.: 175).

The moorland itself, the offstage world into which Janet exits
and which she makes her own, also contributes towards the
significance of her action because it has other qualities apart
from blankness. For Mary, the landscape always represents either desolation or imprisonment. In the first act, she contrasts its
barren sternness with the gentle lanes of her Devonshire girl-
hood, and, in the final scene, she imagines herself living in
Rutherford's isolated house 'year after year, with the fells closed
round her' (ibid.: 189). An alternative vision Janet describes of
the moor takes the form of a dream which she has after Rutherford orders her to leave his house and while she still believes
that Martin loves her. She was in a place with flowers, she tells
Mary. It was summer time and the flowers were 'white and thick
like they never grow on the moor'. But 'it was the moor', close by
Martin's cottage, and, in her dream, Martin came to her 'with the
look he had when [she] was a little lass' and it was 'as if
sweetness poured into' her (ibid.: 177). When Janet leaves her
father's house, therefore, it is to enter simultaneously a blankness and a dreamed possibility of sweetness and joy. She has no
home to go to, no money, and no obvious means of earning any,
so her future may well be a blank. At the same time, the moor,
the 'wilderness' into which she voluntarily goes alone, has, at
least in a dream state, been infused for her with the fragrance of
not-yet-existing, but imagined, flowers.

There is a further aspect of the moorland which, apart from
Janet's dreamed revisioning of it, queries its blankness, and this
is the fact that it is the location of Martin's cottage and the site
therefore of Janet's transgression of Rutherford's rules. This
transgression is active and deliberate for, by her own admission,
Janet was the chief instigator of her affair with Martin. 'Admitting
to a sexual aggressiveness foreign to the period's ideal of female
passivity but linked to the stage adventuress and the "new
woman" of the 1890s, Janet insists that Martin "didn't come
after me. I went after him"' (Stowell 1992: 143). In her partly
self-chosen exile in the ambiguous offstage terrain that borders

Rutherford's house, Janet is at once a blank (the cypher that women have so often been perceived as), the creator of possible fertility and 'sweetness', and a disorderly, subversive force. Her liaison with Martin reveals the limits of Rutherford's power, and, though he casts her out from the domestic space he believes she has contaminated, the wild, chaotic landscape into which she is banished will press against, and perhaps eventually wear away, the walls of Rutherford's house. The sense of threat to the values Rutherford espouses and exemplifies is strengthened by the fact that Sowerby shows Mary and Janet (the woman who remains in the home, and the woman whose place becomes the wilderness) as united by a bond of sisterhood. Even before Martin rejects Janet, Mary pledges her loving assistance to her sister-in-law: 'if ever the time should be when you want help . . . remember that I'll come when you ask me – always' (Sowerby 1991: 178). The woman who sits in the house 'with the fells closed round her' at the end of the play is kin therefore to the woman who has gone out into the wild moorland. The house and the wilderness are linked, not only as sites of women's imprisonment or exile, but also as potential sources of reappropriation and reclamation.

Even more powerfully than *Rutherford and Son*, the action of *Granite* evokes the wilderness that constitutes its imagined offstage world, in this case the granite island of Lundy in the Bristol Channel. The play is set in the second decade of the nineteenth century in a 'large vaulted room' that was originally the kitchen of a twelfth-century castle and is now the living room of Jordan Morris's farmhouse. The action begins on an autumn night when a storm is brewing. The stage is illuminated only by candle and firelight, and three of the central characters are present: Jordan Morris, his wife, Judith, and his half-brother, Prosper. The curtains have not yet been drawn and, through the windows, 'the deep black of the night' (Dane 1949: 2) can be seen. Violent gusts of wind make the casement rattle noisily. The heavy door upstage centre is closed for the night, but, when it is open later in the play, it reveals a 'glimpse of a sheer cliff with blank grey sea' (ibid.: 1). At times restless and savage like the wind, the sea in its periodic blankness reduplicates this aspect of the moors in *Rutherford and Son*. Whereas Janet, however, at least partially refashions the wilderness into a place of her own desiring, Judith's contradictory interpretations of the wind and the sea as, at one moment, her accomplices and, at another, her gaolers, hint from the beginning at her inability to enact a similar transformation.

Close to the start of the play, Judith allies herself to the wind, dancing in accompaniment to its 'wild tune', and holding out her arms to Prosper to join her, but, when Jordan makes her break off her dance and orders her to go to bed, she defines the 'whistle of the wind', 'the beat of the sea' and Jordan's ever-lasting commands: ' "Come to bed, Judith . . . Up with you, Judith!" and "Do this, you fool!" and "Do that, you vain fool!" ' as the voices of her three hated 'masters' (ibid.: 3–4). Jordan, the grim, unfeeling owner of the granite island of Lundy, is himself a man seemingly hewn out of granite. Like the sea, another of Judith's masters, he is also a wrecker, for he uses false lights to lure ships onto the treacherous rocks, where the sea dashes them to pieces. With the help of labourers from his farm, Jordan salvages the cargo – and pushes the drowning men back into the sea.

In defiance of Jordan's commands, Judith remains downstairs when the men go up to bed. Jordan has refused her the luxury of a candle, so, crying out that she wishes that the walls would catch light and the house burn down, she flings log after log on the fire until the room is lit as though by a furnace. But even the walls are on Jordan's side. They cannot catch fire for they are made of stone. For ten years Judith has sat 'between stone walls, beside a stone man' (ibid.: 7). The storm outside the house gathers momentum, and the wind shrieks deafeningly. To Judith, how-ever, it no longer seems a master but instead a poor helpless creature like herself, the 'fool' Jordan termed her. Be still, she admonishes, still as she herself must be. Fashioned out of the granite island itself, the house is stronger than the wind.

Judith is joined in the downstairs room by a young servant girl, Penny Holt. Penny is perturbed because she has heard noises for which she has been unable to account: voices downstairs after everyone (as she believed) had gone to bed, and the sound of someone laughing outside the house. Judith tries to reassure her, explaining that the laughter was in reality the cry of the wind, whilst the voices Penny has heard were simply Judith talking to herself, but, though Penny does find Judith's words somewhat reassuring, the idea of talking to oneself continues to disturb her. Who answers when one talks to oneself? she wonders. She always becomes frightened when she realises that she is talking to herself because it is as if someone else, a stranger inside her, is struggling for freedom. Flinging her arms out wildly, Judith echoes Penny's words: 'A stranger! A stranger in me! And he wants to get out!' (ibid.: 8). The wind takes up Judith's cry and, again, Penny thinks she hears laughter outside the house. To Judith, what Penny has heard is the storm presaging a wreck that night. Judith glories in the storm, which makes her feel alive. 'Oh, how the sea must ease itself', she exults, as it smashes down cliff, ships and men (ibid.). Like the sea, Judith longs for the ease that destruction must bring. Previously a master, the sea at this point becomes a kind of alter ego. It is significant, however, that Judith links the power of the sea, smashing down ships and men, with the 'stranger' inside herself whom she defines as male. It is the gentle Penny, and not the passionate Judith, who first talks about the stranger within. For both women therefore – and they are the only female characters in the play – the inner desiring self is alienated from the conscious self. But it is Judith who determines the stranger's gender. Like the masters who imprison her, the part of Judith that rages most violently against her confinement assumes for her the form of a man.

Her gendering of her anger as male is followed by the entry into the play's action of its other major character. Before returning to bed, Penny has told an admonitory tale about a girl who conjured up a devil-man, and Judith speculates on her own chances of making a pact with the Devil. What she wants from the Devil is the power to keep Prosper, with whom she is in love, on Lundy. In return, she will make the conventional payment of her soul, but, at this notion, Judith begins to laugh harshly because she doesn't own her soul. Jordan owns it, as he owns everything on Lundy, and he would never allow her to sell it. Her laughter turns into bitter sobbing, and, for the first time clearly, the sound of someone laughing outside the window is heard. Momentarily, what might be the moon, or alternatively a man's face, is glimpsed at the window. The wind gusts so violently that the house shakes, despite its roots in the granite, and, as the door bursts open, the figure of a man falls headlong into the room. He is wet to the skin, weak as a baby, and he begs Judith to shelter him, to give him life. At first she watches him dispassionately, for she sees no reason why she should help him, but, when The Man (as he is always called in the play) offers her a bargain, she accepts it. In return for food and shelter, he will be her servant. If she has a wish, she has only to turn to him. If she has a desire, he will fulfil it. What he also adds is that, if a woman angers Judith, that is her own quarrel, but, if a man 'lays a finger' on her, he will kill him (ibid.: 13).

The question of who The Man is and where he has come from is fully resolved only at the end of the play. Entering as he does out of the wind and darkness, his clothes sodden as though he has risen from the sea, like the demonic figure in Penny's story, he seems to be the answer to Judith's desire to make a contract with the Devil. Certainly, the contract appears devilish for its outcome is the death first of Jordan and then of Prosper. Both deaths are occasioned by Judith's jealousy of Penny, whom she fears that Prosper may be beginning to be attracted to. When she first gives vent to her anger over Penny, Jordan seizes, and bruises, her wrist, and The Man follows him offstage and kills him. A few months later, Judith marries Prosper, believing that in so doing she is gaining both the man she loves and her escape from the island. Prosper, however, has come to understand that Lundy is a source of wealth – not because of the opportunities it offers for plundering wrecked ships, but because its granite can be quarried and sold – and, whereas he once thought that Jordan was mad to remain on the island, he has now come to understand the challenge it represents: man's will against the granite. His adoption of Jordan's attitude to the island is followed by a fate identical to his half-brother's, despite Judith's desperate struggle to suppress her jealousy of Penny. Prosper has ordered The Man to leave the island, and, when he changes his mind and allows him to remain at Penny's request, having rejected her own identical plea, Judith once again gives way to anger. Prosper grabs hold of her to calm her down, and, as Jordan did earlier, bruises her wrist. The Man prepares once more to follow his victim offstage, and when Judith implores him to desist, he locks her in the house. From the window Judith screams out a warning to Prosper, but the wind carries her voice away. Sobbing, she collapses onto a chair, and The Man re-enters. 'For food, warmth, shelter – quits!' he says (ibid.: 56).

In her terror at the end of the play Judith is certain that she has interpreted correctly the riddle of who The Man is and where he comes from. He is, she believes, the stranger within her who clamoured for freedom, the anger she nurtured until it was strong enough to kill. She had wanted to conjure up the Devil, and she succeeded. She prayed to the Evil One, and, out of her own heart, he came. This analysis is mistaken, however, for The Man is really a convict who escaped from a wrecked ship in the storm at the beginning of the play. He listened outside the house that night, and, when he heard Judith expressing her desire to make a deal with the Devil, he realised how he could use this to his own advantage. In words more chilling than any hellish imprecations could be, he reveals to Judith finally his true motivation: 'Devil? Devil a bit! I wanted what I wanted, like you. And you gave me my chance to get 'em – a farm and a woman, Come here!' He puts his hand on the terrified Judith's shoulder. 'It's no use your fighting me', he tells her, 'I'm stronger than you' (ibid.: 56).

Judith's weakness, identified by The Man in the final moments of the play, has been implicit from the beginning through her mutually exclusive responses to the sea and the wind. The fact that she characterises these elements as *both* desiring aspects of self and her masters, reveals the depths of her powerlessness, for she can conceive of escape only through harnessing the identical energies that she has identified as binding her in servitude. Later, she imagines the 'stranger' within her, her stormy angry self, as male because power (the chief attribute of storm) is exclusively in the hands of men in the play. Wind and sea express only their own restless rages, however, and The Man merely utilises the role of the devilish stranger that Judith unwittingly offers him. Throughout the play she misreads his words and actions, imagining devilry where there is, in reality, only brutal cunning. By contrast, The Man understands Judith without difficulty. When she claims at one point to feel no fear of him, or of any man, and to be driven only by anger, he tells her to look at her thumbs tucked in with her fingers clenched over them. This is a sign not of anger but of fear. Inspiring fear is the stuff of life to The Man. 'To have someone afraid of you', he says, 'that's to rule a kingdom' (ibid.: 45).

The play's action has the terrifying, inexorable quality of a nightmare. Judith is imprisoned by one man of granite. He dies and she turns to a second man, who proves to be fashioned from the self-same rock as the first. He too dies and in his place rises a third, the essential granite man of whom the first two were merely prototypes – the being without redeeming features of any kind, simply The Man. Even Judith's belief in the power of her own anger proves illusory. Not only has it been merely the excuse for, not the cause of, The Man's actions, it has throughout been controlled, and ultimately possessed by him. Never the male counterpart of herself, the inner stranger that Judith imagined him to be, The Man has instead always been, as he claims, horrifyingly the stronger.

Isolated, utterly negated, denied even the ownership of her own anger, Judith serves as a bleak reminder of entrapment in future pages. Jeanne in Cheryl Robson's *The Taking of Liberty* (chapter three) can find an outlet for her anger at the brutalities inflicted on women only when she becomes a ghost, and, even then, she carries the burden of that anger constantly with her. In *Pinchdice and Co.* by Julie Wilkinson (chapter four) Eleanor of Aquitaine, though a powerful woman of high social status, is visited by intimations of a future imprisoned within a room. Poppy in *Vows* by Louise Warren (chapter two) is likewise imprisoned in the present, though the forces that bind her to the room are different. The majority of the characters I discuss succeed, however, in emulating Nora and Janet in that they leave places of confinement. Whereas *A Doll's House* and *Rutherford and Son* depict only moments of departure, the plays that are my focus concentrate on the nature of the journeys. The landscapes through which the characters travel are various, but essentially they are modelled either on the busy public street beyond the walls of the doll's house or the moorland wilderness surrounding Rutherford's house.

Jo in Rona Munro's *Piper's Cave*, a consideration of which forms the first half of my next chapter, is a traveller in a wilderness space. Better equipped for her role than Janet was, she successfully charts the play's actual and metaphysical settings, the central element of which is a cave – a primordial room. In a number of ways, Jo can be seen as the antithesis of Judith in *Granite* or, alternatively, as Judith translated into a new and potent form. In *Piper's Cave* it is the woman who is the stronger, in that she has a more accurate understanding of her environment, and, so, of how to survive within it. Though visited by memories of earlier versions of self in the role of victim, Jo confronts both a man's violence and the destructive potentialities of her own anger, and, in so doing, affirms her transformation into the powerful self she has become.

In the second half of chapter one I concentrate, as in *Piper's Cave*, on a wilderness, but this time the wilderness is an inner world, that of madness. *Augustine (Big Hysteria)* by Anna Furse is set in a mental hospital in late-nineteenth-century Paris and uses actual historical figures as its central characters. Where Jo in *Piper's Cave* claims the power Judith was denied, Augustine successfully enacts the dance of the desiring inner self that, in *Granite*, Judith was prevented from completing. In the passionate movements of her dance, and their enforced cessation, Judith resembles Ibsen's Nora. When Judith dances to the sound of the wind, Jordan orders her to stop, claiming that she is mad and that, if she were an old woman, she would be ducked as a witch. Torvald in *A Doll's House* likewise cuts short a dance that Nora, his wife, performs. Ostensibly rehearsing for the entertainment she will provide later that night for friends at a party, Nora spins 'wildly . . . as if [her] life depended on it', and, like Jordan, Torvald sees this abandonment to the power of the dance as evidence of madness. 'This is sheer lunacy. Stop it, I say!' he cries (Ibsen 1980: 77).

The dance that Nora performs is the tarantella – the spider-dance. In *The Newly Born Woman* by Hélène Cixous and Catherine Clément there is a description of a southern Italian ceremony known as 'doing the spider' or 'dancing the spider' (Cixous and Clément 1986: 19), the purpose of which is to cure women who are supposedly suffering from the poisonous bites of tarantulas. As tarantulas do not exist in the region, however, the symptoms the women exhibit – 'depression, convulsions, dizziness and migraines' – must therefore be the result of 'psychical phenomena' (ibid.). For a period of time that can last several days, the affected woman performs a frenzied dance, the aim of which is to restore normality. At its conclusion, the 'poison' is drained from the woman's system, and she is able 'to leave risk behind . . . to settle down again under a roof, in a house . . . to return to the men's world' (ibid.: 22). Following her tarantella, Nora does temporarily settle down under the husband's roof, and Judith is imprisoned there, but, in *Augustine (Big Hysteria)*, which takes *The Newly Born Woman* as one of its reference points, the anarchic force of the spider-dance frees the dancer both from the mental hospital and from the role of madwoman within which she has additionally been confined.

From the cave and hospital-room settings of the first chapter I move, in the following chapter, with one exception – Winsome Pinnock's *Leave Taking* – to plays set wholly or partly in environments that are situated close to domestic dwelling places: gardens, a courtyard, a woodland, a wasteground, a hillside. I have entitled this chapter 'Related Spaces, Related Lives' because I see the settings as room-related and because, within them, the characters, many of whom are related through sisterhood or because they are mothers and daughters, also relate stories that enable them to map their pasts and presents and, to some degree at least, their futures. In the importance they grant to personal narratives, the plays in this chapter again implicitly, though, in a sense, paradoxically, evoke Nora – paradoxically because, except for the doll identity conferred on her, first by her father and later by her husband, Nora's past is seemingly devoid of narrative content. She does, however, have one story, a hidden and, as the play's events prove, a subversive one, and this is the tale of her forgery of her father's signature on an IOU. It is this story that is the catalyst for all that follows, and its eventual effect is to blast apart the apparent security of the doll's house, with the result that, at the end of the play, Nora stands on the threshold of the story of self she means to inscribe.

This threshold location is a further point of contact with many of the characters, not only in chapter two but also in other chapters. The motif of a woman poised on the brink of her future life frequently recurs. Nora's determination to write, to enact, her story also links her to my chosen characters from late-twentieth-century plays because virtually all of these are story-tellers. Stories spill out from the characters and the plays, jostling against each other, and sometimes finding interconnection, as the women search for the words, and the voices, to articulate their sense of who they are.

Part of the making of narratives consists of their remaking, and, in addition to the creation of new stories, the playwrights give form to old, largely forgotten tales embedded within the interstices of history (thus transforming them into herstory/her stories) and also imagine old narratives anew. Chapter three, 'Time-Travellers and Disorderly Women', is devoted to the first of these ventures, the recording of herstory. Of the four figures

To Alisdair, too, the place is somehow familiar. It reminds *him* of a sound (like the sea) he heard in his head when, dizzy with food and alcohol, he stumbled through the maze of city streets, and also of a mental picture that accompanied the sound: a huge black shape that grew and grew until it devoured the sky. In their turn, the sound and picture evoke earlier sensations of a time 'before anything happened' (ibid.), prior to the existence of memory, when the sea-sound in his head was all there was. Alisdair has made himself a home of sorts in the cave that is the play's setting and title. Though he knows very little about the cave (including its geographical location), he is certain of two seemingly paradoxical things: it is a source of terror, like the black shape that engulfed the sky, and it is *his*. This is '*my* place' he tells Jo (ibid: 112, original emphasis).

As I indicated in the Prologue, *Piper's Cave* has elements in common with *Granite*. Though clearly not as the result of a deliberate intention on the author's part, the later play in a number of ways reworks the earlier one. Partly, this is because Rona Munro effectively rewrites the relationship between man, woman and place that Clemence Dane establishes in *Granite*. In *Granite*, Jordan defines Judith's place as being with him, and his own place as being the Lundy farm: 'a woman goes with her man, and a man goes with his land' (Dane 1949: 4). At the end of the play The Man steps into dead Jordan's shoes, Lundy becomes *his* place and Judith his woman. Except as his chattel, his thing, Judith has no place. In *Piper's Cave*, by contrast, though Alisdair claims the place as his, it is Jo who grasps its real nature. From the beginning Jo is a map-reader, first a literal one in that she names the cave and gives its precise geographical position, and then, by the end of the play, a skilled interpreter of the imaginative and ideological mindscapes of which the cave is the physical representation. At the end of *Piper's Cave* it is not the woman who is a prisoner, as in *Granite*, but the man. Gender roles are not simply reversed, however. What confines Alisdair is not Jo but his own construction of the cave as both a source of primitive terror and the place that he is determined to own, even though it is the 'last place in the world' (Munro 1986: 131).

The 'maps' by means of which Jo comes to understand the inner significance of the play's setting – and to discover at the same time a topography of self – are primarily four stories: three legendary tales and an autobiographical story that I have called

'The Naming'. The play's major storyteller is Helen. It is Helen who acts as Jo's guide along the pathways of narrative. In *Granite* Judith has no control over any aspect of her life. She owns nothing, not even her soul or her anger. Even the story of the devil-man who came out of the sea, which she tries to appropriate for her own purposes, turns to dust in her hands. The narrative which is at the heart of *Granite* is understood fully by Judith, and the audience, only at the moment of its completion, though all its elements were present from the beginning. It is a story manipulated and controlled by The Man, its subject matter the enslavement of the woman. The four interlinked stories in *Piper's Cave* also depict relationships between a man and a woman (or male and female as in The Creation Story), but in this play it is the man who is imprisoned – within life-denying behavioural codes. For Jo, the stories together create a densely textured, allusive web upon which is written a haunting and deeply moving evocation of the possibility of transformation.

Four stories: (1) The Piper and the Cave (the first version)

This story is narrated twice in the play, the first time by Jo and the second time by Helen. Jo's version concentrates primarily on how the cave got its name. There was 'this guy', she explains, who believed that 'he was the greatest thing that ever blew down a chanter'. He thought that he could make better music than 'anything in this world, or the next, anything above ground or below it . . . and he walked into that hill playing his pipes to prove it.' But 'the hill swallowed him up', and it is said that he can still be heard playing, cursing and shouting as he goes round and round in the hillside, 'forever trying to find a way out' (ibid.: 118–19).

In the course of the play, Alisdair tells a number of stories about his previous life. In one version he is a paratrooper, in another a member of the crew of a nuclear submarine, or, alternatively, a worker on an oil rig or in a slaughter house. Eventually, he identifies himself with the piper whose music 'Made the whole . . . fucking . . . world . . . dance' (ibid.: 139). Unlike the piper, however, Alisdair is afraid to enter the cave fully. He inhabits a limbo space at the cave's mouth, from which he is terrified to move in or out. All around him, he believes, is a destructive power which he identifies as female. Outside the

17

cave is the realm of death. The beach is littered with wrecks of ships, and, on the hillside, there are the carcasses of planes that lost their way in the fog. All these 'dead' things are 'toys' that 'she' has gnawed and then spat out, and Alisdair is determined to remain where he is, so she can't get her teeth into him. The innermost part of the cave is also a source of terror to him, for he genders and personifies this place exactly as he does the outer world beyond the cave, giving to each the same attributes. Physically weakened by alcohol and malnutrition, the helpless prey of a machismo-orientated set of values that have nothing to do with the reality of the options that are available to him, Alisdair is a kind of last man, in this 'last place'. The most terrifying manifestation of the female monster that, for Alisdair, inhabits both the inner recesses of the cave and the world outside, is the darkness that creeps forward, inch by slow but inevitable inch. Over and over again he scores marks on the walls of the cave, so that he will always be on his guard, and, when the dark reaches his marks, he will 'get her'. To his horror, however, the darkness instead eventually obliterates his marks, and, panic-stricken, he concludes that the cave (as in the picture he saw in his head of the black shape swallowing the sky) is 'sending the dark out to swallow' him (ibid.: 130).

In addition to their function of providing him with markers by which to gauge the oncoming dark, Alisdair's scratchings on the cave wall assert his ownership of the place and furnish him with proof of his existence: 'Alisdair MacKerral is here. OK?' (ibid.: 131). An essential component of Alisdair's terror is his belief that 'the sooty rain' of the streets around which he tramped in endless circles has wiped out all trace of his name and voice – as the dark erases his marks on the cave walls. Alisdair has to endlessly make his mark, because he fears that otherwise he is invisible, voiceless, nameless. His only response to what he perceives as a destructive female energy that threatens to swallow him alive, whilst at the same time refusing to recognise his existence, is to tear, gouge, maim, rape, kill – in other words, to mark.

(2) The Creation Story and 'The Naming'

The Creation Story and 'The Naming' explore further the desire to wound, to make one's mark. Helen narrates The Creation

Story in the form of a dream dreamed by Jo. In the dream a figure that is Jo and, at the same time, an elemental female force, lies asleep on a hillside and 'he' comes up the hill. He has torn rocks from the ground to make his legs and fashioned his hands and head out of mud, in which he has 'dug pits' for his eyes. From his open mouth water gushes. He touches the female and splits her, 'like roots splitting rocks, water splitting ice'. He tears her limb from limb, and she yells and shows her teeth because she knows that she is stronger than he is. She knows that everywhere her blood falls she is 'making life'. She is 'bleeding life . . . bleeding the world' (ibid.: 129).

The Creation Story is an account of the origins of life in which male and female energies are inextricably linked in a violence/anger nexus. From this connection the male makes himself while in the process of ripping apart the female, and, out of her mutilation, the female makes the world. 'The Naming' story is the creation legend transposed to a modern setting of mean, night-time city streets, with the difference that the primeval violence this depicts now terrorises both the man and the woman, whilst, at the same time, the woman has misplaced the savage anger that characterised the female force in The Creation Story. At the beginning of the play Jo wears a scarf tied around her bare upper arm. A little way into the action Alisdair aggressively pulls the scarf away, revealing a scar roughly shaped like a letter 'J'. 'The Naming' is the story of how Jo got the scar.

Late one night, as Jo was walking home, a man began to follow her, and, though she screamed for help, no-one took any notice. She managed to reach the building where she lived and to lock the door, but the man kicked the door in and pinned her down on the stairs, with his hand on her throat. For a long time he talked, mostly quite normally, telling her details of his life, but, without warning, he would shake her madly, repeating over and over again that he was a killer, he had a killer inside him. He'd just beaten up his girlfriend, and was so petrified by the violence he'd discovered inside himself that he wanted to let it free to terrorise someone else. Then the man did two things. The first was that he took his hand away from Jo's throat, rested his head on her shoulder and wept, out of his terror at the violence he had already committed, and was likely to commit in the future. The second was that he cut an initial in the flesh of Jo's arm – he marked her. Jo's response to his weeping was to touch the back of his head, to comfort him, because she understood a little of his terror. Along with fear and pain and humiliation, her reaction to the mark on her arm was the sense that it negated her, denied her sense of self. The man had not seen *her*, Jo, an individual woman with characteristic attributes and potentialities, but only a malleable substance on which he could make his mark. He had lost his own sense of self – his identity and name – somewhere within the maelstrom of violence he inhabited and inflicted, and he had written his name on Jo's flesh so 'he could find it again' (ibid.: 134). Later that night, when the man had finally gone away, Jo went into the toilet. She tried to weep, but couldn't. Instead, she watched as the blood from her wound dripped into the bowl. When Jo reaches this point in her recounting of the assault, Helen repeats the final words of the creation legend, 'Bleeding the whole world', then adds, 'What's the 'J' for?' But Jo can't, 'won't remember' (ibid.).

In the two stories the woman/female force assumes a variety of identities: victim, mother, dark Other and the stronger. The bleeding female in the creation legend is the mother of the world. Jo touches the back of the man's head, comforting him like a mother. In The Creation Story the female transforms her dismemberment into an energy that creates her vividly potent anger along with all forms of life, but in Jo's memory of the attack she is unable to escape the role of victim. Jo's remembered self is therefore very different from the Jo of the play who is physically strong and fit, well able to protect herself. When Alisdair threatens her with violence, she responds in kind, at one point, for example, producing from her pocket a clasp knife very similar to the one Alisdair has been flourishing. She is also confident and at ease in the environment that terrifies him. It is the inner terrain, the landscape of her victimhood, that Jo must renegotiate, and part of this involves a confrontation with her own capacity for violence.

At a fundamental level, despite Jo's dissimilarities from Alisdair, there are ways in which the two resemble each other. Like Alisdair, Jo understands the fear of being nameless, without identity. This is clear not only from her description of her understanding of the source of her assailant's terror when he marked her, but from other things she says. At one point in the play she almost drowns when she loses her footing and falls into the sea. Afterwards, her hands are so numb with cold that she is unable to feel them. 'No hands,' she says, and adds, 'no body, no face, no Jo. What's new?' (ibid.: 127). Her job (stacking warehouse shelves) renders her faceless and nameless, partly, she explains, because the overall she is obliged to wear swallows her up and partly because she is constantly moved around in her huge place of work, an identical unit among many others.

Jo also resembles Alisdair in her capacity for violence: like him, she understands the desire to mark. In a moment of scalding rage towards Alisdair she constantly repeats that she will kill him, whilst at the same time underlining her words by pounding the ground with a rock. Shortly afterwards her anger is directed towards Helen, the representative, for Alisdair, of the female chaos that he fears will unmake him unless he first gouges his mark upon her. Unlike Alisdair, Jo respects and values the natural world, seeing it as characterised by both power and beauty. Throughout the play, however, Jo confuses Helen, the landscape, with the woman with whom she is in love, and this leads to a moment of aggression in which she temporarily replicates Alisdair's attitude both to the focus of sexual desire and to the environment. As though she is about to stab Helen, Jo raises a stone above her head, and Helen equates this action with the mutilation of the earth: 'Stabbing it, *marking* it and the earth sprays up like blood around your hand.' In a voice suggestive of a 'small quiet joke', Jo replies, 'Christ, Helen . . . I love you so much I've dug a hole in you' (ibid.: 140).

Jo and Alisdair are linked by their common fear that they could become faceless and nameless, and also by their capacity for violence. What distinguishes them is their differing responses to these shared attributes. Alisdair carries out his desire to mark, whereas Jo does not. In addition, Alisdair constructs a piper self as a form of protection against his terror: Jo's inner self is scarred by a sense of victimhood. Through her role as storyteller, Helen guides Jo into a different inner landscape, narrating first a fuller version of The Piper and the Cave story, then The Story of the Sealwoman. Following this, she asks Jo once again what the J-shaped scar on her arm is for, and, this time, Jo answers.

(3) Helen's version of The Piper and the Cave, and The Story of the Sealwoman

Helen's version of The Piper and the Cave story begins, like Jo's, with the piper who thought he was 'the greatest thing that ever blew down a chanter' (ibid.: 130), but what it then adds is that this belief was correct. The piper could coax music out of everything. For every living thing he could create a voice, but what he failed to see was that he was also a part of everything. Being male and young and 'thirty feet high in pride' he wanted 'to make his mark . . . to conquer the cave' (ibid.), and in his blind arrogance he took the two things he loved most with him into the imprisoning darkness: his music and a little mongrel bitch that followed him everywhere. The music was swallowed up along with the piper, but, howling and with all the hair burnt off her back, the dog managed to struggle free.

Like the little mongrel bitch, to which at one point she compares herself, the Jo of 'The Naming' story is scarred. In addition to her connection with the little dog, Jo has, however, a seal-self, and it is this part of her being that makes her capable of transformation. In the story that Helen tells of the sealwoman, a hunter desires the sealwoman and steals her skin to force her to stay with him. In an attempt to escape from the hunter, the sealwoman transforms herself, first into a tree, then into a rock. She is part of everything – the earth, water, the piper himself, his bones and his blood – but, because he is unable to see her in these things, the man goes on hunting. Quietly, Jo supplies the end of the story. One morning the sealwoman discovered her skin that the hunter had hidden and she returned to the sea and her seal shape. It is at this point in the play that Helen asks Jo for a second time what the 'J' scored on her arm stands for. When Jo answers, claiming that the initial is in fact her own, Helen takes the scarf that Jo has used to cover up the scar, and leaves with it. Now that Jo has become her own storyteller, Helen's presence is no longer necessary.

By concluding the sealwoman story, Jo shows that she has understood its meaning – the interconnection of all living things. The hunter cannot see this. Like the Piper and Alisdair, he makes his mark by destroying, not realising he is part of what he destroys. The sealwoman is representative of both transformation and rediscovery. She can transform herself into all things because she *is* all things. For Jo, the sealwoman embodies both reclamation and possibility. In taking back her name, she rescues herself from victimhood and affirms both the self she is now and other future selves.

At the end of the play, alone on stage, Jo compares herself to a seal, floating in salt water, breathing without gills or lungs. She can hear a beating sound, 'like waves . . . like a heartbeat'. Sleek and silver, she hangs in the darkness. Someone who might be herself or another sings 'in a voice that makes you cry . . . as though it reminded you of something you've lost'. The final words of the play are 'Hanging in the dark, waiting . . . waiting . . . That's all' (ibid.: 142), and then the lights fade.

The voice that Jo hears is both her own and what Hélène Cixous describes as 'the oldest, the loveliest Visitation', the 'first, nameless love' that sings within every woman (Cixous and Clément 1986: 93). Floating in the warm darkness, Jo hears the breathing that is not hers only, the singing of the 'nameless love', that can yet be named as the voice of the mother. Hanging in darkness, Jo waits. The seal represents transformation. Jo will change and grow. Having returned to her place of origin, she will voyage on – into further selves. Through her acquired map-reading and survival skills, Jo has both located the cave and freed it from its destructive burden of imagery. A cave is simply itself, not the site of birth or death, or the lair of the demonic Other. At the same time, we *are* our origins. We are a part of everything and this knowledge has its source in the half-remembered experience of birth.

For Alisdair there is only the terror of the dark, and his endless futile scratchings on the wall of the cave. Jo offers, if Alisdair will only come out of the cave, to be his guide, and lead him to a place where he can be cared for. Alisdair takes a few steps. He almost comes out, but then he stops. This is his place – all he knows – and here he will stay. 'Then I can't help you', Jo tells him (ibid.: 142), and she leaves him, in the literal darkness of the cave, and the figurative darkness of his own making. Self-exiled to the marginalised wilderness that is the masculine-defined site of the feminine Other, he waits – not joyously, like Jo – but with dread. Unlike the granite island of Lundy, the cave is part of the mainland. No-one keeps Alisdair there – no-one but himself, that is – but he cannot move. In *Granite*, Judith claims that her 'tongue', her voice, is her own, only to discover that The Man has used her words, her voice, for his own ends. In *Piper's Cave*, Jo finds her own voice through her understanding of the stories Helen tells. Alisdair's voice, name and face are obliterated by the darkness he has created, and so over and over again he makes his mark – the only sign that he exists.

THE TARANTELLA

Like *A Doll's House*, *Rutherford and Son* and *Granite*, Anna Furse's *Augustine (Big Hysteria)* (1991) takes place within an interior setting that is controlled by a patriarchal figure. In this play the location is a mental hospital, the Salpêtrière, the man Jean-Martin Charcot, described by Elaine Showalter in *The Female Malady* as the 'first of the great European theorists of hysteria' (Showalter 1987: 147). Charcot, Showalter writes, was both an excellent teacher and a gifted showman. At his Tuesday lecture demonstrations at the Salpêtrière, which drew large, fashionable audiences, his 'assistants' were selected women patients whom he hypnotised for the edification, and, in some cases no doubt also the delectation, of his audience. Under hypnosis, some of the patients ate pieces of charcoal they had been told were chocolate, while others delightedly smelled a bottle of ammonia in the belief that it was rose water. One barked like a dog, another reacted to a glove as though it were a snake, whilst a third gently rocked a top hat in her arms under the impression that it was a baby. 'The grande finale would be the performance of a full hysterical seizure' (Ibid.: 148). The theatricality of 'Charcot's hysterical stars', plus the fact that the symptoms they displayed were 'rarely observed outside of the Parisian clinical setting', opens up the possibility that 'the women's performances were the result of suggestion, imitation, or even fraud' (ibid.: 150). Charcot, however, denied that he had any controlling function, claiming that he was simply a 'photographer' who registered what he saw.

Literally, as well as figuratively, Charcot was a photographer and he made extensive photographic records of his patients. During the late 1870s the chief 'star' of Charcot's demonstrations and the subject of many of the photographs he took was a young girl called Augustine who was admitted to the Salpêtrière in October 1875. In *The Female Malady* Showalter includes three photographs of Augustine, each with its original caption.

The date of the photographs is 1878, so Augustine would have been seventeen or eighteen at the time. In the first, which is entitled 'Supplication amoureuse', she is seated on a rumpled bed. Her hands are joined in prayer and her face is lifted heavenward. The second, 'Extase', shows Augustine, now with hands and face raised as though in an excess of delight. Her nightgown has slipped down to partially expose her right breast, and one leg is uncovered as far as the thigh. The final picture, 'Erotisme', depicts a supposedly sleeping Augustine. Her arms are crossed over a still partially uncovered breast. Her face is turned towards the camera, and there is a look of (sensual?) fulfilment on her face. These histrionic poses, which, from the evidence of the captions, were clearly interpreted by Charcot in sexual terms, are reminiscent, Showalter notes, of the 'exaggerated gestures of the French classical acting style, or stills from silent movies' (ibid.: 154). In her early years at the Salpêtrière Augustine was an enthusiastic photographic model, but later she developed a strangely apposite symptom: she lost her sense of colour and saw all objects in black and white. The world, in other words, assumed for her the characteristic qualities of the photographs into which she was repeatedly being turned. In 1880 she rebelled against Charcot's methods and became violent, tearing her clothes and breaking windows. She was put in a locked cell, but managed to turn the acting talents she had displayed in her photographic career to her own advantage in that she escaped from the Salpêtrière dressed as a man. No record exists of what happened to her afterwards.

The 'theatricality' of Augustine's 'incarceration', and the dramatic nature of her escape, fascinated Anna Furse, the artistic director of Paines Plough theatre company. How 'on earth *did* [Augustine] escape', she wondered, 'and in which man's clothes?' (Furse 1991: 16). Her research into Augustine's background took her to the Charcot Library in Paris, and there she found photograph after photograph of Augustine, plus a record of her words during her attacks and under the influence of the drugs with which she was treated. Augustine's story was a horrific one. From the age of six to thirteen she was placed in a convent where she was often severely punished by being thrown in the 'slammer' or doused with icy water to exorcise the devil that was believed to be possessing her. At the age of thirteen she was taken into the household of Monsieur C, where her mother was the housekeeper, and, almost certainly, also Monsieur C's mistress. While Augustine was still only thirteen, she was raped at knifepoint by Monsieur C who continued to abuse her throughout the time she spent in his house, and threatened to kill her if she told anyone what was happening to her. She began to suffer from fits, in the course of which she experienced hallucinations, and a feeling of being suffocated. She also exhibited hysterical symptoms: numbness, paralysis and pains in the abdominal region. When she was fifteen, her mother took her to the Salpêtrière, where Charcot diagnosed her as a classic 'Grande Hystérique'. In the record that was made of Augustine's words at the Salpêtrière certain images recur again and again: fear of eyes, of snakes in trousers, and rats in her 'bottom' and 'tummy', terrible dreams of revolution, fire and blood. Prior to her actual escape, she 'performed regular mini-escapes: sorties into the hospital gardens at night in the rain' (Furse 1992: 5).

As a result of her research, various images of Augustine began to take shape within Anna Furse's mind: Augustine the traumatised child, Augustine the rape victim, Augustine the 'star', and Augustine the drag artist, the hypnotist's assistant turned conjurer – now you see her, now you don't! Augustine's translation of her emotional distress into physical symptoms, her conversion of her body into a 'theater for forgotten scenes' (Cixous and Clément 1986: 5) led Anna Furse to include the young Freud as one of the characters in the play she eventually wrote. Freud, in fact, never met Augustine as his studies at the Salpêtrière took place from October 1885 to February 1886, five years therefore after Augustine's escape. Freud's encounter with Charcot's use of hypnotism on hysterics was however, as Furse notes, a formative experience. It was as a result of this 'that Freud began his own private practice in Vienna two years later', where hypnosis 'would give way to simple "stream of consciousness" talking therapy' (Furse 1991: 17). In *Augustine (Big Hysteria)* Freud is the 'listener' and Charcot the 'seer'. Like the camera he used so extensively, Charcot is an eye, constantly observing and recording. A cartographer, he charts Augustine's body, noting its hysterogenic points that constitute for him 'secret geysers in the landscape of hysteria' (Furse 1996: *). What he does not do is listen to her words. 'See how hysterics scream and shout?' he comments. 'Much ado about nothing!' (ibid.). Freud, on the other hand, takes note of Augustine's stories of rape, but, though he is initially inclined to believe what he hears, he moves rapidly to the view that Augustine is recounting what she secretly wanted to happen. Like Charcot who sees without really understanding, therefore, Freud adopts the role of listener but does not truly hear.

Furse distinguishes four layers of text in her play. The first is the authoritative, scientific, yet popularising language of Charcot's lectures. The second layer is composed of arguments between Freud and Charcot as Freud, the younger man, the student, struggles discreetly for the validation of his view of Augustine. Third, there are the dialogues between Freud and Augustine, in which Augustine is alternately child, coquette and the object of psychoanalytic enquiry; and, finally, 'Augustine's monologues, hysterical, liberational or confessional' (Furse 1991: 17). These separate layers are intercut, so that they comment on each other. Interwoven among them, in performance, there was a seventy-cue soundtrack, composed by Graeme Miller, from sounds that evoked Augustine's inner and outer worlds: rainfall, for example, slamming doors, a ticking metronome, and live music provided by a violinist who functioned as Augustine's alter ego. The 'nerve gut' of the violin, which sang, screamed and celebrated, was Augustine's Other voice.

The setting (designed by Sally Jacobs) was a white 'plastic-sheeted triangle' (ibid.), which both facilitated speedy entrances and exits, and could, when required, create a sense of claustrophobia. The main item of furniture was Augustine's bed, which, with its white calico curtains that could be drawn and closed, resembled both a four-poster and a small booth-stage. This was the site of Augustine's hysterical seizures and also the place where she practised her histrionic skills. At some points the bed curtains became screens on to which blown-up images of the historical Augustine could be projected. The plastic curtains of the set could also be used as screens, with the result that Augustine, the object of the camera's, and Charcot's, gaze could be shown to be trapped by and within the photographs that had become her substitutes. In this way, members of the audience also became complicit in the objectification of Augustine. At times their gaze, at Augustine, the photographic model, became that of voyeurs.

The complex nature of the hospital bed – prison, arrangement of objectifying screens, and yet also a three-dimensional stage upon which scenarios and selves can be rehearsed – provides the key to an understanding of Augustine's self-transformation from victim to escapee. This transformative process is enacted not by one but by several routes, each of which affirms Augustine, and not Charcot or Freud, as the person in control. The first route follows the switches she makes from photographic model (and alongside this, object, specimen) to photograph, eventually becoming the camera itself, and, finally, the person who holds the camera, and therefore takes the pictures. Augustine, Furse writes, takes on the qualities ascribed to her by others. She goes 'further into an idea than was ever intended': her art is the art of 'self-parody'. Like Genet, whom Sartre described as 'first an object – and an object to others' and as having 'to make himself become the Other that he already was for Others' (quoted in Furse 1992: 5–6), Augustine becomes that 'which Others condemn her to' (ibid.). At a number of points in the production she toyed with brightly-coloured ribbons, tying them into bows on the frame of her bed, or knotting them around her wrist and trying to ascertain which colour Charcot and Freud liked best. The moment when the stage lights suddenly bleached out the colours from the ribbons and Augustine's scream of distress was picked up and extended by the vibrato of the violin demonstrated the fact that she was 'writing her body', which, in bold theatrical terms, was 'saying *I am a photograph*'. It was also saying '*I am a camera and I see you out there in black and white*' (ibid.: 6, original emphasis). At the end of the play Augustine wore a mixture of Charcot's and Freud's clothes. She had stolen their authority along with their costumes, for they looked 'vulnerable, like babies' (Furse 1996: *). They sat in their shirtsleeves and longjohns, unmoving as figures in a photograph. Augustine was now their photographer, not their model. 'No more emotion pictures!' she told them, before she vanished from the scene.

The second route by which she gains control, and thereby freedom, is her transformation of what Charcot describes as the 'lascivious choreography' of her seizure into 'a spider dance' of her own choosing (ibid.: *). When Charcot brings her hysterical fit to a close, he claims that Augustine will forget all the obscenities she has uttered and will 'be charm itself'. His words were undercut in performance, however, by the violinist, Augustine's alter ego, whom a lighting change suddenly revealed 'stamping a wild tarantella out on Charcot's desktop' (ibid.: *). Later, in her mini-escape into the rain-washed garden which precedes her final departure, Augustine claims: 'I'm an upside down festival! I'm the impossible dance! I'm the sabbat! I'm the spider dance! I'm a Tarantella!' (ibid.: *). In addition to becoming the transgressive rhythms of the tarantella, she rewrites the fairy-tale role assigned to her by Charcot, that of Sleeping Beauty, and this rewriting becomes her third escape route. Charcot, the hypnotist, puts Augustine into a sleep from which he believes he is the only 'prince' who can 'kiss' her awake, but Augustine is tired of sleep. She has slept for a hundred years. Now it is time to awake of her own volition.

Through her reappropriation of the fairy story, and her 'art of self-parody', Augustine transforms her situation. She becomes the photograph, and then the camera. She *is* the wild, anarchic tarantella. The hypnotised patient is first that desired object of the male gaze, the unconscious, silent woman. But Sleeping Beauty awakes without kissing the prince, camera in hand, and the tarantella in her blood. Through her tarantella, Augustine appropriates also the power of the witch/sorceress to whom Charcot has earlier likened her. In his demonstration of the hysterical origin of the partial paralysis of Augustine's right side, Charcot, in performance, pricked the skin of her arm and slightly drew blood. 'We are reminded of the skins of sorceresses', he told his audience when she made no response. 'Scratch an hysteric, find a witch!' (ibid.: *). Witches also fly, however, and, at the end of the play, Augustine does precisely that, leaving Charcot behind.

According to *The Newly Born Woman* one characteristic of the sorceress is laughter, and, like Medusa's laugh, the laughter of the sorceress shatters 'constraint' (Cixous and Clément 1986: 32). Near the end of the play, Charcot sculpts Augustine into one pose after another, which he then photographs. Placing her in 'a praying position', he asks her what she sees. God, Augustine answers, and Jesus – and the Virgin Mary. There's 'a rainbow above her head . . . [and she's] stepping on a snake'. 'Anything else you'd like to tell the audience?' Charcot asks. 'She's talking to Magdalena!' Augustine answers, '*And she's laughing*!!!!' (Furse 1996: *) In Augustine's vision, the Virgin, the 'sterile woman' (Cixous and Clément 1986: 32) bonds with the whore, and the sign of the their pact is their transgressive laughter. It is immediately after her perception of a possible sisterhood between Mary and Magdalena that Augustine leaves the stage to don the clothes of the patriarchs who have observed her actions without understanding them and noted her words without appreciating their significance.

To Charcot, the masculine scientist and rationalist, Augustine is the 'feminine', because she is both, in his words, 'Nature herself' and the irrational Other. Furse provides a surname for Augustine, Dubois (from the woods), to draw attention to Charcot's designation of her, but also to Augustine's reclamation of his ascription for her own purpose. It is in the rainy garden that she rehearses her escape. Like the sealwoman in *Piper's Cave*, Augustine is in, *is* everything: 'bad smells', 'sour milk', 'a feast of roses', 'tears and snot and the wet from inside', 'the flood', 'a volcano', with hot annihilating lava, 'a bird' and 'a snake' (ibid.: *). At the end of the play she prepares to disappear, but she will return. Potent shaman that she has become, she will reconstruct herself. Then, she 'will tell everything'. The doctors 'will listen, really listen, and [they] will believe every word' she says (ibid.: *).

Meanwhile, she escapes, into the wilderness, not of a remote and desolate place, but into the streets of Paris and an unknown, uncharted destination – uncharted, that is, by possible pursuers. What happened to Augustine is not known and maybe it was not good. One can take heart, however, from Judith Walkowitz's description of the streets of another city, London, in the 1880s. Marginalised groups, she writes, 'repeatedly spilled over and out of their ascribed, bounded roles, costumes and locales . . . engaged on missions of their own' in a manner that 'rendered the streets of London an enigmatic and contested site for class and gender encounters' (Walkowitz 1992: 41). It may be that Augustine, the spider dancer, sorceress, and purloiner of men's clothes and status, found a terrain which she traversed skilfully and with ease. In Anna Furse's play, this seems certain. Augustine 'leaves the stage by a window of light, as though performing a conjuring trick' (Furse 1996: *). Sleeping Beauty is now thoroughly awake and she exits to write her own stories in her own words.

* Not published at time of going to press

2

RELATED SPACES, RELATED LIVES

The room-related setting on which I focus first in this chapter is a garden; the related characters, three sisters. The play is *Vows*, by Louise Warren, toured by Scarlet Theatre in 1991; its subject matter the narration, and investigation, of a fairy-tale-inspired story. Once upon a time, so the story relates, there were three little girls in a magic childhood garden who made a solemn vow to be married, each of them on the same day. First, in order to try to escape the identities others had imposed upon them, they renamed themselves. The middle sister became Pasha, a name soft as a breath, yet with 'long and exotic roots' (Warren 1991: 4). The youngest sister would have chosen Rose as her name, but Pasha suggested Poppy instead because roses have thorns and the youngest sister hadn't, 'at least not yet' (ibid.). Besides, a poppy is not only beautiful, but also tough, despite its apparent fragility. It grows in rubbish tips as well as cornfields. The eldest, who took Pandora as her name, was the sister who organised the ritual of the vow. She took off the red cardigan she was wearing, and told Pasha and Poppy to take off theirs. Then the three of them placed their arms in the sleeves of each others' cardigans, so that they would be joined together as they promised to be true to their names, their hearts and their sisters. One day, Pandora told them, they would stand in 'white dresses and from out of the tree a nut [would] fall and out of the nut [would] step three princes', one for each of them (ibid.). Pasha was unimpressed by this story of her future destiny, and asked if she could have the nut instead, so that she could grow another tree, but Pandora was adamant that she must have a prince like her sisters. They must all be married on the same day, so that no-one would be left behind.

Through the promise she extracted from her sisters, Pandora attempted, despite their claiming of individuality through their choice of names, to structure their futures. Each of them would have a role in life as the equivalent of a fairy-tale princess, and a place within a magic future garden which would replicate the security of childhood. At the beginning of the play, however, when the sisters return to the garden to fulfil their vows, only Poppy is still convinced that marriage to the fairy prince will lead to the fulfilment of desire. Even as a child, Pasha had been sceptical of the desirability of the fairy-tale prince in his shiny nutshell, and, though she struggles to remain true to her promise, Pandora now, too, feels certainty slipping away. Each sister is searching for a way of reaffirming, or alternatively re-envisioning, the childhood promise in order to find, through the sense of dedication this will bring, a shape to adult life. In their separate ways, Poppy, Pandora and Pasha have 'set sail across the world. [In] their . . . shaky boats . . . looking for something . . . A meaning . . . To be fished up from the bottom of their souls . . . A creed to live by' (ibid.: 23). At the play's opening, they meet on the eve – the edge – of the remaking of the promise, the taking of vows.

In performance the garden was represented by a free-standing, mobile structure composed of two cupboards connected to a chest of drawers, the drawers, when opened, acting as a staircase that the sisters could ascend or descend. At the start of the performance, the three actresses entered and took up positions on this staircase. Momentarily, the stage darkened, once they were in place, and then light flooded out from one of the cupboard doors, revealing gardening implements: a spade, a hoe, a rake. Pasha stepped out of the door, wearing a large raincoat tied at the waist with string, and carrying a torch in her hand. To the sound of rain, she knelt and began to press earth down into a flowerpot. Throughout, Pasha was closely connected with this cupboard, while the second cupboard, which resembled a miniature room, was identified with Poppy. At one point, to the toylike sound of a musical box, the cupboard-chest-of-drawers structure was spun round, and Poppy was revealed standing by her open cupboard door, the door of her 'doll's house'. Inside, she promised Pandora, were all the good things they had always wanted: 'Sieves, soup tureens, cut glass and china and mirrors and spoons and vases full of flowers and warm towels' (ibid.: 14). This was her chosen space in which, four times a day, she drank tea and sang, in a voice 'sugary and crumbly like a sweet biscuit', to remind herself why she was there 'shining and bright in [her] shining house' (ibid.).

Whereas Pasha and Poppy were connected more with cupboards (Pasha's cupboard garden-related, Poppy's room-related), Pandora was more closely associated with the staircase chest of drawers, and, through this, with the concept of journeys. All the sisters opened and closed the drawers, and, through the objects they discovered there, reached into their past selves and inner lives – the secret places of their yearning. Near the beginning of the performance, Poppy and Pandora opened a drawer containing the red childhood cardigans, whilst Pasha opened a drawer full of dolls. Following their choice of their new names, the sisters had placed the dolls' dresses ceremoniously in a drawer full of leaves. Perhaps the dresses would grow, Pasha had speculated. After all, feet grew. Pandora had been sceptical. Feet were alive, dresses dead. Magically, however, the dresses had lived and grown, for, when Poppy and Pasha opened the leaf-drawer on the eve of the wedding, they drew out three, white, adult-sized dresses: a wedding dress, a fairy-tale-princess dress and 'a soft, habit-like dress' (ibid.: 16) – garments representative of their present desires.

Each dress was eventually identified with one sister. In addition, each sister had a specific object, or objects. Pandora's were a suitcase (the counterpart of the box associated with her mythical namesake), and shoes, symbolic of journeys, and, in some fairy stories, also of transformation. Poppy's object was a tablecloth. At one moment, she wrapped this around her doll, thus affirming her choice of marriage and domesticity. At another, she fed it through her fingers like a rosary, transforming it into a sanctified object, an altar cloth perhaps, the cloth of her marriage ceremony. Pasha was characterised by her garden implements and a drawer full of earth. When Poppy told her that she must pack the essential things she needed for the wedding journey, Pasha transferred the earth from the drawer to a suitcase. At the moment of choice as to whether or not she would marry, she ran with the suitcase to the top of the stairs. The lights dimmed around her until only she was lit. To the sound of running water, she described a voyage of discovery she had made the previous evening. She recalled stepping barefoot on to the path that led from the house, away from the 'safe and contained into the unknown', then leaving the path and running wildly 'looking for clues' (ibid.: 12). She could smell the wet earth, feel the growing things around her in the darkness, and she knew that she must free herself from 'the tiny brightly lit house' (ibid.) and remain in the garden where there was so much to do. As a sign of her decision not to be married, but, instead, to dedicate her life to singleness and the care of growing things, she emptied the dark fertile earth down the staircase. Pandora and Poppy then entered as their childhood selves. 'Where are you, Pasha?' Poppy asked, and, from the top of the stairs, Pasha, also now a child, replied, 'I'm in the tree! I'm so big that I'm splitting out of my nightdress, my head is wearing the moon for a hat and stars are in my eyes!' (ibid.).

Telling her sisters that she would not, after all, be married alongside them was difficult for Pasha. The words were hard in her mouth, like stones, but she knew that, if she swallowed them, and they remained unuttered, she would die. It was Pasha, who found words in general alien, who nevertheless rewrote the fairy story and transformed the vow, finding in her life of solitary dedication sources of joy. In Pasha's version of the fairy story there was once a little girl who was told that she must grow up to marry a prince who would step, ready and waiting, from a nutshell, and then she would live happily ever after in her little nutshell house. But Pasha knew better, and, from the beginning, she wanted, not the prince, but the nut itself, whole and complete, because out of the nut another tree would grow. Her farsightedness as a child about her deepest needs was demonstrated by her image of herself bursting through her nightdress – the childhood 'skin' that had become too small and tight to contain her. Whilst Pandora and Poppy still nursed their dolls, Pasha envisioned herself wearing in her hair the moon (symbol of Diana, goddess of the single life) and poised in the tree like a witch ready for flight. The adult Pasha was, at one and the same time, gardener, nun and sorceress. *Her* garment, when it emerged from its nest of leaves, was the 'habit-like dress', and its soft pallor and classical simplicity transformed her into a moon goddess. In her self-chosen life of solitary dedication, Pasha brought into a fruitful conjunction passive and active aspects of the 'feminine'. Her life as a nurturer of growing things consisted in assisting, allowing, enabling – for her plants dictated 'their own vocabulary and [had] more say in the shape of things than [she could] ever plan' (ibid.: 24). At the same time, in her role as wisewoman, she was powerful and witchy. Pasha also remade the magic childhood garden so that it became a meaningful place within which to live her adult life.

Poppy, the youngest, and therefore, within a traditional fairy-tale format, the favoured sister, chose to remain true to her childhood promise and to exchange her role as fairy-tale princess for that of a bride. Her leaf-drawer dress was therefore the wedding gown. Immediately prior to the moment of her marriage, wings sprouted from her shoulders, but, whereas Pasha had split out of her childhood nightdress into a new self, Poppy's wings of desire that burst through her dress reaffirmed her commitment to the vow she had made as a child. Poppy's bridegroom never appeared on stage. His presence was apprehended only through the ecstatic language in which Poppy heralded his approach. In words taken from The Song of Songs, than which, Marina Warner writes in *Alone of All Her Sex*, there 'has never been a more intense communication of the experience of desire' (Warner 1976: 126), Poppy reassembled the childhood garden into a garden of delight which she figured as both all around her and as the substance of her body: 'Awake O north wind, and come thou south, blow upon my garden, that the spices thereof may flow out. Let my beloved come into his garden and eat his pleasant fruits' (Warren 1991: 22).

Poppy's sensuous image of her body as a source from which abundant sweetness flowed for the bridegroom's pleasure was permeated with a sense of holiness. (As Warner notes, the lover in The Song of Songs has been interpreted both as Mary and as a nun at the time of her consecration when she becomes a 'bride of Christ', Warner 1976: 128.) For Poppy the marriage vow was a positive and responsible act through which she consecrated herself to her chosen life. At the beginning and end of the performance, however, when the sisters expressed the state of their lives following their moments of choice, Poppy's language was characterised by images of loss and constriction: shivering in the aisles of shops, bumping, in the street, into people who were replicas of herself. The grown-up version of the doll's-house cupboard, in which she had joyously enumerated spoons and mirrors, sieves, cut glass and soup tureens, and had sung in her sugary voice, had proved to be a place of confinement. Once upon a time, she had been 'carried like a full blown rose over the threshold of [her] choosing', but the garden of delight had led to a room in which she had become 'pressed against the wallpaper'. Her solace now was to dream of other rooms, 'quiet, southward facing', permeated perhaps by the sunshine which for Poppy had always been a characteristic of the childhood garden, but without sunshine's vivacity: still and tranquil, untroubled by desire (Warren 1991: 23).

Unlike her fairy-tale equivalents, Poppy, who married the fairy prince, did not live happily ever after. Her status as the youngest did not, as so often in fairy stories, protect her from danger or ensure that she made a wise choice. Pandora, the eldest sister, and the one who originally formulated the vow, found herself drawn to a life of wandering, but she longed also to conform to the life she had mapped out for her sisters and herself. For Pandora, fairy tales were that desired 'distant country' which, Toril Moi writes, in the context of Cixous's work, 'is perceived as pervasively meaningful, as closure and unity' (Moi 1988: 116). The irrelevance of the fairy-tale ending – marriage and a life of happy-ever-after – to Pandora's real needs was demonstrated by the fact that, when the dresses emerged from the leaf-drawer, she quickly pounced on the fairy-tale dress, only to discover that it was too small for her. She had outgrown the fairy tale, though not the desire to be made somehow to 'fit' its pattern, for, as a fairy-tale princess, she would be made 'whole' by the magic prince. When she realised that the dress was the wrong size, Pandora begged Poppy to exchange dresses with her, and, on Poppy's refusal, she rushed at her and tried to grab the wedding dress. 'I want to trip you up', she cried. 'I want to tear your dress . . . I want to clip your wing . . . I want . . .' and then she was silent. 'What do you want?' Pasha asked, and it was then that Pandora understood what she *didn't* want. 'I don't want to get married', she replied (Warren 1991: 21). She took off the fairy-tale dress and wrote a letter to her projected bridegroom, whose name she could remember only with extreme difficulty, cancelling the wedding. Then she posted it in one of the drawers, from which she also took her silver wedding shoes and placed them on Poppy's feet. Pandora's future life would be spent journeying, placing one foot in front of another (without any certainty as to her destination), but she would not walk down the wedding aisle. That was Poppy's choice but not hers. Apart from her

suitcase, shoes had always been the objects most closely associated with Pandora. The gift of the wedding shoes therefore
signalled clearly her disengagement from the land of fairy tale.
The only shoes she would need to retain were ones suitable for
her journey.

The performance had begun with a speech from each of the
sisters, and it ended with the same speeches, though in reverse
order, Pasha, who had spoken first, also speaking last. Pasha and
Poppy spoke from what the text defined as 'a state of being',
Pandora from 'a state of becoming' (ibid.: 23–4). At the performance's end, as at its beginning, Pandora stood poised on the
threshold of her future. As had Pasha, so she too had rejected the
childhood vow. Unlike Pasha, however, Pandora existed only in
a state of immanence, of future possibility. Pandora's dedication
was to the journey, to an acceptance of the fact that there would
be no 'happy ever after'. Like her mythical namesake, Pandora
carried a box (suitcase). When the original Pandora opened her
box, against the strict command of Zeus, she let loose disease
and evil into the world. No patriarchal prohibition guarded this
Pandora's box. She could open it as and when she chose. But,
though its contents were less terrifying than those of the original
box, they were also more nebulous, for they were change and
the challenge of the unknown. Pandora stood ready to take her
first step into a terrain for which, now that she had closed the
book of fairy tales, she had no map.

Pandora's beginning and ending position was, both literally
and figuratively, a liminal one. She existed on the edge of
possibility, though a possibility of her own choosing. Pasha and
Poppy had passed their thresholds of choice in the course of the
performance. Poppy was carried over hers, only to find herself
cut off from the desiring self she had once been. Her 'state of
being' was a limbo-space, isolated from past and future. The
framing speeches, spoken from states of 'being' and 'becoming',
demonstrated the production's investment in traditional con-
cepts of the 'feminine', as the siting of the action within the
magic garden revealed its concern with the ways in which the
child's sense of what she is and might become permeates adult
choice. Of the sisters, only Pasha, who married within herself the
traditional images of nurturer and wisewoman, found a deep
sense of fulfilment. It is noteworthy, however, that Pasha's form
of dedication was to singleness. She did not attempt to live with

a husband, like Poppy, or to journey into the outside world like Pandora. The 'threshold' which she passed was into an inner space and a secluded life. Only within a reformulated, self-chosen version of the childhood garden could a life of purpose and (quiet) joy be clearly envisaged.

Bryony Lavery's *Two Marias*, first performed in 1989 by Theatre Centre Women's Company to teenage schoolgirl audiences, has a certain similarity to *Vows* in that it too dramatises the undertaking of emotional journeys within a secluded setting. A dusty Spanish courtyard replaces the garden of *Vows*. On three sides of this courtyard there are chairs, benches and terracotta pots, and, on the fourth side, the house. 'There is fierce light and heat in some of the courtyard, deep cool shade elsewhere' (Lavery 1991: 57). A further connection between Lavery's play and *Vows* is that the two Marias of the title, though not actual sisters, are united by a bond as deep – or deeper – than sisterhood. The play's action, which is based on an actual occurrence that Bryony Lavery had read a newspaper account of, arises from a strange and dreadful coincidence. One hot June night in 1987 two seventeen-year-old girls, both named Maria, were driving from opposite directions towards the beach. Without warning, a car swerved close to the car driven by one of the Marias, and threw up a shower of gravel. Unable to see what she was doing, the young driver (Maria del Morte) tried frantically to brake, but lost control of the car, and slammed into the oncoming vehicle driven by Maria del Amor. Her chest was crushed by its impact with the steering wheel, and then she was hurtled, face first, through the windscreen. That Saturday night the road was packed tight with pilgrims on their way to visit the shrine at El Roscio and it was an hour before the ambulance could get to the scene of the accident. When it did eventually arrive, Maria del Morte was dead, and Maria del Amor only just alive. The two girls were laid beside each other in the ambulance, and in 'the confusion and pain and blood' (ibid.: 62), their handbags containing their names were switched, with the result that, when they reached the hospital, Maria del Morte was wrongly named as the living girl. The parents of Maria del Amor were informed of their daughter's death, but, as they were advised against seeing the body, because of its badly mutilated state, they did not discover that a mistake had been made.

As the supposed Maria del Morte began to recover members of her family were baffled by changes in her appearance, but doctors put these down to the traumatic experience of the accident and the cortisone injections with which she was being treated. The girl's own belief that her name was not del Morte was attributed to loss of memory. It was only through a further coincidence that the truth was eventually established. Though he was himself from a distant part of Spain, the therapist who was treating the living Maria just happened to know a doctor in the little place from which Maria del Amor, the supposedly dead girl, came. He was puzzled by the fact that the living Maria knew certain facts about the 'dead' Maria: her address, for example, and the fact that she was studying beauty therapy. He came to the conclusion that she must have heard these details in the immediate aftermath of the accident, and subliminally taken on aspects of the dead girl. In order to help him to understand the case, the therapist asked his doctor friend to see her, and so the truth was discovered. Maria del Amor was returned to the family who had believed her to be dead, and the body of the real Maria del Morte was reinterred near the home of her parents.

Maria del Amor, Maria del Morte – a girl of love and a girl of death. Death is the Other that shadows not only love in *Two Marias* but also birth and life. A supposedly dead girl is reborn; another, who had been believed to have been rescued from death, lives now only in her mother's heart and in the newspaper cuttings that that mother (Marguerita) carries always with her. From a seemingly endless supply of newspaper, Marguerita performs the conjuring tricks (turning one newspaper into a tree, for instance, and pouring water from another) with which she used to entertain her daughter – tricks which of course the girl falsely identified as Maria del Morte does not recognise. Maria del Morte makes her first entrance in the play from a disordered heap of newspapers in a darkened area of the stage, thus emphasising the fact that she now inhabits chiefly a two-dimensional newsprint world. Marguerita is haunted by her love for her lost daughter, but the dead Maria is haunted also – by her living counterpart who has been given her name. She begs Maria del Amor (or Maria as she is simply termed in the play) to lend her her heart and warmth so that she can make the emotional journey back to her final moments of life. In unison, the two girls create the time and place of the accident, viewing it with the eyes of the living Maria. Within the present tense of the courtyard they reanimate the moment that decided which of them would live and which would die. They conjure up the smell of pine trees through the open window of the car, see 'the long long bend' of the road, feel panic as the wheel refuses to turn out of the path of the oncoming car. There's 'a girl coming at me through the windscreen', both Marias cry together; then, as the windscreen goes blank, becomes snow, ice, they continue: 'it's burning my face . . . it's slicing my brain into pieces of gravel, what is happening? Where am I? Who am I? I am in pieces all over the road!!' (ibid.: 71).

From the pieces on the road only one living body can be assembled. So, too, out of the play's four characters (two mothers and two daughters) only Julia and Maria (del Amor) have the opportunity to form a living relationship. Even after her reconstruction (with Maria del Amor's help) of the moment which severed her from life, Maria del Morte finds it difficult to rest in peace. She is unable to 'lie down in [her] blackened, stinking, decomposing body in the graveyard' (ibid: 81) because over and over in her mind she questions how it could have happened that her mother mistook another girl for herself. This is the question that Julia also asks of Marguerita. For seventeen years Marguerita has held this girl, 'looked with wonder on her every day', been gripped with fear when she was in danger. How could she not know that this was not her child? 'How could I not know?' Marguerita repeats 'I *knew*! I knew the first day it wasn't my daughter. How could I not? (Pause) But . . . I couldn't bring myself to let her go' (ibid.: 79 and 82). In order to reanimate the corpse of her daughter, to reassemble the pieces on the road into *her* Maria, Marguerita accepted the child she had been given in her dead daughter's place. She slept beside her, comforted her, took off the paint that should not have been on her toe-nails, ignored the fact that a mole that used to be on her daughter's hip had disappeared, planned to have her nose changed by plastic surgery, would have agreed to the sending of volt after volt of electricity through the girl's brain until, like Frankenstein, she reanimated the dead. At the end of the play, however, Marguerita accepts the fact of her loss and blesses the living. Marguerita's is the first line of the play: 'This house here is full of pain' (ibid.: 57). Immediately prior to her final exit, after expressing her happiness that the living Maria has forgotten the time she spent with her, she adds: 'I'm not her mother, you see. I lay my hand upon the forehead of this house. Let it be free of pain' (ibid.: 83).

The pain that Marguerita attempts to exorcise from the house is caused by an estrangement between Julia and her daughter which arises from the fact that Maria is in love with a girl – an orientation of desire that Julia considers to be both unnatural and sterile. At various points in the play newspaper stories have been read out that tell bizarre and horrifying tales of mothers imprisoning their daughters within the home in an attempt to protect them from the dangers of the outside world. In an extreme form, these stories represent both Julia's and Marguerita's desire to hold on to their daughters. Marguerita comes eventually to an acceptance of her child's death, but Julia is unable to allow the living Maria to develop into a self she cannot recognise and approve. Though, near the play's end, there is a rapprochement of a kind between Julia and Maria, the mother still attempts to contain the daughter within what she perceives as the safe space of the home. She will use her traditional skills as provider and carer, will make Maria a delicious supper of tortilla de patatas, tomato salad and chorizo, after which, surely the girl will be too full and contented to want to go off roaming with her girlfriend. Maria temporises – perhaps she will stay at home – but, when her mother goes into the house, she lives in anticipation of the coming evening: first dancing, then driving with her girlfriend to the beach, along the 'twisty road' where the accident occurred.

At the end of *Two Marias*, the beach road, the site of death, is transformed into the site of pleasure and life. In contrast to Maria del Morte, who rests now in the still places remaining to her, the grave and her mother's heart, Maria del Amor will go out from the secluded courtyard adjoining *her* mother's house to claim her right to life. A play therefore which has been primarily concerned with the past and with death, ends poised on the edge of the future and of life. The Otherness of death and loss is not forgotten – there were once two Marias, and the mothers' pain is only partly healed – but the major emphasis is on the living Maria, and on what her name promises – amor, love.

Like *Vows*, *Two Marias* ends with one of its characters poised on the brink of change. Like *Vows*, too, dramatic time in *Two Marias* is plastic and malleable, with the result that the linearity of performance time is confused and enriched by frequent slippages between present, past and future. The secluded setting that is characteristic of both plays becomes the site of memory, possibility and loss. Louise Page's *Real Estate* also dramatises the impingement of past and future on the present, but, in contrast to *Vows* and *Two Marias*, its form is largely naturalistic, and the action unfolds within linear time. A study of reviews of the original production reveals that it was the naturalistic quality of the play that frequently muted the enthusiasm of those critics who were otherwise well disposed towards *Real Estate*. Both Susan Todd (*New Statesman*, 18 May 1984) and Jane Edwardes (*Time Out*, 10 May 1984), for example, responded sympathetically to the play and its production, but Susan Todd found the 'conventionality of the play's form . . . unsatisfying', while Jane Edwardes considered the ending 'improbable', a view that in all likelihood arose out of a response to expectations raised by *Real Estate*'s naturalistic form. Michael Billington, though expressing the wish that he had enjoyed more the excellent performances of 'visibly real people fighting to penetrate each other's defences', complained of its 'goldfish-bowl quality'. *Real Estate* was, he wrote, 'one of those hermetic psychological dramas in which nothing much seems to exist outside the closed-in world of the play' (*Guardian*, 8 May 1984). Giles Gordon in the *Spectator*, on the other hand (19 May 1984), pointed to the Chekhovian nature of Page's approach. 'If this sounds dull and mundane', he wrote of *Real Estate*, 'try Chekhov's plots', and his assessment is borne out by Page herself, who, in an interview with Elizabeth Sakellaridou in *New Theatre Quarterly* (1990), has confirmed her commitment, as a writer to the 'minutiae' of people's lives, because 'it is those moments that actually do radically affect people' (Page 1990: 174).

Interestingly, even those critics who were not particularly enthusiastic about the play or its production were excited by Ellen Cairns's set which cleverly brought together Page's various settings: an office, Gwen's and Dick's Oxfordshire home and the wood behind the house. Victoria Radin writing in the *Observer* (13 May 1984) commented that the 'unexpected set suggest[ed] the oblique, unpredictable surrealism of Ms Page's *Salonika*' which Radin hoped the playwright had 'only temporarily . . . abandoned'. In my view, the qualities Radin admired in the set are also characteristic elements of the scenes that take place in the wood. The woodland setting, and the action that takes place within it, complicates and deepens our response to the rest of the play, with the result that the minutiae of people's lives are informed by something beyond the simply naturalistic or psychological.

Real Estate begins, as it will end, in the wood. The time is late dusk on an autumn evening and there are dead leaves on the ground. A ball crosses the stage and then, from offstage, a woman shouts for a dog to come back. The woman, Gwen, enters with a dog lead. She rattles the lead, whistles and again calls the dog's name. She calls out to someone offstage and then picks up an acorn with a small root and exits. A younger woman, Gwen's daughter, enters with the ball. 'She is dressed almost identically to Gwen except that she is wearing silly shoes' (Page 1990: 134). These moments in the darkening wood – the throwing of the ball, Gwen's entrance with the dog's lead, her picking up of the acorn, and the entrance of the younger woman – small and mundane as they are, are the immediate successors to an extraordinary happening that precedes the play's beginning, though it is only gradually established by its action, and that, in its turn, was preceded by another, much earlier, out-of-the-ordinary event. Twenty years ago, after a disagreement with her mother and her stepfather, Dick, Jenny ran away from home. For the whole of that time Gwen and Dick have had no knowledge of her whereabouts, or even whether she was alive or dead. Immediately prior to the opening moments of the play Jenny has turned up on their doorstep, unexpected and unannounced.

The refutation of the expectation that the future will be as the past has been, and that the long-vanished Jenny will remain lost to Gwen and Dick, acts therefore as the catalyst for a play which, as Jane Edwardes noted in *Time Out*, 'confounds expectations'. This refutation of expectation is, Elaine Turner writes, characteristic of Page's work. 'In plays as different in form as *Tissue*, *Salonika* and *Real Estate*, the most frequent single word is "expect"', and the 'background of expectations' against which the action of the plays occurs alerts the audience to 'the contradictions, deviations, limitations and distortions these ingrained preconceptions place upon individual behaviour' (Turner 1994: 555). In *Real Estate* expectations cluster around the mother-child relationship, and it is these expectations that Page questions and unravels. At the age of twenty-eight Jenny has become pregnant, and her visit to her mother is ostensibly caused by the fact that her lover's daughter, Lottie (with whom Jenny has recently been in contact) has developed German measles. Jenny therefore needs to know whether she herself had German measles as a child. As the play's action develops, however, it becomes clear that Jenny wishes to re-establish herself in the home she left so abruptly twenty years earlier, and to co-opt Gwen's services in caring for the child when it is born. In the years following Jenny's departure Gwen has built up a thriving business as an estate agent, and it eventually becomes evident that Jenny expects effectively to take over the business while Gwen plays the role of nurturing grandmother at home.

These expectations are frustrated because, despite her fear of losing her daughter for a second time, Gwen refuses to give up the life she has made for herself. In addition, the act of nurturing is itself freed from its traditional burden of expectations because the desire to love and care for a child is not seen as tied to the maternal function. In the event, it is Dick, who has always longed for a child, who offers Jenny a home and help in looking after the baby. Dick retired early in order to spend time with Gwen, only to find that the estate business, into which she had apparently entered so casually, is now very successful and consumes the majority of her time and energy. Dick has developed traditional 'womanly' skills. He cleans, cooks, shops, even embroiders. Jenny's lover, Eric, is also a gentle, caring man. He passionately loves the daughter to whom he has access only every other weekend. Although he cares far more for Jenny than she does for him, he refuses (in the course of the play) to continue to see her after the baby is born, unless she is willing to make a permanent commitment to him, because he cannot face the thought of relating to a child again in the piecemeal, unsatisfactory way that is all that is available to him with Lottie.

Near the end of the play Eric leaves intending never to return, and Dick prepares to become both the surrogate father Jenny rejected twenty years earlier, and the carer of her unborn child. The final moments focus on Gwen, who is alone on stage, first in the house and then in the wood. Before leaving the house Gwen performs a sequence of actions that signify the end of her life there. She cuts from its frame the tapestry that Dick had been making as part of a set for the dining-room chairs, but later decided, against Gwen's expressed desire, to give to Jenny, and puts it in her briefcase. She collects the dog's lead and bowl, takes from its glass the little oak tree she has grown from the acorn she found in scene one, and leaves her house key on the table. When she enters the wood, it is almost dawn. As in the first scene, she is wearing smart office clothes. She carries with her a briefcase, and the oak tree, which she plants 'using her hands to dig'. She crosses the stage, looks back at the house, then exits. From offstage she whistles to the dog. 'Dawn breaks' (Page 1990: 214).

From a strictly naturalist perspective Gwen's final moments in the wood, and her departure from the house in which she has spent so much of her life, carrying with her only a few symbolic objects, may perhaps, as Jane Edwardes comments, have an air of implausibility, but, as I noted earlier, the whole play is based on two equally extraordinary events: Jenny's total disappearance from Gwen's and Dick's life and her unheralded re-entry into it twenty years later. The other factor that makes Gwen's final actions both credible and powerful is their location within the wood which is at once adjacent to, and Other than, the house she has left, and has also, in the course of the play, been revealed as a place that links past and future, meetings and departures, birth and death, possibility and loss. Though the actual moment of Jenny's re-entry into Gwen's life is not shown, mother and daughter are first seen together in the wood. It is in the wood too that Jenny tells, first her mother, then later, individually, Dick and Eric, that she is pregnant, and the wood is also the place where Dick has buried the evidence of his own and Gwen's past grief, and of his hopes of becoming a father.

Though Jenny did not know this at the time, when she left home her mother was pregnant. When Jenny went, Dick tells Eric, Gwen's 'womb let go ... Bleeding and bleeding and bleeding. Everything in it. No torrent just oozing, like the sap from a tree. Day after day. A slipping away. In clots. [The baby] could have been any of them' (ibid.: 167). Gwen told Dick to soak the sheets in cold water and then boil them, but he didn't want to 'see the froth on the top of the pan like boiling bones' (ibid.) and, instead, he buried the bloody sheets in the wood. Beneath the earth, the past has bled into the present. The young woman who left home twenty years earlier, knowing nothing of the child her mother was carrying, or of its slow seeping away from her mother's body, returns, at the play's beginning, now of an almost identical age to that of her mother when she left, and, also, like her mother was then, pregnant.

In addition to its function as a place in which meeting and departure, birth and death can be brought into close conjunction, the wood is a childhood-linked space. The unseen Lottie is first mentioned in the wood, where Eric is collecting chestnuts to take back for her. It is in the wood that the normally brittle and self-absorbed Jenny is presented at her most vulnerable and childlike. The scene which ends the first half of the play takes place in the wood late on Christmas Eve. Jenny has recently had an amniocentesis, but has not yet received the results, and she is anxious as to whether all is well with the baby. She enters, alone, in her nightdress, and speaks to the foetus inside her. 'Child? Can you hear me?' she asks. 'Please. Move. Quicken. Just once. Something. It's Christmas. Do you know that? Christmas Eve' (ibid.: 172). Eric enters and tries to get her to come back into the warmth of the house. What will Christmas Day be like? Jenny wonders. What will its rituals be? The same as they were before she left, Eric suggests, and Jenny comments, 'Like being a child again' (ibid.: 173). The remembered security of childhood acts as a form of reassurance in the face of her fears about the fate of her child. Half jokingly, half seriously, Eric begins to tell her a fairy tale, Lottie's favourite, and in the process leads her back into the house. The scene ends with an evocation of Western culture's most famous story of a pregnant woman. Gwen enters, and standing alone on stage, she sings of the Angel Gabriel who came from heaven with 'wings as drifted snow', eyes like 'flame', to honour the 'lowly maiden Mary' (ibid.: 174).

Partly, this evocation of the meek and compliant Mary who was honoured because she obliterated self in the fulfilment of her role as nurturer, is ironical, but the haunting loveliness of the carol's words and tune in the night-time Christmas wood, where the roots of trees merge with sheets bloodied by a miscarried child, and Jenny speaks to *her* unborn child, also extends the play's exploration of the desire for, and the necessity of, nurturance beyond the domain of the naturalistic or psychological. Gwen's own attitudes to motherhood are complex and, in some ways, contradictory. Her original intention in having Jenny was to hold on to a man she was afraid of losing, and, despite her later love for her daughter, one of her most vivid memories as a young mother is of her distress when the baby was sick on a new black angora cardigan. Everyone had cooed at, and admired, the baby and Gwen had worn the cardigan because she too wanted to feel special. When it was ruined, she knew that she would be unable to afford another. Years later, she became pregnant by Dick more for his sake than her own, and the bloody sheets in the wood signify his loss rather than hers. Yet, at the same time, Gwen has longed for twenty years for the return of her daughter. The carol does not reconcile these different elements of experience. Rather, it adds its own distinctive and bell-like note. The first half of the play presents the desire for a child as an entity that exists beyond the confines of character or gender. Like a kaleidoscope, the play's action shakes this desire so that it forms varied and contrasted patterns: a barely recognised young woman who returns after twenty years, the new life within her, a coveted cardigan ruined, collecting chestnuts for a daughter in the presence of a lover, the anguished longing for a child who does not return, the bleeding away of another potential child and the loss of a man's hopes of fatherhood.

The second half of the play maps the choices the various characters make: Jenny to have both a successful career and a carer for her child, Dick to be that carer. Eric and Gwen leave, Eric to be available should Lottie need him, and Gwen to focus on her own life rather than be sucked into the orbit of Jenny's needs and demands. She takes with her the dog that, near the beginning of the play, Jenny mistakenly identifies as primarily Dick's. It is Gwen who has always cared most for the dog. Though it needs walks and food and affection, the dog does not require the moment-by-moment expenditure of effort and love that a baby would, and Gwen's taking of the dog with her signals the limited space now available in her life for the nurturer role. Before she leaves, she plants the little oak tree. She has cared for it while it began its initial task of sending out the shoots from which one day the vast trunk and lofty branches will develop. Now it can manage on its own, or, if it can't, she has done her best. Though the play's overall concern is with the joys and problems of nurturing, it focuses finally on Gwen's right to her own life. In interview, Louise Page has described *Real Estate* as 'a subversive play' because 'it says that the mother should be free to live her own life and not bring up the grandchild'. Some people have criticised what they have seen as her lack of support for

'women who don't have partners to have children', she continues, but she does 'absolutely' support Jenny's right to do that.
What she doesn't support is 'her right to do it and expect her
mother to change the nappies' (Page 1990: 181). Gwen hopes to
maintain loving contact with both Jenny and Dick. At the end of
the play, however, she leaves the house and the wood, having
first planted a growing tree in the earth where, somewhere, the
bloody sheets lie buried. The past is unalterable. Gwen will give
what she willingly can to the future. The remaining spaces in her
life are her own. At the age of sixty she moves into her own self-
chosen place.

Place, in a number of its attributes: birthplace, home, making a
place for oneself, feeling displaced, and also the problems of
survival in an inhospitable place, are fundamental aspects of
Winsome Pinnock's *Leave Taking*. Like Gwen in *Real Estate*,
Enid Matthews is a middle-aged woman, but, unlike Gwen, she is
black and poor, and the spaces to which she is able to lay claim
are therefore more restricted.

As a young woman Enid left her home in Jamaica and settled in
England. Later, when her husband deserted her, she managed,
by dint of taking cleaning jobs, to bring up her two daughters on
her own. Now, her energies are mainly directed towards trying
to ensure their continued survival. Enid's attitude towards England rests upon a basic contradiction of which she is only partly
aware. On the one hand she claims that England has been good
to her and that this is the place she now identifies with: 'I love
England an' I bring up the girls to love England because they
English' (Pinnock 1989: 152), and, on the other hand, that
England is a white man's country: 'a black woman less than
nuttin' (ibid.: 148).

In their different ways, her daughters view the problem of
being black, female and English with a clarity that derives from
the fact that they have lived all their lives in a country that
grudges them a sense of belonging. Del, the elder daughter,
rejects the accommodations Enid has made in order to ensure
her own and her daughters' survival. When Enid reminds her
that she has managed always to keep a roof over their heads and
to put food in their bellies, Del retorts that she doesn't give them
anything they 'can use out there'. People 'can do what the hell
they like with' them. Enid is always telling them to 'be grateful',

but 'For what?' (ibid.: 156–7). Enid is locked into a bitter feud with Del, who rejects the careful, careworn life her mother lives and insists on her own right to a fullness of life, love and sexuality.

The focus of Enid's pride and hopes is her younger daughter Viv, who is still at school and predicted to do well at A level. Viv, however, finds her mother's hopes for her burdensome and rebels also against an educational system that constructs her as something other than the person she feels herself to be. Enid claims that the daughters she has brought up as English are not confused as to their identities: 'They know who they are.' Asked to identify 'who she is', Viv stands up and recites from Rupert Brooke's poem, *The Soldier*: 'A dust whom England bore, shaped made aware . . . A body of England's breathing English air.' Enid is nonplussed by this at first, but eventually rallies, and responds, 'See. *That's* all you need to know, English' (ibid.: 153, original emphasis). The irony escapes her, but not Viv, who recognises that this is *not* all she needs to know. Despite her partial Englishness, she is shaped also by a different dust and is the inheritor of the blessings of another and warmer sun than 'the suns of home' Brooke's poem commemorates. Later in the play, she describes how she has walked out of an exam. She knew the answers to the questions but felt that it was pointless to write them down because they would change nothing.

Viv and Del have direct experience only of England, but Enid's early life was lived within a different country and culture. That other place, and earlier home, enters the play most vividly and poignantly through a letter that Enid receives from her sister. She puts off opening this letter because other things intervene, but also because she is afraid of what it may contain. While the letter is still unread, she puts it to her nose, and inhaling its smell, which reminds her of home, she is assailed by memories of her mother. When she left Jamaica, her mother refused to stop her work in the fields and take leave of her. 'She must be never want me to go', Enid explains, but, when she finally had to give up and walk away without any acknowledgement from her mother, she 'had this . . . big dark hole inside' (ibid.: 160). When she does at last open the letter, Enid learns that her mother is dead. It is Enid who speaks the final words of act one: 'I want to go home' (ibid.: 166).

Enid's articulation of her desire to return to her place of origin, and to the mother for whose love she still aches, is made in the context of a bitter row with Del, as a result of which Del packs her suitcase and leaves. The beginning of act two finds Del established in the bedsit of an obeah woman called Mai, who serves for Enid as a link with a culture she has largely rejected, but for which she nevertheless yearns, and, despite Mai's avowal that she will not do this, acts for Del as a kind of surrogate mother. Mai repeats Enid's insistence on the importance of survival, and tells Del that it is her own, and her mother's, joint task to help each other to survive. The end of the play restates Pinnock's linked themes of survival and the quest for 'place'. Enid did not send money back to Jamaica for her sick mother when she was asked to by members of her family there, and consequently she blames herself for her mother's death. What the audience learn at the end of the play, however, is that her mother made her promise, during Enid's last visit to Jamaica, not to send money because she wanted to die. To Enid, this request, and her mother's advice that Enid should forget the family she left behind and get on with her life in England, amounted to rejection. 'How can a person forget?' she cries out to Del. Forgetting would necessitate tearing one's 'heart out' (ibid.: 188). But for Del the fact that her mother has not made a leave taking of her previous home has inhibited Del's own ability to become the strong woman she wants and needs to be. Enid claims that her daughters are weak but the cause of this, Del tells her, is that Enid kept so much of herself back when her daughters needed her. It's as if the mother is an empty shell because she has left a vital part of herself behind in the past. Survival isn't enough, Del explains. She has no sense of belonging, is constantly 'running around trying to find a place to fit in' (ibid.: 189). Del is pregnant, and unmarried, and, for the sake of her unborn child, she has to stop running. Economic necessity forced her mother to leave Jamaica for England, just as in the 1920s her grandmother had to go to Cuba to cut sugar cane. Del knows that the time has come to stand her ground and claim the place where she is as her own.

The play ends partly with a leave taking but also with a bonding of women across the generations. Del's assertion of her right to a place of certainty is followed by an appeal for her mother's love. Every night when she curls up in bed she remembers how her mother used to hold her as a child and whisper secrets in her ear. 'And don't I need to curl up in somebody's lap and to be told stories to make the sun shine?' Enid asks (ibid.). Enid never felt able to be the child her mother wanted. She was too black and her hair was too dry – the things her mother disliked and rejected in herself. Only once did she feel really close to her mother and that was when her mother took her on a long walk 'to all she secret places . . . [where] she would just sit, think and dream' (ibid: 160). Del's memory of the secrets her mother whispered in her ear as a child connects with the secret places her grandmother showed *her* daughter. These places create, within a play that is set entirely within rooms, an alternative space that has similarities to the garden of memory, loss and possibility which forms the setting in *Vows*. The secret-ness of these places and their link with 'home' constructs them also as inner spaces – places of the heart. The end of the play enacts a form of leave taking in that Enid's final words and gesture relocate her loving and needy younger self that was denied the emotional sustenance she longed for from the past into the present. She opens out her arms to Del. 'Come hold me' (ibid.: 189), she says, and through this request for Del's em-brace, tacitly accepts the fact that she can never now be em-braced by her mother. Yet, because Enid holds her mother inside herself in the form of her knowledge of her mother's secret places, the final moments of the play are also a meeting, a bringing together. In her neediness Enid offers herself to her daughter both as a mother and as a child. The fact that she contains her own mother's secrets, and that Del carries within her her unborn child, brings into conjuction within the present moment four generations of a family in a way that works to undo the linearity of time.

Winsome Pinnock's exploration of the interconnected lives of grandmother, mother and daughter, and her re-examination of the impact of the past on the present, links *Leave Taking* to a play that received its first production in February 1987 (i.e. nine months prior to the initial performance of *Leave Taking*), Char-lotte Keatley's *My Mother Said I Never Should*. In the Prologue I quoted Charlotte Keatley's comparison of a play text to a map. Though not the earliest of the plays discussed in this chapter (*Real Estate* was first performed in 1984) *My Mother Said I Never*

Should can valuably be viewed as the text that explores most extensively a stretch of terrain that the other plays also partially chart, and, though each cartographer's perspective is somewhat different, the maps they make are recognisably of the same country. All give form to an emotional landscape, the contours of which could be named expectation, and its fulfilment or denial; past pain and anger and the necessity of making accommodations with these experiences; the reaching of thresholds of possibility; and the manner in which the present moment can be irradiated by the past and, perhaps, the future. *Leave Taking* and *Two Marias* embody inner landscapes within the defined locations of, respectively, rooms and a courtyard. *Real Estate* intersperses scenes set in rooms and an office with others that take place in the stranger and more potent space of the wood. The staircase setting of *Vows* links childhood and fairy tale with the possibilities and results of adult choice.

The action of *My Mother Said* takes place in Manchester, Oldham and London; in domestic rooms, an office, gardens and a childhood-linked space known as the wasteground. As Keatley makes clear in her stage directions, the setting is not meant to be naturalistic, but should instead 'be a magic place where things can happen' (Keatley 1990b). Within the present moment of theatre time and the actuality of the stage space the play's time and locations shift and jumble so that past and present events become neither linear nor 'strictly simultaneous, but something in between' (Keatley 1990a: 131). The wasteground is the most magic of the play's locations, and it is here that the play begins. In the wasteground, the play's characters, Doris, Margaret, Jackie and Rosie (four generations of women) come together, not as great-grandmother, grandmother, mother and daughter, but as children. The erasure of the mother/daughter status in the wasteground scenes and the plasticality of time throughout *My Mother Said* have the effect of giving the play equally to all four characters. No single perspective predominates. At the same time, there is a sense of moving forward. Part of the play's emotional power arises from the pattern of repetition it establishes. Incidents in the lives of mothers are replayed in the lives of daughters, but with crucial changes of emphasis. In Keatley's words, 'the same thresholds are reached in every generation, though very different choices [are] ultimately . . . made, largely due to the different social expectations directed at women in each generation' (ibid.). Holding all these different events and time-scales together, earthing them, as it were, are the objects that create the varied locations: a piano and a swing, for example, white wax flowers, a wartime Utility mug, a transistor radio, a baby's red sock, a doll, a pile of sheets. Always present – always there to be handled by the actors and seen by the audience – these objects are at once solidly real and enablers of transformation. Their time is always identical with the time of the performance, and yet they are the means by which the play's various time-scales are given form. Through them memory is evoked and change made palpable.

Among the most powerful of these objects (because of their malleability) are the various sheets that are used in the course of the play. A moment of especial theatre magic – of which a sheet is the agent – occurs in act one, between scenes six and seven. Scene six is set in a council flat in Mosside, Manchester, in early December 1971. Jackie is nineteen and her mother, Margaret, is forty. Jackie has a three-month-old daughter, Rosie, whom she loves very much, but finds desperately difficult to care for as a single parent. For this reason she agrees (albeit unwillingly) to Margaret's suggestion that *she* should bring Rosie up as her own child. The scene ends with a blackout in which the sound of a crying baby can be heard. Then, in a dim light, Margaret is seen rocking and comforting the 'baby', which gradually quietens and begins to coo. As the lights come up brightly for the next scene, 'Margaret turns and billows out the sheet' (Keatley 1990b: 15), that has represented the baby, transforming it into an item of washing that has been hanging on a line to dry. The place becomes the garden of Doris's and Jack's house in Cheadle Hulme, Manchester; the time a hot, stormy August day in 1951. Margaret is now the daughter, a young woman of twenty, engaged to be married. Her mother, Doris, is fifty-one.

As the scene begins, the sound of light aircraft can be heard overhead, and Margaret identifies the planes as American B29s, not the RAF Lancasters Doris takes them to be. Perhaps one of the planes will be Ken's (her fiancé's), she speculates. The two women meticulously fold the sheet, and, at the same time, Margaret tries to share with her mother her excitement at the married life that she is about to enter. She 'can't wait to live in London', she confides. She is 'in love' (ibid.: 16). Doris makes no reply to this. Instead, her words focus on a threatened downpour that she fears may deluge them before they can get the washing safely inside. As Margaret continues to try to engage her mother's interest, her hands mechanically shake, pull and fold the sheet, but her words negate the value of the domestic task in which she is engaged. She is going to learn to type, she tells Doris, so that she can get 'a *proper* job' (original emphasis). She's not going to waste her life. This rejection of the values by which she has lived her life finally engages Doris's full attention. The sheet has at this point been folded into a long narrow shape, and, angrily, Doris orders Margaret to pull it taut. Margaret's response is to pull so hard that the two women jerk away from each other and Doris is forced to let go of her end of the sheet. The moment of disjunction when the sheet no longer physically unites them embodies the severance of sympathy between the women. As they resume the act of folding Margaret informs her mother that she and Ken have decided not 'to have a family, babies and all that'. Then, as though to underline her determination to order her life differently from her mother's, she, 'grandly' explains how she will avoid pregnancy: 'There's THINGS you can get . . . I've heard about them' (original emphasis). Doris's response is to cradle the folded sheet in her arms and to inhale its scent of lavender. It's not simply a matter of 'rubber things', she tells Margaret. 'Mother Nature' is a powerful force to be reckoned with. Will Margaret be able to resist the desire 'for little arms . . . round [her] neck'? (ibid.). She holds out the sheet for Margaret to smell it too, but Margaret rejects once again the idea that her life will be like her mother's. Little arms are precisely what she doesn't want: her generation will organise things differently.

The dual use of the sheet in act one, scene six and act one, scene seven – as both a child-related object, and a sign of external connection, yet emotional disconnection, between mother and daughter – physicalises motifs that recur throughout the play. The moment of stage time when Doris cradles the sheet in her arms infuses events in a summer garden in 1951 with others that, within the play, have already taken place, yet, in chronological time, have yet to happen in a council flat in winter time twenty years later. The sheet that Doris holds in her arms is the same one that represented Rosie, the grandchild whom Margaret took/will take from Jackie (the daughter whom in act one, scene seven she plans never to have) to bring up as her own child. The two moments of cradling the sheet (by Margaret at the end of act one, scene six, and by Doris in the next scene) are together the centre of a ripple effect that spreads through the play: an exploration of the yearning and pain the mother experiences in relation to the daughter. In act one, scene five, the audience learns of an important underlying cause of Margaret's need for another child: a miscarriage she suffers when Jackie is nine, a miscarriage furthermore that her mother informs her is the result of her haste in going after a temping job. Jackie's anguish at giving up Rosie is established in scene six. Through her brief role as a single parent, Jackie extends the ripple effect into events preceding the play's action in that she acts as a connection backwards in time to Doris's mother who, it is eventually revealed, was also unmarried. Like the sheet that Margaret and Doris shake and stretch and fold, time is pulled taut, then separate, yet related, moments are placed edge to edge. Sometimes, as when the sheet is jerked from Doris's hands, the smoothness of time is fractured and then, like Doris cradling the sheet, moments of particular significance in the lives of the various women are brought into conjunction.

Time is at its most obviously pliable in act one. The action in act two is continuous and, in act three, apart from the final scene and the wasteground scenes, events occur within chronological time. In the later acts, however, as in the first, the past insistently infiltrates the present. Act two takes place on a wintry day in December 1982 in the Cheadle Hulme house where Doris and Jack have spent their married life. Jack has recently died, but his offstage presence is strongly felt, and the truth about who is Rosie's mother hovers in the interstices of the dialogue waiting to speak itself. At one point, Jackie almost articulates her need to have Rosie back. In a sequence of action that has echoes of the sheet-folding in act one, scene seven, Margaret and Jackie wrap and pack crockery and ornaments, but, though their hands perform related actions, their minds fail to connect and Jackie does not, in the end, bring up the subject of Rosie.

A few moments later, however, the use of an actual sheet in a new way opens up different possibilities of communication between the generations of women. Rosie, who is eleven in act two, comes bursting into the room with a sheet draped over her head, pretending to be a ghost. She and Doris (the youngest and the oldest characters) have been sorting out bedlinen upstairs, and, in the process, Doris has cut holes for eyes in a couple of sheets in order to make ghost costumes for herself and Rosie. This ability to have fun together forms a continuing bond between Rosie and Doris. Later in the play, Rosie moves in with Doris, and, in the penultimate scene, which takes place on Rosie's sixteenth birthday, the old and the young woman sit together in the sunny backyard of Doris's new home, an end-terrace house in Oldham. Rosie has set up a kite-making business, and, at the beginning of the scene, Doris enters holding up the tail of a kite on which she has been working. Rosie meanwhile concentrates on, and eventually succeeds in solving, a Solitaire puzzle that once belonged to Doris's mother. Both women are engaged therefore in occupations that are at once purposeful and playful, the kites additionally connecting the old woman with the world of children, while the Solitaire puzzle links Rosie to the foremother she has never known.

Like the sheets that are used variously by all the characters, the Solitaire puzzle and the kites become imbued with significance, the former acting as a promise that problems are solvable and family herstory contactable without attendant anguish, the latter, through their sky-soaring properties, imaging the possibilities that can exist despite grief and loss. Other stage objects also accrue layers of meaning. When Rosie tips out a jumble of clothes from a binliner in act two, discovering in the process one of her baby dresses, her action recalls Jackie (her mother) sorting through a bag of clothes and holding up the identical dress in act one, scene six after Margaret's exit. The use of a pair of red baby socks at the end of act one similarly evokes Jackie's loss of Rosie. As a baby, Rosie had to hold one of her red socks in order to get to sleep, and, when Margaret left with Rosie, she took one sock with her, while Jackie kept the other. The final scene of act one, which takes place on Rosie's eighth birthday, begins with Rosie burying, in a tub of earth, a doll that belonged originally to Margaret, when she was a little girl. She is doing this out of a sense of anger that she feels towards Margaret, whom she believes to be her mother, but she is also conscious of an animosity she doesn't understand towards Jackie. At the end of the act, Jackie digs up the doll and discovers that it is wearing a red sock. She take the sock's twin from her pocket and puts it on the doll's other foot. As the lights fade, she lifts the doll tenderly to her cheek in memory of the baby she lost.

The doll that Rosie buries in the final scene of act one makes its initial appearance in the second scene of the play, which takes place at Christmas time in 1940. The setting for this scene is created by a baby grand piano, underneath which Doris has made a bed for Margaret as some protection against falling bombs, and on top of which stands the only Christmas decoration, 'a vase of white, wax Christmas roses with a red bow' (ibid.: 3). Scentless and lifeless, these roses connect both with real flowers in the play and also with Margaret's dying search for a desired garden. In act two Rosie brings in from Doris's garden a frozen flower that the author specifically likens to the wax flowers in act one, scene two, thus linking events in the wartime Christmas of 1940 with others in the same house that Doris is leaving forty-two years later. It is Margaret who names the dead flower Rosie finds as a Christmas rose, and it is Margaret who, in her bed beneath the piano in 1940, is most closely connected with the wax roses. Though this is only hinted at in act two, Margaret is suffering from cancer. Five years later she dies, and in her death scene (act three, scene four) the icy coldness that has been connected with the two versions of the Christmas rose is contrasted with the fertility that flowers usually represent.

Act three, scene four consists of a monologue spoken by Margaret, who, under anaesthetic, has become attenuated, almost substanceless, simply 'a voice'. The setting is not a room or a garden, as is generally the case for the non-wasteground scenes, but an inner space, a place of the mind. A room and a garden form, however, the main subject matter of Margaret's speech. On the brink of death, she journeys mentally through an arctic, barren landscape that is the terrain of her childhood. She is searching for a way into a garden, but can find only a door into a bathroom where, even in summer, a cold wind blows on her bare flesh. This frozen, sterile room is the only place to which she can retreat when she feels the need to cry, but, even here, privacy is impossible because the roar of water rushing down the plughole gives her hiding place away. Margaret contrasts the cold, comfortless room (frozen and life-denying as the Christmas roses) with the garden to which she is seeking entrance, and the fact that the garden represents the desired, but never achieved, loving childhood relationship with her mother is suggested by the pattern of thought at the end of the speech. Her parents' names, Margaret explains, are 'Guilt and Duty'. By contrast, when she grows up and has children, she will call them 'Sugar and Spice'. She 'will give them everything they want, and they will love' her (ibid.: 46). Her own desperate need to receive reassurance and love is revealed by the repetition of a question she asked in 1940 when, after settling her under the piano, her mother began to leave the room where Margaret would then be alone for the night. Fearful of the bombs, against which she realised the piano would be little protection, Margaret asked, 'Mummy . . . What happens when you die?' (ibid.: 6). Her echoing of this query near the end of her death speech is followed by a final reference to the longed-for garden. If only she could find it! Surely she will if she 'just keep[s on] going' (ibid.: 47).

As Margaret speaks these words, the lights fade and the sound of first a baby and then a child crying is heard. The end of act three, scene four evokes therefore a number of earlier images: the adult Margaret nursing baby Rosie; Margaret's own needy childhood self; her dying quest for the garden of the mother; and the 1951 garden in which she and Doris folded a sheet together, while remaining emotionally apart, and Doris then lovingly cradled the sheet as though it were a baby. Within a few seconds of stage time other, yet related, moments are simultaneously given life.

Though the sound of the crying child suggests that Margaret does not find her way into the imagined garden, an earlier scene (act three, scene one) depicts a coming together of Margaret's adult self and Doris within a garden setting. This scene takes place in the backyard of Doris's Oldham terrace house. Doris and Margaret are planting geraniums together, and the first part of the scene follows the established pattern whereby the women work jointly on a task while mentally following their separate concerns. Doris, however, realises that something is worrying Margaret and eventually gently elicits from her the information that her husband has left her. In her turn, Doris offers confidences of her own – the fact that Jack stopped 'wanting' her many years previously, and a memory of her father who, briefly and disturbingly, made an incursion into her childhood life. She remembers the disfiguring marks on her mother's body when she took a bath in front of the fire and how her mother explained that these were caused by Doris's father who 'loved her so much he hugged her too tight' (ibid.: 40). The reality – that these marks were the result of beatings – remains unspoken, but this long-ago pain connects with the unhappiness the two onstage women have experienced. Doris asks Margaret to come with her into the house so that she can give her a photograph of the grandmother she never knew, and the two women exit arm in arm. Along with other scenes it invokes, therefore, Margaret's death scene also has echoes of the loving contact mother and daughter make in act three, scene one. Though Margaret fails to find her way into the childhood garden, other loving encounters have proved possible.

In all the mother–daughter relationships in the play love exists alongside frustration and anger: each of these emotions is inter-woven so tightly that it is frequently difficult to separate them out. Unkindness does not preclude tenderness but co-exists, and is often infused, with it. The character who has most diffi-culty in expressing her anger – and perhaps also her love – towards her mother is Jackie. But though this is true of the scenes that take place in the more naturalistic environments, in the wasteground things are different. At once secret and childhood-linked, the wasteground is Other than the neater, more contained room and garden settings. In the wasteground Jackie's usually suppressed anger towards the mother who took Rosie from her is given form. In act three, scene three, which takes place in near darkness so that the audience sees only 'the glint of faces and hands' (ibid.: 45), Jackie casts a magic spell that will make her mother 'die and rot'. Worms will enter her nose and wriggle out through her eyeballs.

This scene is followed by Margaret's death speech, but in act three, scene six (the last of the wasteground scenes) Margaret and Jackie are reconciled. The wasteground functions as a magic space in which otherwise unexpressed desires can be articulated and transformations enacted. Here, Jackie has expressed the bitterness of her anger towards Margaret, and here too, fittingly, the breach between mother and daughter is healed. Margaret reassures an anxious Jackie, telling her that the spell she at-tempted to cast didn't work after all. Then, in words that link with Enid's mother's 'secret places' in *Leave Taking*, she offers to take Jackie to her 'secret, secret hide' (ibid.: 49). In the waste-ground, therefore, Margaret, who, in her death speech, failed to find the sanctuary she sought, shares with Jackie her secret place of safety. The fact that the children in the wasteground scenes are played by adults extends Margaret's and Jackie's reconciliation beyond the world of childhood. It is the figure of an adult woman who reassures, and offers to share what is precious to her, and the figure of another adult woman who takes her hand and accepts her offering.

The final scene, which is chronologically the earliest one, takes place on a May day in 1923. Doris, whose scene this is, is a young woman. She enters breathlessly. 'Mother! Mother?' she calls excitedly. 'Oh, what do you think! It's happened, happened to me!' (ibid.: 52). The 'it' that has 'happened' is that Jack has asked her to be his wife. As the lights fade at the end of her speech, Doris exclaims jubilantly, 'Oh Mother, I'm so happy. SO HAPPY! I suppose, really and truly, this is the beginning of my life!' (ibid.: 53, original emphasis). The fact that Doris's eventual life with Jack was not very happy does not negate the value of her belief in the possibility of happiness: one effect of the play's meshing of past and present is to give equal validity to different points in time. At the play's end, Doris is both an old woman with a long life behind her and a young woman at the beginning of her adult journey. Additionally, the placing of the play's chronologically earliest event as the culminating point of its action, plus the fact that Doris addresses this final speech to her (unseen) mother (parts of whose story have gradually been made known to the audience), extend the pain and love and yearning that characterise *My Mother Said I Never Should* further back into time. The thresholds the four women reach, the choices they make, are revealed as part of a fabric that knits together their lives with those of their foremothers. Decisions made in the course of the play, opportunities lost – and found – are seen to be haunted by earlier choices and longings in the lives of women who are both other than, and yet integrally connected to, Jackie, Margaret, Doris and Rosie.

Like *My Mother Said I Never Should*, April De Angelis's *Iron-mistress*, a play for two actresses and three characters that was first performed by Resisters Theatre Company at the Young Vic Theatre Studio, London, in January 1989, is haunted by the lives of other women – in this case women marginalised and abandoned by mid-nineteenth-century industrial 'progress'. In contrast to *My Mother Said*, one of these women, a character called Shanny Pinns, physically invades and fundamentally affects the action. The other two characters in the play are Martha Darby, who has taken control of her husband's ironworks after his death, and her daughter Little Cog, so named, by her father, because to him she was the 'sweetest . . . littlest cog in his machine' (De Angelis 1990: 5). It is Little Cog who at certain points in the play transforms herself into the accusatory, sub-versive figure of Shanny Pinns, thus establishing a vital connec-tion between the daughter of the wealthy Martha Darby and the despised woman whose only home is a windy hillside, and who scrapes a living by washing the ironstone that feeds the furnaces and by selling herself to men.

Through her enactment by Little Cog, Shanny Pinns becomes a kind of unacknowledged daughter of Martha Darby, somewhat reminiscent therefore of Angie, the rejected daughter figure in Caryl Churchill's 1980 play, *Top Girls*. Martha resembles Mar-lene, the successful Thatcherite businesswoman who is Angie's mother in Churchill's play, for, like Marlene, she is a top girl. The inspiration for *Ironmistress*, April De Angelis writes in her After-word to the play, came to her when she read about a 'Sarah Darby who had inherited her brother's ironworks at Coalbrook-dale in the early nineteenth century'. What were the 'implica-tions', she wondered, of such a woman having 'power in a "man's world" . . . [particularly] for the women around her?' (ibid.: 28). In her determination to hold fast to the power that control of her ironworks affords her, Martha turns her back on the neediness of Shanny Pinns, who becomes, in her turn, a suppressed, yet anarchic, force that constantly threatens to dis-rupt Martha's world.

Shanny Pinns is further linked to ironmistress Martha Darby because she was used to create the mould for an iron statue of a woman. One cold night, men pressed the body of Shanny Pinns down into the muddy earth. Then, into the imprint her body had left, they poured molten iron which later solidified. 'Like lovers', the men polished and cared for it. Abraham Darby attempted literally to behave like a lover. Hearing sounds that she couldn't account for one night, Martha crept downstairs to find her husband trying to consummate his passion for the substance he manufactured and traded in by copulating with the statue – his ironmistress. Martha's connection with the statue is emphasised by her initial description in the stage directions as 'frozen and statuelike' (ibid.: 3). Additionally, though she owns the iron-works after Abraham's death, she is not a master of iron, but a mistress (with all the word's problematic connotations). In a variety of ways she and Shanny Pinns, from whose muddy imprint the iron woman was fashioned, are kin.

Little Cog is also connected to the statue, partly through her enactment of Shanny Pinns and partly through the fact that she narrates the story of the statue's creation. The Resisters' production of *Ironmistress* emphasised the link between the statue, Little Cog and Shanny Pinns through their use of the shadow of the actress who played Little Cog and Shanny Pinns (Louise Waddington) cast on to a sheet of corrugated iron to create the statue. A further effect of this decision, April De Angelis writes, was to locate the statue within 'the partial world of fantasy' (ibid.), thus underlining the play's often dreamlike quality. Like the wasteground in *My Mother Said*, the setting for *Ironmistress* is an amorphous, yet potent, space where transformations can occur. The home of Martha Darby merges into the furnace of the ironworks and into the nearby hillside which is the terrain first of Shanny Pinns and, later, also of Little Cog, the sound of wind mingling with the roar of the furnace. Darkness rapidly alternates with light, and shadows assist the process of transformation. It is from the half-world of shadows that presses in on the central area of light that Little Cog first enters when she dons the work boots and shawl of Shanny Pinns.

Ironmistress begins on the eve of Little Cog's wedding, as Martha instructs her daughter in the decorous arts of a Victorian wife – arts which Martha herself has rejected. Alone on stage near the beginning of the play, Martha studies a small portrait of her dead husband. 'I'm not rubbing you out,' she tells her husband's image, 'I'm only dusting, darling' (ibid.). But Abraham Darby *is* rubbed out, cancelled, deep underground in an iron coffin. When her husband first died Martha sat watching the rain stream down the windowpanes and thought of the coffin sinking deeper and deeper into the mud. Then a different thought came to her. She realised that there was no new ironmaster to take her husband's place. There was only herself, and so there was nothing for it but to do her duty and accept the burden that had been laid upon her. Rapidly, the burden became a source of pleasure as she discovered the joys of being a business woman. Martha had always longed to enter the masculine world of authority and power. As a little girl, she would creep into the room where her father did his accounts and get her hands all covered with ink from his quill pen. She was scolded for this, and the pen was confiscated, but she sneaked back later and swallowed it so that no-one could take it away from her ever again.

Martha swallowed the pen, and other things, because she had herself been swallowed. Throughout her childhood, it seemed to her as though she were a prisoner in a keyless box that engulfed her like a stomach. Marriage simply strengthened this sense of entombment. Her experience of childbirth was of terror and obliteration. She knew the baby was coming from inside her, but not from which part of her. Her body was not her own, but, instead, an alien machine that was switched on by others when the time came for the baby to be born. Once she became the ironmistress, she was determined to mould herself from the substance in which she traded. An iron woman, she gloried in her connection with 'the perfect machine', the 'market' 'where everything in the world is bought and sold' (ibid.: 6). Iron became her model for transactions between human beings, for these, she believed, should be 'Grey and free of feeling' (ibid.: 22).

Little Cog comes, however, to different conclusions about the nature of iron and the value of machines. When Martha visits her after she is married, Little Cog draws her mother's attention to the iron gates that imprison her within her husband's home. In horrifying terms, she describes her husband's use of her, on her wedding night, as though she were a machine, a 'bad machine' that was difficult to start. The pain and fear she experienced she expresses through imagery of the furnace and of molten iron. She was 'in a dark place', she tells Martha, 'Amongst the furnace ash / Where things burn in the dark', and inside her was a burning sensation as though she was filled with hot metal. When her husband had finished, there was blood, red like 'melted iron' on her nightdress, and 'Bright' between her legs. This pleased her husband, and Little Cog concluded that, as a machine, she 'must have worked' (ibid.: 23).

Little Cog as sexual machine resembles Martha, the childbirth machine whose knobs and levers were pressed by hands other than her own, but whereas Martha's response was to wish to become a master and control the greatest machine of all, Little Cog's experience leads her to ally herself more closely with Shanny Pinns. Shanny longed to escape from the freezing hillside that was her home, and the hand-numbing water in which she washed the ironstone. She asked Martha to allow her to work in the fiery heat where machines stretched and shaped the metal, and, when Martha refused this request and sacked her because she wouldn't go on washing the stones, Shanny vowed that if she starved to death she would come back as a ghost and haunt Martha. In addition to a ghost, Shanny cast herself, in her desires, in the role of witch. Desperate for warmth, she dreamed of dropping down the chimney of the ironworks into the middle of the furnace, where, witchlike, she would burn. Little Cog's wedding-night experience is of a searing, furnace-like heat that comes close to burning her up. She survives, however, and takes on something of the anarchic power of the witch to whom Shanny likened herself. Using this witch-power, Little Cog enters into verbal battle with Martha as to which of them will tell the end of Shanny Pinns's story, and so decide her fate.

For the last time, Little Cog puts on Shanny's clothes and, as she does so, Martha tells her that she can't create the image of Shanny Pinns anymore because Shanny Pinns is dead: 'she starved on the hill' (ibid.). When Little Cog refuses to accept this ending, Martha provides others. Shanny, she says, rotted to death from the pox, or, in a story that an anguished Little Cog almost accepts, was shot by soldiers as she took part in a food riot. When she hears this ending, Little Cog whispers 'No' and drops her head, but then she rallies, looks up and claims that the soldier missed, or shot himself by mistake. It was his body that Martha saw fall and mistook for that of Shanny Pinns. 'And then . . . What?' Martha asks. There could be no future for Shanny Pinns. What was she, after all? Only a 'ghost on a hill' (ibid.: 24), a piece of the machine that didn't fit.

It seems as though the final words have been spoken regarding Shanny Pinns but, suddenly, Little Cog finds the answer she has been seeking. Near the beginning of the play, as she explained the operations of the market, Martha laced Little Cog tightly into a corset. Little Cog tried to escape from the constriction of the corset, and of Martha's concept of freedom, by pretending to be a powerful horse, a mare named Alf that galloped at enormous speed. Martha vetoed this game, but, in her search for an alternative ending to Shanny Pinns's story, Little Cog revives Alf and, in imagination, places Shanny on her back in the guise of a highwayman. The lighting changes to represent a dark, stormy night, and Little Cog tells and performs the story of daredevil Shanny Pinns who holds up the coach in which Martha is travelling, robs her of money and jewels whilst laughing 'evilly' and 'piratically', then leaps on to the back of the 'faithful Alf' and gallops off into the darkness.

Through her translation of Shanny Pinns into highwayman, Little Cog transforms Shanny's life, at least in imagination, from one of helpless privation to a tale of heroic daring and rebellion. Shanny as female highwayman on her valiant mare also provides an alternative possibility to the ghost and the witch – the only subversive role-models Shanny could envisage for herself. At the end of the play Little Cog, speaking now also as Shanny Pinns, tells a further story that links with, and comments on, the opening speech that is spoken by Little Cog alone. *Ironmistress* begins with Little Cog staring down at the ironworks and telling the story of how Deadman's Hill, on which she is standing, got its name. A dead soldier was found there once, she explains. She found him. He'd been shot in the face and he had no nose. He was covered in rusty blood and his arms were twisted in a strange way, as if he were dancing. The dead man had returned to the place where the bullet that shot him was made. The play's final story is set over a hundred years in the future. In this story, a girl walks on the hill and is haunted by its past. She sees a 'metal woman' (reminiscent of the iron statue) 'Lying in the earth / With one arm stretched out,' as though she were 'asking for something' (ibid.: 27). Birds are wheeling and swooping around the girl and she watches them with pleasure and wonders how they are made. The story of the dead soldier comes into her mind and the fear that he will grab hold of her arm and hold her fast causes her heart to beat in her ribcage like a bird struggling frantically for freedom. One day, on the hillside, she discovers an answer to what the metal woman's hand is reaching out for, and an alternative function for the machines that made the bullet with which the soldier was killed. This answer has been around her all the time, in the sky above the hillside, and within her own body when the desperate 'bird' trapped inside her attempted to get free. At her feet, she finds a bird's wing which she takes apart, cleans and reassembles. She delights in the skill and beauty of the 'machine' she has discovered and realises that it is the model from which she dreams of building, one day, 'a metal bird machine' that will fly 'in the sky' and give 'people lifts' (ibid.).

In her highwayman story Little Cog reinvents Shanny Pinns and in the final story Little Cog and Shanny Pinns together imagine future innovations, both in the making of machines and of possibilities in people's lives. The Little Cog/Shanny Pinns story also transforms the hill from a place of death to one of life and freedom. From the hillside, the inventors will one day watch their bird machine rise into the sky. As the hill forms their imagined launching pad, so *Ironmistress* acts as mine into the following two chapters. *Ironmistress* is a mother/daughter play, a play about 'related lives', but, like the plays discussed in my fourth chapter, it is also a play about the retelling of stories. Shanny Pinns and Little Cog provide the additional service of leading me into my next chapter, the former as a subversive, disorderly woman, Little Cog through her identification with that subversiveness, and both characters by way of their roles, at the end of *Ironmistress*, as time-travellers into a future where their capacity for invention will have greater scope.

3

TIME-TRAVELLERS AND
DISORDERLY WOMEN

In *A History of Their Own: Women in Europe from Prehistory to the Present: Volume One*, Bonnie S. Anderson and Judith P. Zinsser quote a handful of exquisitely lovely, yet deeply disturbing, lines from a Celtic lyric in which the imagined speaker, Eve, describes what the world would have been like if she had not picked the apple. 'There would', she says, 'be no ice glazing ground . . . no glistening windswept winter . . . no hell . . . no sorrow . . . no fear, were it not for me' (Anderson and Zinsser 1990: 335).

Given the desolation conjured up by these words, it is hardly surprising that so many of Eve's female descendants down the ages eschewed her rebellious example and did their best to accept the passive, subservient role a patriarchal culture enjoined on them. This is not of course to say that they all succeeded, while some, the active, disorderly women who kept escaping from their allotted place, were determined not to try. Yet so many past women's voices were muted, their lives, in Sheila Rowbotham's memorable phrase, 'hidden from history' – in the case of poor women, doubly hidden, by reasons of class as well as gender. The names and stories of a few women who, by an accident of history, found themselves in positions of power have come down to us, but, for the most part, the rest are lost in silence. Even those women who, against all the odds, managed to establish a public voice for themselves through the medium of print were usually quickly forgotten, particularly when they were transgressors in the more public, male-dominated world of theatre rather than remaining within the private, domestic space of the novel. So, until fairly recently, such names as Catherine Trotter, Mary Pix, Delarivier Manley, Susannah Centlivre (even, perhaps, Aphra Behn), Elizabeth Baker, Cecily Hamilton, Elizabeth Robins and Githa Sowerby had slipped from view. An important aspect of feminist scholarship has been its unearthing of writers well known in their day, but whose mouths had long been stopped by the dust of neglect. Feminist historians have likewise worked to piece together the few remaining fragments of women's hidden lives, those lives the pattern of which, in Virginia Woolf's words, is 'locked in old diaries, stuffed away in old drawers' (Woolf 1966: 141).

From the early years of the twentieth century women's herstories have formed the subject matter of a good number of plays by female writers. Early-twentieth-century plays of this kind celebrated chiefly the invigorating and empowering example of the few women from the past whose names were still relatively well known. Cicely Hamilton's *A Pageant of Great Women*, for example, first performed in 1909, had a cast list of nearly fifty that included writers, painters, actresses, queens, saints and other assorted heroines. Clemence Dane's *Wild Decembers* (a play about the Brontës) and Gordon Daviot's *Mary Queen of Scots* were just two of a number of between-the-wars plays on the subject of famous women. More recently, women playwrights have widened the focus of their enquiry into the past, to include dramatic studies of 'ordinary' women's lives in addition to the better recorded narratives of their more famous sisters. A list of recent plays about historical women would include a number by writers, other examples of whose work are discussed in these pages: Liz Lochhead's *Mary Queen of Scots Got Her Head Chopped Off* (1987), Sheila Yeger's *Self Portrait* (1987, about Gwen John), Winsome Pinnock's *A Rock in Water* (1989, about Claudia Jones, the woman credited with having started the Notting Hill Carnivals), April De Angelis's *Crux* (1990, centring around the life of Marguarite Porete, the thirteenth-century advocate of the Doctrine of the Free Spirit who was burnt at the stake), and Sarah Daniels's *The Gut Girls* (1988), which explores the lives of women slaughterhouse workers in late-Victorian Deptford.

Actual, or imagined, narratives of real or fictional women from the past jostle against each other in so many contemporary plays by female writers, their stories spilling out from the equivalent of Virginia Woolf's 'diaries' and 'drawers', that it was difficult to decide which plays to focus on in this chapter. Eventually, however, the voices from five remained with me especially distinctly, either because of the clamour they set up within my mind or because I found them particularly haunting. In the latter category are the characters from Sue Glover's *Bondagers* (1991), who step out of the misty obscurity of a Scottish Border farm of the 1860s wearing the full petticoats, the boots or clogs, the 'head-hankies' (kerchiefs that covered the head and could be tied over the chin or lower face as protection from dirt and dust), and the black straw bonnets with red trimmings, to tell the stories of the griefs and pleasures that interlaced their daily toil. Cheryl Robson's *The Taking of Liberty* (1990) hooked me with its opening lines, addressed directly to the audience: 'While you've a voice, you can speak / You can make yourself heard' (Robson 1991: 224). *The Taking of Liberty* is based on real events that happened during the French Revolution. The women characters begin by accepting their ascribed, gender-defined roles, but later they institute their own revolution, speaking out against their marginalisation and working towards a more truly free society. Marie, Agathe, Jeanne and Catherine in *The Taking of Liberty* become representatives of the subversive figures Anderson and Zinsser describe in *A History of Their Own*, 'Women out to place, women unchecked, [embodiments of] disorder' (ibid.: 257). A further character, Thérèse, an ex-prostitute turned soldier, is, through her initial profession and her appropriation of male clothes, a doubly transgressive figure.

Cross-dressing features also in Sarah Daniels's *Byrthrite* (1986) and in Shirley Gee's *Warrior* (1989). The female soldier, Jane, is just one of the disorderly, seventeenth-century women in *Byrthrite*. Hannah Snell (1723–92), deserted wife, sailor, combatant on board a man o' war, theatrical performer and denizen of Bedlam, is the central character in *Warrior*. Both a disorderly woman and a time-traveller, Hannah is also woman and 'man', a marginalised, permeable figure, a kind of shaman at the mercy of alternative places and times. Haunted by nightmares of a nuclear future she does not understand, she transmutes her affliction into a battle against war. In her availability to ghosts of the future, Hannah resembles 'daftie' Tottie in *Bondagers*, whose lack of 'normal' intelligence leaves her similarly unprotected against outside forces. The characters in the fifth play, Jackie Kay's *Chiaroscuro* (1986), are also marginalised, this time because they are lesbian and black. Perceived by 'straights', and often by whites, as disorderly, their own search is for the validation of herstories. Reaching into their joint pasts, they hunt words and stories that have been lost. What, they ask, was the name for a woman who loved another woman in Ashanti, in Yoruba, in patois? Naming and narratives are central to *Chiaroscuro*. 'If we should die in the wilderness', the four characters sing near the end of the play, 'let the child that finds us / know our names and stories' (Kay 1987: 80).

Stories and names, of unseen but powerfully felt people and places, are vital threads in the distinctive fabric of *Bondagers*. The setting is Blacksheils, a Border farm of the 1860s, but, within the precision of the play's time and place, other locations are verbally created and stories of unseen characters surround and invade those of the figures on stage. The latter are exclusively women: Liza, the very young bondager hired by the unseen Andra as his co-worker in the fields; Maggie, Andra's wife; Sara and her 'daftie' daughter, Tottie; Jenny, a farm worker who is slightly older than Liza; Ellen, the former farm worker who is now the 'maister's' wife; and, briefly, Bella, a parlour maid, and two (non-speaking) warders from a mental asylum. Photographs of the original production at the Traverse Theatre, Edinburgh, published with the text of the play in *Theatre Scotland* (1993), capture the characteristic costumes of the Bondager women: the stiff skirts that don't quite reach the ground, the shawls and aprons, the high-fronted bonnets and the kerchiefs over the foreheads. Each woman appears separate, locked into her own thoughts, yet the positioning of the various figures suggests their interrelation.

Apart from the Hiring Fair that opens the play, the first act takes place in summer, the second in winter, and the action follows the seasonal activities of the women's lives. Traditionally, the Hiring Fair, where farm workers vied for employment for the next year, was held on the first Monday in February. Each hind (male farm worker) was obliged to engage to bring a female worker (a bondager) to work alongside him in the fields. Sometimes his wife or daughter was able to fulfil this function. Failing this, he had to secure the services of a bondager at the Fair, and, later, lodge her with his family. Hard on the heels of the hiring, came the flitting, with carts 'Bung fu' [full]: beds, bairns, clocks, dressers, grandpas, geraniums' (Glover 1993: 35), everyone desperately hoping that the rain would hold off, so that people and belongings would remain dry. The necessity of abandoning their old homes and moving to new ones each year has made the characters in Sue Glover's play both resilient and somewhat restless, and their frequent flittings have resulted in a lively interest in news and gossip – 'crack' – about the doings on surrounding farms. Ties of affection and memory also link the women with emigrés who have left for Canada: Steenie, Liza's brother and Ellen's (rejected) lover; Patie, Tottie's father, who was 'handfasted' to Sara; Walter Brotherston from Coldstream, who once, for a joke, swapped the bonnets and shawls worn by a group of babies so that the babies all went home with the wrong mothers.

In addition to being her brother's home, Canada exists for Liza as a possible future, a place to which she, too, might emigrate. For Tottie, Canada is the magic country of her father, 'Sas-katch-e-wan', his destination, a whispered talisman that she hopes will protect her from dangers and unkindness. Apart from Canada, the place Tottie is chiefly connected with is the nearby moor she both fears and is drawn to. Once, the maister sent her up there with a message for the herdsman, but a mist came down, obliterating everything: the land, herself, even her voice. Then, in the stillness, she heard, close at hand, the sound of a plough moving through the earth and the voice of a man calling to his beasts. She could smell the oxen, feel them through her feet, but later the herdsman told her: 'Naebody ploughs there, Tottie – the only rigs there are the lang syne rigs. Ye can see the marks still. Hundreds of years old. But ye'll no see ony plooman, and ye'll no see ony plough' (ibid.: 34). The ghostly moorland, Canada, Sas-katch-e-wan, and the various Border farms on which the women have worked, or may work in the future, constitute alternative offstage spaces and realities that press upon and fold into those of the play. Like the marks of the abandoned lang syne rigs, other lives score themselves on the lives around which the play takes shape.

Tottie's experience of the ghostly ploughman, recounted in the form of a story that she tells Maggie's baby to stop it from crying, is just one of the play's many descriptions of offstage events, some past, some present. Liza is attracted by Kello, the ploughman on the Blacksheils farm with his curly hair and his laughter, his way with horses and women and his skill as a dancer. With the economy and precision of a snapshot, Liza verbally captures an image of the dancing Kello. 'Tappity with his clogs – and a kind of singsong he makes all the while – right there in the glaur, at the tweak o' a bonnet' (ibid.). Sara's longer account of the day she travelled with Patie to Greenock, intending to continue on with him to Canada, has a similar vividness and clarity. There was a sudden silence, she remembers, before everyone put up their hands to signify their decision to leave and, in that silence, the sound of a Highland lass singing was heard. Sara was carrying baby Tottie and, when the forest of hands shot up, the baby screamed as never before. The scream stabbed Sara's heart and the milk spurted from her breast. The sound of the girl's singing and of the crying baby, the spurt of her milk, have become for Sara the indelible traces of her decision to remain on the land she loved in spite of her other love for Patie. Together, these events create a narrative that encapsulates and gives repeatable form to memory.

A letter that arrives for Liza from her brother in Canada is also the source of stories, and the other women gather round as she opens it, like children waiting for a storyteller to begin. The major narrative of the letter – Steenie's experiences in Canada – contains within it other narratives: of Donald McPhail with his sixty acres and Walter Brotherston (muddler-up of babies) with his hundred; of ice, big as a house, floating on the lake in winter; and of the Indians with their own stories of a hell composed of snow and ice and of heaven filled with buffalo. Stories such as Tottie's encounter with the mist-enveloped oxen and ploughman, Sara's abortive trip to Greenock and the North American Indians in their frozen hell and buffalo-filled heaven, along with 'crack' and the occasional festivity, such as the 'girn' when the harvest is safely gathered in, are the leaven in the women's daily round of toil. The bondage is an old, seemingly immutable, custom. Though the maister is a favour of progress, he won't put an end to the bondage. Women are a vital part of the farm economy. Who else would work as hard as they do for so little pay?

Though the women complain about the hardness of their lives, they are proud of their skills and the play endorses and celebrates that pride. Liza refuses Jenny's offer to teach her to spin, and so enable her to work inside, because she prefers farm work to the conventional domestic tasks of women. Though she is pleased to be warm and dry in the maister's house, Ellen misses the powerful pleasure she used to feel in her skill at harvest-time. She loved the whisper the corn made when it was ripe for the sickle, the speed and fury of the shearers, herself among them like 'yon Amazon in the Bible' (ibid.: 37).

Maggie and Liza, briefly, criticise the system of bondage, but the character who chiefly disturbs and disrupts the established pattern of the women's lives is Tottie, marked off and separated from this pattern (despite her mother's love for her and the others' tolerance) by her differentness. Tottie wants to be like Liza and Jenny, to dance at the girn and flirt with the men. When Liza stares into a looking-glass by candlelight hoping to see the face of the man she loves, Kello, reflected there, Tottie pleads, unsuccessfully, for a turn and, when Liza laughingly refuses to go to Coldstream with Kello after the girn to be 'married', Tottie goes along instead. The next morning she explains what happened. Kello said Coldstream was too far, so they 'were wed in the rigs. Lift your claes! Woosh!' (ibid.: 38). Tottie is both distressed by what has happened and triumphant, because she believes that she is now married and will have the things a woman gets when she marries: a clock, a dresser, a bed and a baby.

Tottie longs to be married because she sees this as the sign of an adult woman. Though Sara is unmarried, Maggie's marriage problematic, and Liza, who doesn't want bairns, plans to defer marriage for a good time yet, the recurring song the women sing reveals the established basis of their lives: 'Woo'd and married and a' / Kissed and carried awa' / And is no the bride well off / That's woo'd and married and a'' (ibid.: 42). After the first time, Kello wants to have nothing more to do with Tottie. He promises to meet her on the moor, but fails to turn up, and, instead, Tottie finds herself time-travelling – not into the past as she did when she heard the ghostly ploughman, but into the future. In the story that Tottie later tells of this experience, she saw an unknown man who stood in the lang syne rigs, between herself and the sun. 'We don't need you now', he told her. 'We don't need folk', or horses. The man had machines in place of horses, and there was plenty of bread: 'Too much bread' (ibid.: 39). Tottie wasn't afraid, as she was when she heard the ploughman, because, this time, the man wasn't the ghost: she was, and this gave her a sense of power and control.

Unfortunately, it is only as a ghost that Tottie has any power. Her pursuit of Kello ends in a tragedy, which is not staged and which the audience encounters through two stories – two versions of the event: the first told to the maister by the parlour maid, Bella; the second, to the baby, by Tottie. In Bella's version she was on her way past the stable when she heard a noise of shouting. She went into the stable, and saw Kello, lying, all twisted at the bottom of the ladder with blood on his head. Tottie was half-way down the ladder, and Bella heard her say 'it serves yourself right'. She pushed him off the ladder, Bella claims. 'I could tell by her face' (ibid.: 43). In Tottie's story, Bella was up in the chamber at the top of the ladder, making love with Kello. Tottie climbed the ladder and Kello tried to kick her off it, with the result that she, the ladder and Kello fell down to the stable floor. It is Bella's story that is heard and believed. As Tottie tells her version, the two warders creep up on her with a sheet that they plan to wrap around her like a straitjacket. When Tottie realises what they mean to do, she tries to use her narrative gifts to distract them. Backing away, she says, placatingly: 'What fettle? Do you want a story? I'll tell you a story. I'll tell you a story of Jackanory' (ibid.: 44).

While Tottie is being imprisoned in the 'straitjacket', Sara is in the fields trying to work. As the sheet goes round Tottie, Sara feels it on her own body, and, as Tottie desperately cries out 'No', Sara makes the same sound. Though Tottie's mouth is silenced in the mental asylum, Sara, at the end of the play, takes over her narrative voice. 'She would tell me these stories', Sara tells Liza, 'she said they were true'. Then Sara recounts Tottie's premonitory vision of a future in which the bondagers will be ghosts in fields empty of folk or horses, where a whole week's harvesting will be done in a night 'By the light of great lamps' (ibid.). The sense of the ending of a way of life that this conveys is strengthened by the fact that Ellen has just told Sara and Maggie that she and the maister will themselves be obliged to leave because the owner of Blacksheils disapproves of the maister's more progressive policies and has given them notice to quit. The final words of the play are Liza's. The young woman who has insistently asserted that she prefers farm work, despite its back-breaking nature, to the domestic task of spinning asks

Sara, if they find themselves on the same farm after the next hiring, to teach her to spin.

Stories in *Bondagers* connect the characters with a wider community on the surrounding Border farms and in Canada. In addition, through the agency of Tottie, they assert a continuity, albeit a disturbing one, between the lives of the farm workers, their forebears and the future of the land. In *Chiaroscuro*, stories are the means by which the four black women explore and celebrate their roots. Whereas *Bondagers* ends, however, on the edge of a fraying apart of a way of life over which the women have had very little control, *Chiaroscuro* depicts an attempt to take control of, and responsibility for, individual and related futures. Aisha, Beth, Yomi and Opal, the four characters, come from varied backgrounds that form part of the play's exploration of chiaroscuro (light and shade). Near the beginning of the play, each woman recounts the story of her naming. Aisha was named after her grandmother who 'was born in the Himalayas, at dawn', Beth after the great-great-great-great grandmother on her father's side who was taken from Africa to be a slave in America. Beth is 'the name the white people gave her with welts in her black skin'. But Beth, as her namesake explains, 'was one strong woman . . . like Sojourner Truth or Harriet Tubman' (Kay 1987: 59). Yomi, the heterosexual member of the group, is of Nigerian ancestry. She is called after a foremother who was born without a tongue, but who told her own stories through the wonderful pictures she painted. The origin of Opal's name is uncertain. She was brought up in a children's home and doesn't know her parents. To the best of her knowledge, her name was the suggestion of an old nurse who always wore opal earrings. Opal and Beth (who has a white mother) are lighter skinned than the other two women. They are linked, too, by the sexual relationship they establish in the course of the play. At the beginning of the play, Aisha is conscious of the possibility that she may also be gay, but is alarmed by the prospect.

The setting for *Chiaroscuro* is simple: a grey floorcloth, two black, high-backed chairs, two white stools, an old chest and a largely pale grey backdrop created from photographs and pictures of landscapes. The chest, in Jackie Kay's words, functions partly as 'the past' – the repository of various objects that are part of the women's heritage – 'and also as the chest in the human body. In order to breathe, these four women have to get things "off their chest" ' (ibid.: 82). The characters are dressed throughout in all-in-one jumpsuits, black for Yomi and Opal, red for Aisha and Beth. Occasionally, they add other items of clothing over the suits: a red belt, for example, a yellow skirt, colourful African wraps, a white T-shirt. The four characters are all onstage before the entrance of the audience, and the objects – a cushion, a photograph album, an oval-shaped mirror and a black doll – are all spread out on the floor. After an opening piece of music, each woman, seated by her representative object, narrates the story of her origin. Aisha's object is the cushion, which she uses to demonstrate the way in which her grandmother made her entrance into the world. Beth's is the album that contains the photographic record of her childhood: her friends – all white – and her pale 'frightened-looking' mother. Opal's object is the mirror. As a little girl, she was haunted by glass, which seemed to her to be everywhere and to be filled with images of faces that were both herself and Other. Yomi uses the doll, her object, to recreate her birth, when she was cut out of her mother at midnight after a protracted labour. As a little girl, Yomi used to play with the doll, which she called Amanda, until, one day, some white children shouted after her that she didn't have to have 'a darky doll' just because she was a 'darky' herself. In response, Yomi vindictively gave the doll new names: 'Nigger. Wog. Sambo. Dirty doll' (ibid.: 60 and 61). Along with the names that connect them to their foremothers, there are therefore also the abusive, racist epithets that hook the women into a culture they often want to reject, and yet, as Yomi's choice of the white-sounding name, Amanda, for her doll, and the faces of the white girls in Beth's album demonstrate, are also part of. Like Opal, haunted, as a child, by the faces in the glass that seemed to be all around her, they are surrounded by spectral images and names, some of which are empowering, whilst others seek to marginalise and diminish them.

A means of traversing the bewildering landscape of the present, formed as it is by topographies of past heroisms and brutalities, and by continuing injustices and new possibilities, is offered by Opal's attitude to naming. Unlike the other women, Opal's genesis is cloudy, rather like her namestone, and uncertain, but her response is to assert that names are 'chance' entities: butterfly-light, ephemeral structures that can change or take wing. Though the burden of other people's (and their own) inherited prejudices is difficult to shake off, the women eventually learn to play with the light and shade of possibilities, trying out new names, reinventing themselves in the process. As Jackie Kay explains, self-invention is the characters' goal. The play is a repeatable ritual, a journey, partly pleasurable, partly painful, that the women have already gone through and are in the process of going through again. Each of them is 'in flux, reassessing her identity, travelling back into memory and forward into possibility' (ibid.: 82).

Interestingly, it is Yomi, who, throughout the play, has been most certain of her own values, criticising Beth and Opal both for their sexual orientation and for their insistence that they should be termed 'black' rather than 'coloured' or 'half-caste', despite the lightness of their skins, who makes the crucial journey into memory. Yomi has been embarrassed by the relationship between Beth and Opal, expressing surprise that such an entity as a black lesbian even exists. Near the end of *Chiaroscuro*, however, Yomi recalls something her mother once said about a group of Nigerian women, who, though they lived with their husbands, loved each other. To her amazement, her mother had felt that it was a pity the women had to hide their feelings, and couldn't just live together openly. Opal, the woman who was named after a pair of earrings because she had no known foremother whom she could be called after, then sings of the 'nameless ones', the women who love other women. She longs to discover the name – the secret, hidden, empowering name – of such a woman in all the languages of the world. She wonders, too, if her mother is still alive and whether she would like to have a daughter who is lesbian. Would her mother call, know, *her* name?

Memory and past stories offer a partial answer to what the women are searching for, but the present, and through this, the future, must also be rethought and remade. At the end of the play, the objects that signified the women's herstories are redistributed and their meanings alter. This time, Yomi gets the mirror, Aisha the album, Beth the doll and Opal the cushion. Yomi needs to learn to see herself, and the other women, afresh. Aisha, who is afraid of her desires, needs to allow all the separate images, the parts, of herself to be expressed. The doll is an affirmation of Beth's desire for a child; the cushion, signifier of the birth process, represents Opal's need to give birth to, to invent, herself. At the end of the play the characters exit, leaving the four objects in the positions they were in at the beginning. They then re-enter and repeat their actions from the start of the play as the lights fade. The performance will have to be repeated a good many more times before the interplay of light and shade exhausts its possibilities.

In *Chiaroscuro* the characters journey through memory into the past, seeking a life source that will enable them to move into the future. The initial aim of the majority of the women in Cheryl Robson's *The Taking of Liberty* is not to find new ways forward but to return, in a time of turbulence and bloodshed, to the relative stability of the past. The play is loosely based, as its author explains, on actual events that occurred between September 1793 and March 1794 'in Saint-Germain-Laval, a small commune near Lyon, in a deeply conservative region of France which rebelled against the Revolution and fought to keep the institutions of the Monarchy and the Church alive' (Robson 1991: 222). In a time of war, bad harvests, mass executions and general turmoil, the women in the play try to hold fast to the certainty offered them by their religion, in spite of the 'dechristianisation rulings' promulgated by the revolutionary authorities. The play begins with a flash-forward into a future when Agathe, the character whose voice is heard most forcibly in the play, has learned to think and speak for herself. Scene two returns to the past, to the moment that was the genesis of the slow growth of new ways of seeing and thinking. The setting is the market-place in Saint-Germain-Laval during the winter of 1793. Centre stage stands a stone cross on a plinth. Two women, Jeanne and Catherine, are sweeping up autumn leaves and putting them into a brazier. Agathe enters, goes over to the cross and, having brushed away the leaves, puts a little bunch of winter flowers at its base. She then makes the sign of the cross and the other women react anxiously to her dual defiance of the ban on religious observances. They're not allowed to place flowers near the cross anymore, they tell Agathe. The priest has sworn an oath and she will get him into trouble. Jeanne picks up the flowers and Catherine puts them in the brazier to burn.

From the beginning of the play, Agathe is the inhabitant of Saint-Germain-Laval who most clearly rejects the Revolution. In place of the promised new world, all Agathe can see is men who want to destroy. How, she wonders, can 'paradise break out of the belly of this age of killing?' (ibid.: 228). Her rebellion is initially expressed as a desire to return to the past, to the values of her father who made the stone cross and who would never have vowed 'to love Robespierre before God', but an event that occurs almost immediately after she has thrown the flowers on to the brazier acts as an early signpost on the journey she eventually makes into a previously unknown world where women may find ease of movement and freedom of voice. Agathe tells Catherine and Jeanne to stop sweeping up the leaves, to let them rot like the horrors the Revolution has given rise to and that can't be swept away. The two women continue with their task, however, and uncover in the process a fugitive hidden under a pile of the leaves. Marie Lebrun is the wife of a Royalist captain whom the revolutionary forces are engaged in hunting down. Worn out by hunger and terror, she has crawled with her baby under the leaves. When she is discovered, she begs the women to find a new hiding place for herself and to take the child, but the entry of Javogues, Proconsul for the Loire region, and Commissioner Lapalus foils any possibility of aid the women might have been able to give. Jeanne does manage to hide the baby under her shawl, but she is frightened by the men's brutal behaviour and eventually hands it over. By threatening to drop the child into the fire in the brazier, Lapalus terrifies Marie into signing a document that will condemn her friends to the guillotine. When she realises the full horror of what she has done, Marie throws the document, and herself, on to the brazier. As Lapalus drags Marie away, Javogues decrees that the act that she has begun should be completed. They will burn Marie, and, in addition, they will squash any possibility of rebellion in Saint-Germain-Laval by smashing symbols of revolt, notably the cross in the market-place.

Marie's moment of rebellion is abortive: it saves neither herself nor her friends. What it does do, however, is to serve as an example of defiance that will haunt Agathe. When Marie signs the document, Catherine and Jeanne have to support Agathe, who almost faints. After Marie has been taken away, Agathe seeks a means of further connection with her. 'What was her name?' she asks (ibid.: 228) At the end of the scene, she is still trying to find words to express the enormity of what has happened.

'There was a woman here . . .' (ibid.: 229), she begins, but then she falls silent. As yet, there are no words, there is no way through the rotting mounds of leaves that represent the grim, chaotic time in which Agathe finds herself.

Agathe's inarticulacy over Marie's fate will be followed by her finding of a voice in which to express the pain of all women. The name Agathe did not know will give birth to a multiplicity of names. For Jeanne, too, Marie serves as an indication of her future, in that Jeanne will follow Marie in becoming, like her, a ghost, though a ghost who, like Tottie in *Bondagers*, moves backwards and forwards in time. Marie, by contrast, is tied, to the place where her discovery beneath the leaves led to her execution. She is indissolubly connected for ever to everyone there who let her burn. The living Jeanne is also bound by a sense of place, and this is reinforced by her religious beliefs. When the corpse of her soldier brother is delivered to her, she is determined to bury it in consecrated ground, despite the penalties against this. In act one, scene six (immediately after Marie's ghost lays claim to the place that it will haunt for ever) Jeanne is discovered, painstakingly demolishing a wall in the church crypt by the light of a lantern. Through the hole she makes in the wall, the lantern light reveals the ghostly whiteness of bones: her 'people stacked and stored with care. Their limbs and ribs woven together to hold in place for centuries' (ibid.: 242). Jeanne's intention in taking apart the wall is to add her brother's mouldering remains to those of his ancestors, so that he, too, will be held in place for all time, but when she enters as a ghost near the end of the play, it is to articulate and embody an alternative vision to this earlier belief in the rightness of inhabiting one's ascribed place. Jeanne's ghost is wrapped in a large fishing net, which drags behind her as she walks and which is full of bones and bits of women that the world has thrown away as valueless: bound feet from China, genitals cut off in Africa, 'ovaries destroyed in Germany, bodies, burned in India, minds, blanked in America' (ibid.: 266). Jeanne has collected these fragments and now she wanders backwards and forwards in time, seeking a way out for herself and the mutilations she has rescued. A ghost herself, she is haunted by barbarities that, although enacted within individual places and times, interconnect with each other beyond the confines of these specificities. Where Marie's ghost could express only her own suffering, Jeanne's gives form also to that of others. In her dead state she cannot, however, effect the changes that need to be made. This is Agathe's task. Agathe, Jeanne tells her, is able to speak out and sway the crowds. If she uses this talent, people will listen.

Agathe's public voice is first heard in the context of an image that is erected in the market-place as a substitute for the stone cross: a statue of a naked woman dressed in a red bonnet and tricolour sash. In one hand it holds a stone tablet on which the Declaration of Human Rights has been engraved, and in the other a pike, painted red. When it rains, red paint trickles down the statue, collecting in the navel and then running down the legs. The men are first amused by what has happed to the statue and then alarmed and disgusted by the 'obscenity . . . [the] filthy waters that pour from the devil's gateway' (ibid.: 243). For Agathe, Jeanne and Catherine the men's reaction presents a possible means of getting rid of the statue, which they see as a symbol of the iniquities of the Revolution, and they therefore stress the fact that the blood-coloured disfiguring pigment is a sign of God's anger at events in Saint-Germain-Laval. Jeanne explains that God has sent the rain that has caused the statue to be stained blood-red. He is crying out, Catherine warns, for the dead, and Agathe adds: 'Murdered in the name of Liberty' (ibid: 244). When the men decide only to clean the statue, or to hide it away, the women determine to destroy this sign of a spurious liberty. Under cover of fog and darkness, they loosen the statue from its plinth with a crowbar and sledgehammer, then smash it to pieces which they throw in the river. In the subsequent meeting in the Town Hall, organised by the men to elicit what has happened to the statue, Agathe asserts her right to be heard. When will women be allowed to speak? she asks Lapalus who has been addressing them from the podium. When will women get their 'chance to be represented up there? . . . You'd better change or we'll change things for you' (ibid.: 251 and 252).

Alongside her taking of the statue of Liberty, Agathe begins to clarify her sense of her own, and other women's, entitlement to freedom. The character who aids her in this understanding is Thérèse, a once-famous courtesan who fell foul of certain powerful personages and was condemned to rot in prison. Liberated by the Parisian mob when the Revolution began, Thérèse determined to protect herself by dressing as a soldier. In this guise she met, and formed a friendship with, Jeanne's brother, and when he was wounded she dragged him home to Saint-Germain-Laval on a cart. On the way the brother died, but Thérèse continued with her self-imposed task. Though she returns her dead friend to his home, Thérèse advises Agathe to let her own 'dead man', the husband who cares nothing for her, go. What are things like for you in bed at night? Thérèse asks, and Agathe replies that she lies there aching, with, beside her, 'an ocean of room' that can never be filled. Sometimes she finds herself looking down into the river, staring at the ice as it is 'washed downstream' (ibid.: 240). It is winter time and the ice is real ice, but it conjures up, too, the 'ice glazing ground' that, in the Celtic lyric quoted by Anderson and Zinsser (see p. 67), Eve saw as the punishment for her sin. For Agathe, however, the ice that has held her to old ways of seeing and responding melts. Imprisoned after the Town Hall meeting for her part in the statue's destruction, she takes, as her example, not the Eve frozen by a sense of sin, but the Eve who ate the apple. Freedom, she has come to realise, can be gained only by grabbing it, as Eve grabbed hold of the apple.

The character who takes upon herself the role of sinful Eve is Jeanne. Shortly before she dies in the freezing prison cell, Jeanne speaks of herself, and of all women, as beings entrapped in ice. Every night, Jeanne feels the ice growing between her ribs, choking the breath from her body, and this arctic entombment is emblematic for her of all women, for 'Woman was born to serve . . . serve the ice, serve the cold, serve the darkness' (ibid.: 259). After she helped to destroy the statue, Jeanne affirmed her belief in the rightness of what she had done, even though her voice was shaking with fear at what might happen to her, but, in prison, her voice dwindles to a thread as she whispers a prayer for deliverance. As the ice spreads through her body and mind, she tastes ashes in her mouth, remnants perhaps of the burnt body of Marie. Jeanne's ghost, however, is more powerful than Marie's. After her death, Jeanne rejects the silent, subservient role she had come to believe was enjoined on her. Though she is lost in a wilderness from which she can find no way out, Jeanne gives form and voice to age-old, and still continuing, cruelties inflicted on women.

As a ghost, Jeanne rebels against the bondage she came to see as women's lot by deliberately burdening herself with the atrocities enacted on women to confine and silence them. In place of an ice-serving Eve, she becomes a fearsome, Lilith-like figure who will roam the wastes that exist beyond the confines of time. Thérèse, too, inhabits a marginalised wilderness, but in her case this is at the edges of social space, rather than of time. In life, Thérèse takes on something of the demonic, Lilith-like quality Jeanne assumes in death. To the priest, Father Tiquet, who recognises her from her former existence as a prostitute, Thérèse is the 'bloody whore', the living manifestation of the statue that has ousted the symbol of God from the market-place. In act one, scene eight, Tiquet uses this substitution of the 'devil's gateway' for the cross in order to justify his rape of Thérèse, but, though Thérèse lacks the physical strength to prevent his violation of her, it confirms her resolution to strive, through every means available to her, against the culture that has sought to destroy her. It is Thérèse who offers an alternative interpretation of the statue that has been branded an obscenity. What is the statue, after all, she tells the other women, but a huge, potent, naked woman with blood between her thighs. They should rejoice to see this image raised up to public view.

Foiled in her attempt to protect herself from abuse by putting on the clothes of the dominant sex, Thérèse determines to use the statue as her model and become herself a force for revolution. Her ally in this is Cristophe, an ex-slave who once belonged to the nobleman who also originally owned the statue and who, like the statue, has been 'liberated', though in his case all this means is that he is free to wander in the wind and snow seeking food and shelter. In prison, Thérèse refuses to give up her belief that there is some way out of her predicament, and, in the event, she is proved right, because Javogues, who is toppled from power by Lapalus, reacts to his demotion by freeing the prisoners in the hope that they will turn on Lapalus and kill him. The actual agent of Thérèse's (and also Agathe's) delivery from prison is Cristophe, who finds his way into the prison after it has been deserted by the guards, and who is first seen in the cell silhouetted in light like a biblical angel. Thérèse, the embodiment of the statue, the whore, the bloody devil's gateway, and Cristophe, the dark-skinned angel of light, therefore subvert the biblical basis of the patriarchal culture that has used and despised, then forgotten them. At the end of the play, the two of them leave for Cristophe's earlier island home, where Thérèse also once lived with a planter. There, a former slave, a 'black prince', is leading a revolt, and Thérèse and Cristophe plan to join him. They try to persuade Agathe to go with them, but she knows that their dream cannot be hers. The 'hell' inside her would destroy their projected 'heaven within a week' (ibid.: 267).

Though she recognises that the island paradise can never be her country, Agathe, earlier, uses a similar but dreamed landscape to try to woo Jeanne away from her nightmare vision of women trapped in icy darkness. In imagination, Agathe conjures up soft sand and pure, white light glistening against a turquoise sea. Jeanne dies from the cold, however, and Agathe learns what has happened to Catherine in the separate prison in which she has been kept. Pregnant when she was imprisoned, Catherine lost the child and then had to watch in horror as a fear-and-hunger-crazed woman licked its blood up from the floor. Catherine's and Jeanne's experiences become for Agathe the measure of dreams which, for a time, seem to serve only to dazzle the eyes and mind and, in so doing, to blind people to the realities of the chains that confine them.

At the end of the play, Agathe rediscovers her belief in the transformative power of dreams, but in the context of what she has learned from Thérèse and from Jeanne's ghost. From the former she has understood the necessity of fighting if one wants to change things, and, from Jeanne, the interconnection of women, all of whom are 'stitched together', like 'a puzzle of knots'. If one woman 'is murdered for what she believes, we're all violated' (ibid.: 268). Alone now on stage, Agathe leaves her cell, that extreme form of the room in which so many women have been imprisoned, and steps forward into 'blinding whiteness'. The 'guards', including those of 'home, family, duty', and also the security of her 'father's wishes and husband's convictions and God's commandments' (ibid), have gone. The steps she imprints now in the whiteness of the unknown will be new, 'Dangerous . . . Nobody ahead and nothing behind' (ibid). With her, journey all the unseen women – the imprisoned, the hidden, the dispossessed – on whose behalf she will speak out. The village that used to be her home, Saint-Germain-Laval, has twice been renamed by the Revolution. Its name was changed first to Montchalier, then to Montpurifiée. Agathe will seek a new name that will give form to the experiences and yearnings of women. When she begins to speak her words will sparkle and shine, 'and a sigh of pleasure will breathe from the throats of women because their world has finally been named' (ibid).

The Taking of Liberty ends on the edge of possibility as Agathe imprints her feet in virgin snow, journeying towards a future that is still to be made and named. *Warrior* also ends with a female character beginning a quest on behalf of the future, but the task that faces Hannah Snell is very different from that which confronts Agathe. Hannah, alias James Grey, combines elements of Agathe, Thérèse and Jeanne. Like Thérèse, she wears men's clothes. Like Jeanne, she is haunted by the victims of past and future horrors and, like Agathe, she escapes at the end of the play from imprisonment. Hannah's quest, however, is for a means of averting the nuclear disaster (of which she has had premonitions in waking nightmares) of a planet peopled only by white shadows and composed of barren rock over which the wind howls endlessly. Shirley Gee's Hannah is heroine, woman-warrior and visionary. Narrators of Hannah's exploits in her own lifetime concentrated on her heroism, along with firm assertions of the propriety – and chastity – she maintained throughout her exploits. Gee's character is more complex. For one thing, her self-construction as a man presents her with near-insoluble problems as well as benefits. For another, her author, as Gee herself explains, 'has pressed Hannah into [her] service, made her sail [her own] troubled seas' (Gee 1991: xi). The reasons for the historical Hannah's incarceration in Bedlam are unknown, but Gee locates them in the 'seeing' with which she afflicts her character. Her shaping of Hannah's story articulates, in addition to a narrative of female heroism, a twentieth-century 'shadow' and nightmare. At the end of *Warrior* Hannah voyages, not into an unknown and unmade world, like Agathe, but towards a future that will be the outcome of present actions. The task that faces her is the alteration of a possible future nightmare scenario, through the reconstruction of present-day attitudes.

Structurally, *Warrior* consists of a 'giant flashback, bracketed' by scenes set in Bedlam, until Hannah's committal, from which point the play 'continues in a straight line until the end'. The overall pace is swift, one scene flowing continuously into another. 'Naturalism', Shirley Gee writes, 'is not important', 'the style is tuppence coloured and vividness and colour should swirl throughout' (ibid.: xii). The first half of the play chronicles chiefly Hannah's desertion by her husband, Davey, her assumption of men's clothes in order to go in search of him, and her enlistment and experiences aboard a man o' war. In the second act Hannah is on dry land and has of necessity therefore to resume women's clothes. In order to support herself, she teams up with two other ex-members of the ship's crew, Cuttle and Godbolt, to present a theatrical version of her naval exploits. One night, however, when the King is watching the performance with a view to presenting her with a pension at its close, Hannah is overwhelmed by the premonitions that have increasingly troubled her and she loudly denounces the supposed justice and glory of war, calling out the words of a song that have been sung earlier in the play: 'Oh never be as silly as to fight for kings and queens – For none of them is half as good as half a pound of greens.' 'Glory?' she continues. 'It don't amount to a horse's fart' (ibid.: 46). Though she loses her pension, Hannah escapes any worse consequences at this juncture, but, when she and her fellow performers switch to a mind-reading act, in the course of which Hannah prophesies a 'pillar of cloud' that will annihilate history, she is deemed mad and sent to Bedlam.

Hannah is defined as mad because, to her contemporaries, her descriptions of her 'seeings' are incomprehensible. 'Senseless', Godbolt terms them, 'Shadows. Danger from the sky, rain that eats forests, dead seas. Babble' (ibid.: 47). For Hannah, however, her visions are both fearsome *and* enabling. They are a source of dread and, eventually, of her being locked away, but they are also both the dark, yet vital, threads that connect her to the web of time, and, in addition, the impetus that first leads her to lay aside the constrictions of being a woman and assume male disguise. In Hannah's eighteenth-century world women have value only through their relationship to men. When Susan, Hannah's sister-in-law, discovers that Hannah has been deserted by her husband, her response is that Hannah is now nothing, without place or identity. Immediately upon hearing these words, Hannah is overwhelmed by a premonition of Davey's fate. She sees him, standing on the rim of a wide expanse of sea, staring at her with sad eyes. Then, his shadow detaches itself from his body, turns white and is lost beneath the waves. Hannah's response is to go in quest of Davey, to attempt to save him, and, in order to protect herself against the danger of sexual molestation, she disguises herself as a man. It is when she is enquiring about ships on which Davey might have sailed that she is herself persuaded to enlist. Her counterfeit presentation of a man is taken for the real thing, and one of the results of this is that aboard the man o' war Hannah finds, at least to some degree, a place that seems to her worth having. She discovers comradeship there and, though the life is very hard, she develops a pride in her 'seaman's' skills and her ability to survive the harsh discipline of the ship. One part of Hannah identifies with, and rejoices in, her new role as a warrior. Before the first military engagement with the French forces, for example, she asserts her determination to 'fight like thunder' (ibid.: 20), and, in an interpolated scene in the madhouse, she still calls out that the seas belong to Britain, as of 'right'.

Hannah's new identity as a warrior is, however, inherently unstable, because, to the men, war and the weapons with which it is waged are female. Hannah is taught that her musket is her girl that she must oil, polish, wrap in flannel, find in the dark, sleep with. As the French bombardment of the ship begins, Godbolt orders the men to wait for it 'nice and easy. She's coming to us', he tells them. 'Oh, but she's grand. She's coming – STAND HARD AS DOGS' (ibid.: 21, original emphasis). In her warrior role, therefore, Hannah is pitted against herself as a woman. The 'place' she has discovered aboard ship is also difficult to sustain because the men simultaneously view the ship as a refuge and as a source of danger. Like war and its weapons, both the whirling unstructured chaos beneath the ship's planks, and the ship itself, are defined as female – hence the aggressive sexual language the men frequently use in connection with the ship. Their safety depends on something that in their heart of hearts they believe to be part of what threatens them. A real woman on board would underline the ship's insecurity, and would, as Hannah well knows, be first sexually abused, to demonstrate their desired mastery over chaos and death, and then rapidly thrown overboard, to become a feast for the sharks. What remained of her would be left to rot and to return to the structureless darkness of which she was anyway believed to be a part. Hannah's place aboard ship can be maintained only by the successful continuation of her impersonation.

The ambiguity that the ship assumes for the sailors, its dual role as protector and traitorous fellow-conspirator with the sea, fills them with terror. Locked within a rigid set of beliefs and thought patterns, their only response to what they fear is to attack. By contrast, though she searches for the security of a 'place', Hannah, from the start, tolerates the existence of a quality of doubleness within things, the imminence of Otherness. Fearsome though they are, her visions are the incentive that starts her off on her actual and inner journeys. Unlike the men, who fear what protects them, Hannah accepts from the start the necessity of nurturance. She starts on her quest in order to save Davey from the 'white shadow' that waits for him. The link between this shadow and connection with others is stressed when Hannah befriends Cuttle, a simple, gentle man who is being tormented by the other sailors, and Cuttle vows eternal friendship and loyalty to Hannah with the words 'if you'll have me, sir, I'm yours. Bone to bone. Shadow to shadow' (ibid.: 16). This speech is followed by the sound of a wind blowing and a persistent 'throbbing beat'. The mournful, insistent wind and the beat that resembles variously a drum, a clock and a heartbeat are heard, first intermittently, then with increasing frequency in the play. Along with the recurring references to shadows, bones and place, the wind and the beat 'thread' through the play, providing aural confirmation of Hannah's journey towards the future she both fears and increasingly struggles to refashion.

Act one ends with a horrifying evocation of the relationship between the beat and the wind, bones, shadows and place. The final scene of the first half of the play begins with Hannah sitting with three other members of the ship's crew in a cove to which they have been sent to bury the dead from the battle. In the sand is a piece of driftwood that they have dressed in a dead enemy's coat and, from time to time, they idly stone this. In contrast to the rapid, forward impetus of the majority of the play's action, the rhythm here is slow and reflective. The men are drinking from a bottle they pass round between them. Cuttle plays on a whistle. One of their number wanders away and, when he returns, he holds a seashell that he plans to take home for his young son. The other men handle it with delight, commenting on its beauty, and war seems a very long way away. Then Hannah hears, although the others cannot, a distant drum beat, and from this point in the scene the mood begins to change, a mounting sense of horror and panic gradually erasing the meditative feeling of the opening. Cuttle discovers a dead body from an earlier campaign and, believing at first that it must be a British

corpse, they decide to give it an honourable burial. The realisation that the remains stink of garlic leads to a change of mind,
and the corpse changes from that of a 'true Britisher' to that of a
'Frog', a 'foreign buggeroo'. It should therefore be 'hanged like
a dog' (ibid.: 28 and 29).

As she had earlier protected Cuttle, Hannah now defends the
body's rights to a decent burial. Nationality is unimportant, she
insists. British or French, he was a man. The same wind blows on
us all. Awed by her determination, the men begin to dig a grave,
but Hannah stops them. The ground at that point, she tells them,
is already choked with bodies. The men move to another place,
then another, and yet another, but everywhere Hannah senses
the presence of death. The earth is full of white shadows from
the future, clustering so thickly that there is no place free for the
existing dead. In terror, the men point out possible burial sites.
Here? they ask. Here, here? But each time Hannah answers 'no'.
'For Christ's immortal sake, then, where?' Cuttle pleads, and
Hannah cries out in desperation, 'There's nowhere. Nowhere.
NOWHERE' (ibid.: 30, original emphasis). Her words are followed by darkness, in which the beat can be heard strongly, and
the sound of wind howling. The wind that blows alike on the
British and the French blows equally also on the present and the
future. Beyond time, it howls over a void, seeking time's
obliteration.

Though Hannah is frequently disoriented, unplaced, to Cuttle
she represents always a fixed point, even when he doesn't know
what name to give to that point. When Hannah is wounded in
the groin, she insists that Cuttle should cut the shot out for her
so that the doctor won't find out her true sex. Cuttle's response
to his discovery of her identity, 'But you're a woman, sir' (ibid.:
24), encapsulates his dilemma, while, at the same time, pointing
to what is for him a solution. Though Hannah is a woman, he will
continue to accord her the respect due to a man and a superior
officer. Even though he is almost overwhelmed with anxiety by
Hannah's inability to find a place to bury the dead soldier, he still
looks to her as the only person capable of finding a way out of
this dilemma. Cuttle is Hannah's comrade, and also her disciple.
He insists on accompanying her on the mission she starts out on
at the end of the play, despite Hannah's objection that he doesn't
believe what she believes. He'll learn, he promises. He feels 'like

a crusader', and though he's not sure yet what he's 'crusading about', he'll 'soon get the hang of it' (ibid.: 60).

The relationship between Hannah and Godbolt, the third member of the theatrical trio that is formed in the second half of the play, is less straightforward. Godbolt, Sergeant of Marines, is an excellent soldier, but a complex, difficult man. Like Cuttle, Godbolt reacts to the discovery that Hannah is a woman by attempting to retain the fiction that she is a man, but his feelings are complicated by the unexpressed but powerful sexual magnetism that exists between himself and Hannah, and by his own imprisonment within a rigidified sense of his, and Hannah's, place within the hierarchical order. King and Country have been the reference points by which Godbolt has set his life's compass. Aboard ship, he drilled Hannah into a sailor and a soldier, and it is he who suggests that they should continue to enact this transformation before a paying public when their sailing days are over. Hannah's outburst in front of the King fills him with a sense of shame. 'I made you', he tells Hannah, 'steeled you, kept you in best order. For all you're a woman, I thought you was my man' (ibid.: 48). His further suggestion that they should substitute a mind-reading act for their military performance is subconsciously motivated partly by a desire to contain Hannah within an assigned place. In the course of the act he draws a chalk circle around her and tells the audience that she will remain in this spot, 'fixed precisely half-way between Heaven and the Hereafter' (ibid.: 50). This designation of Hannah's place points, however, not to fixity but to fluidity. Half-way between Heaven and the Hereafter is not a precise point of definition. Hannah's role as time-traveller also negates any easily definable relationship between herself and place.

On the eve of Hannah's removal to a part of the madhouse set aside for confirmed lunatics, who are chained down like wild animals, Godbolt breaks in and rescues her, but he is unable to free himself from established ways of seeing. If she will give up her foolish stories of 'Some cannon-ball headed our way that'll drive the earth out of its orbit round the sun' (ibid.: 59), he will go with her, he promises, anywhere that she wishes. When Hannah counters his offer with the suggestion that their life together be predicated on Godbolt's leaving behind the obsolete values that confine him, Godbolt replies that she marches alone, as does he. He cannot accompany her into the unchartered regions to which her voyaging will take her.

Hannah's rescue by Godbolt is preceded by her rejection of medical attempts to cure her of her 'delusions'. The madhouse doctor, Dr Kemp, is a caring, moderate man who genuinely believes that Hannah's only salvation lies in her accepting the fact that the sights that press in on her are the product of her own imagination. The end of the world, he tells her, is a common fantasy among lunatics. It is impossible that a single weapon could destroy a city or that shadows could be white. Bones cannot speak. 'All's well with God's world' (ibid.: 56), and Hannah must accept this fact if she wishes to return to the world. The alternative is life imprisonment among men and women so debased that they try to destroy both their companions and themselves, to the extent of tearing at, and eating, their own flesh. As all other forms of treatment that have been used on Hannah have failed, Dr Kemp places his hopes of recovery on a contraption called the swing, a large, heavy structure resembling a see-saw. At one end there is a weight, and at the other a chair to which the patient is strapped. When the swing is in motion, the patient is jolted high up into the air, and down again, with a terrifying velocity. The resulting nausea and dizziness are so dreadful that the patient is (theoretically at least) unable to concentrate on her 'hallucinations'. For Hannah, however, the sickening disorientation the swing causes leads to an intensification of her visions, and, though initially her terror causes her to recant, a few moments later she reaffirms the truth of her 'seeings'. Perched high on the swing, as she is flung repeatedly into the air, she grasps the totality of the obliteration that is to come: first, 'Heat like light', and then the erasure of place and time – dead sea, dead moon – and 'On the rim, nothing. No history. No moments. Nothing. And the stars fall' (ibid.: 54 and 55). The annihilation of the future entails the cancellation of the past. In the nadir of nothingness that is to come, memory is wiped out as though human lives had never been lived.

After her rescue from prison, Hannah's quest clarifies itself as a rewriting of the future that is, at the same time, a retention of the past in the form of 'moments'. To Godbolt's questioning of what she means by moments, she replies that a 'chain of moments' is what our lives consist of: the smell of morning, a baby's hand closing on one's fingers, a breeze lifting the blossom. If we lose these, we can never be forgiven because there will be no-one 'left to forgive us' (ibid.: 59).

Hannah's exit from the prison, along with that of Cuttle and Godbolt, is presented through the use of a lighting effect that creates the illusion of water. The three of them dive and swim through the fluidity of water until, gradually, the lighting changes so that it represents sea and sky. Then, the setting becomes a quayside and Hannah and Cuttle are in a small sailing boat. A 'good wind' is blowing and Cuttle, who, for the first time, calls Hannah 'ma'am' rather than 'sir', tells her that this wind will blow her words around the world. On the rim of the world, Hannah can see a faint star which will serve as the guide by which she will steer her course. The star is the one essential fixed point in the fluid, changing, and therefore changeable, world into which she will journey. So long as its steady beacon of light remains, so, too, do the future and the past. 'Hold to the star, Hannah', Godbolt admonishes (ibid.: 61), and Hannah promises that she will, so that everyday, human moments and lives can continue to succeed each other. It is close to midnight, nuclear as well as diurnal, when Hannah and Cuttle sail. The play ends on the rim of loss, and of hope. The star is shining brightly and in the distance a wind can be heard. Whether the wind will remain the good wind that blows Hannah's message around the world or the nuclear wind that will moan over the dead planet only time can tell, and time is precisely the entity that Hannah has set out to rescue. Should she fail, time itself will fall into an abyss.

Agathe in *The Taking of Liberty* and Hannah Snell in *Warrior* are visionary time-travellers, engaged in missions that take them beyond the confines of chronological time. Within the immediacy of stage time, they give expression to an engagement between past and present that has profound implications for the future. Though it has no time-traveller figures in the sense of Agathe and Hannah, *Byrthrite* also explores the effect of the past on the present and the likely implications for the future. The action takes place in Essex during the Civil War, a tumultuous time in English history when great barbarities were committed and, yet, when a far-reaching and potentially beneficent re-structuring of society also seemed possible. Sarah Daniels uses this explosive historical moment as a kind of crucible within which to explore both the oppression and disempowerment of women and, at the same time, their *em*powerment as they begin to articulate their herstories. In addition to the age-old privations women have suffered within all patriarchal cultures, the late sixteenth and early seventeenth centuries were infamous for the number of women who were executed as witches, and this is the fate of some of the characters in *Byrthrite*. Disempowerment in the play arises from the fact that, as Sarah Daniels writes in her Foreword, the seventeenth century was 'the time when control over women's reproductive processes began to change hands from women to men'. It was a 'changeover' that 'began with the introduction of new technology by male doctors, the use of forceps in childbirth' (Daniels 1991: 331). Seeds of empowerment exist because the chaotic, iconoclastic period of the Civil War was also a time when previously silenced voices, including those of women, were sometimes able to make themselves heard. Within radical religious sects, such as the Quakers, it was possible for women, in the guise of preachers or prophetesses, to disregard St Paul's injunction on female silence and to speak out publicly. In *Byrthrite*, Helen takes on this role, becoming first a Quaker and then a preacher, and using this sanctioned form of public speech to articulate both women's suppression and their rebellion.

A young woman called Rose transgresses still further into the traditional space of men, for Rose is engaged in writing a play that aims, through entertainment, to aid women in their task of self-education. Rose has been taught to read and write by an elderly healer and midwife called Grace who, from the beginning of *Byrthrite*, asserts the importance of the word, both spoken and written. Grace knows that women must not only learn to read and write, but must also acquire skills in the dissemination of the written word. When one of the women claims that printing is a 'curse', Grace explains her mistake. 'Printing is not the curse', she tells her, 'but them who decide what's on the lines' (ibid.: 344). Women must somehow ensure that they have a part in the decision-making process. Rose's play, both in a printed and acted form, will, it is hoped, contribute to the destabilisation of patriarchy.

Taking Rose's projected play as its model, Sarah Daniels's play shows women rejecting the constructions of self that have been foisted on them and restructuring their pasts and futures along with the present. *Byrthrite* begins literally with a birth rite, one that subverts the West's most famous birth story. The child whose birth is celebrated at the beginning of *Byrthrite* is not a boy, like Jesus, but a girl – the daughter of a woman, not the Son of God. In their 'Birthing Song' the women adopt a well-known hymn to their own purposes: 'Unto you a child is born / Unto you a daughter given' (ibid.: 335), and this appropriation of the language of Christian worship continues to reverberate later in the play. In part two, scene two, which is set in a church, the Parson tells his wife (Helen) that he is engaged in writing history, a task for which he informs her, women are unfitted because (a) they can't write, (b) their emotions would get in the way of their intellects even if they could write and (c) 'women don't make history' (ibid.: 381). Shortly after he makes this latter pronouncement, an old woman who is kneeling in the church begins to mutter a mixed-up, only partially remembered version of the Lord's Prayer that begins 'Our father witch chart in heaven' (ibid.: 382), thus neatly subverting the notion of sanctified patriarchal space by placing an 'evil' woman at its heart. The old woman's words suggest, moreover, that, in order to journey through a male-defined heaven, one needs a witch's map as guide. Her words appear to perform a related navigational function for Helen, for it is immediately after the old woman's prayer that Helen announces her conversion to the Quakerism that will subsequently enable her to tailor her 'visions' to the needs of women.

The opening subversive lines of 'The Birthing Song' are followed by an injunction to women to pass on knowledge and skills from one generation to another. 'From this time forth go', the characters sing, 'and to all women tell / That the daughter's inheritance shall pass / Through you all, to be kept forever' (ibid.: 335). The sustaining interconnection of women in the present moment and down the ages is a central concern of the play. Even though some of the women are executed as witches, the remainder refuse to be browbeaten into accepting a marginalised or victim status. The passing on of inheritance is itself subversive, for its aim is to enable women to take control of their lives. The skills that the women hand down are of two kinds: the traditional arts of healing and midwifery, and newly acquired, speech-based skills. An important source of both these areas of expertise is Grace, and Rose, along with another young woman called Ursula, is the chief inheritor of Grace's skills, Rose becoming a carrier of the new forms of knowledge, Ursula of the old. Ursula has learned the healing arts, not from Grace, but from her own mother, who, in the course of the play, is hanged as a witch. Before she dies, the mother implores the daughter to keep her dangerous knowledge a secret. Secrecy comes easily to Ursula as she is dumb, but, towards the end of the play, she reveals her skills when she uses them to cure Grace who has become sick. Through her curing of Grace, Ursula takes over Grace's, and her own mother's, roles as healer.

Ursula and Rose are daughter, or, given their youth and Grace's age, granddaughter figures whose task will be to pass on their inheritance to future generations of women. Though Rose is present in more scenes than is Ursula, her voice is not privileged over the other woman's silence. Indeed, Ursula's 'silence' is anyway notional as she is skilled in a language of signs and gestures. In addition, like Rose, she creates a piece of theatre: not a play, in her case, but a seemingly spontaneous enactment. Ursula's theatre piece records the punishment of a witch-finder by a group of women, an event that has recently occurred in actuality. It is acted out in three different ways – through dumb show (using a dummy of the witch-finder), in sign language, and by means of a taped voice-over – and the fact that all these narrative forms are employed simultaneously means that no single one has precedence over the others. Signed speech and mimed action are accorded equal status with the spoken word. To Grace's earlier insistence on the importance of women's becoming skilled in the use of oral and printed language is added therefore a sense of the need to understand and respect other languages, the language of the Other.

In the context of the multiple nature of language, Rose's play becomes an entity that can be viewed from a number of perspectives. In part two, scene eight, Grace, though expressing admiration for what Rose has achieved, subjects the play to a process of criticism. Her depiction of cunning women 'is too glowing for truth', Grace tells Rose. 'So many have been killed in this purge who didn't know a sprig of dill from a cauliflower.' The reason they were chosen was not that they were 'special' but that 'they were women' (ibid.: 410). Grace stresses the commonality of women, their similarity as the focus of male violence. For Rose, however, 'the condemned woman is special' because she 'has freed herself as much as possible and will not keep her

mouth still about it' (ibid.: 411). The debate between Grace and
Rose concentrates eventually on the latter's own appropriation
of the role of special woman. For a large part of the play Rose
dresses as a man, a disguise she adopts after meeting a woman
soldier named Jane. Out of love for Jane, and a desire to live the
freer life of a man, Rose also becomes a soldier. When she
returns to her village, she discovers that, in her absence, a
number of the women have been hung as witches. The news
causes Rose to take off her soldier's uniform, though she continues to wear men's clothes, and it is this continuing male
impersonation that Grace objects to, along with her criticisms of
Rose's play. What is at issue is not only what the play 'says' but
who, as playwright, is speaking and also to whom, and on behalf
of whom, speech is being uttered.

Despite the cogency of Grace's criticism of author and text,
Rose's arguments do have weight and substance. She is not
trying to record 'exact history', she tells Grace. She has created,
out of her imagination, a play 'to entertain. Not a bible' (ibid.).
Rose's male disguise has in fact been of vital assistance to Grace,
for it was Rose's men's clothes that enabled her to rescue the old
woman from prison when she was condemned as a witch. Rose
continues to wear men's clothes as a form of protection, but also
in order to hold down a 'man's' job. What matters is not her
clothes, she additionally informs Grace, but her play. Not long
after this debate Grace dies and a copy of Rose's play is buried
beside her. When Rose expresses anxiety because her play is
being hidden away before it has had a life, Helen reassures her
that, even if the play remains unperformed in Rose's lifetime, it
will be found one day. 'But s'pose it never gets unearthed?' Rose
objects, and, in response, Jane speaks the play's final line:
'You're not the only woman in the world, Rose' (ibid.: 420). In
Jane's summing up, whose play it is becomes irrelevant. In*her*it-
ance *will* be passed on. If one play is lost, another woman will
make a new one. At the same time, Rose's play is crucial because
of what it promises. Grace – healer, midwife and teacher – will lie
in the ground down the ages alongside the text of her friend and
pupil. Together, the dead woman and the buried play will act as
linked sources of knowledge and potency for future generations
of women. Rose's text will be constantly refashioned to give form
to other women's lives, but a first text as model and guide was
necessary. An understanding of both the commonality of women

and of the 'special' woman has validity if the result is the unlocking of voices that have previously been silenced.

From one perspective or another, each of the plays I have discussed in this chapter forges a link between past and present, and often also the future. The plays considered in the next chapter also bring past and present into conjunction in that they are retellings of existing texts, sometimes plays, sometimes stories. I begin with three plays from the late 1980s that re-examine tales of silenced women. *Lear's Daughters* (1987), by the Women's Theatre Group and Elaine Feinstein, gives distinct and individual voices to the daughters whom Shakespeare polarises as the good Cordelia and the wicked duo, Goneril and Regan. Julie Wilkinson's *Pinchdice and Co.* (also 1987), though less firmly based on a source text than *Lear's Daughters*, has important similarities with Brecht's *Mother Courage and Her Children*. Like Courage, another 'canteen woman', Pinchdice, lives off war – though the battlefields on which she plies her trade are those of the Crusades, not the Thirty Years' War. Yvette, the prostitute in Brecht's play, becomes Kisspenny in *Pinchdice and Co.*, and Courage's dumb daughter, Kattrin, is transformed into Cleverlegs, whose name attests to a physical dexterity that, along with her growing attachment to Kisspenny, is the crucial factor in her developing ability to chart the actual and ideological landscapes in which she finds herself. Timberlake Wertenbaker's *The Love of the Nightingale* (1988) reworks Ovid's horrifying story of the rape of Philomela and her subsequent silencing by the cutting out of her tongue. In Ovid's version Philomela can articulate her violation and mutilation only through the woman's art of weaving, which she undertakes in her secluded prison. In *The Love of the Nightingale*, Philomele's revelation of her story is, by contrast, doubly located within a public space. Not only is Philomele a character in a play, she also herself utilises the public nature of the theatrical event to enact her tale. Chapter four ends with two reworkings of a text by a woman, Mary Shelley's paradigmatic exploration of monstrosity and of the interconnection of creator and created.

4

RETELLINGS

Mother Courage is first seen in Brecht's play lolling at her ease in a covered wagon pulled by her sons, Eilif and Swiss Cheese. Beside her in the wagon is her dumb daughter, Kattrin. A Sergeant and a Recruiter challenge Courage. Who is she, they ask, and what is her business? By reply, Courage sings her selling song, defining business – the selling of food and other provisions to the soldiers – as precisely the reason for her presence. *Mother Courage and Her Children* focuses primarily on the central figure of Courage: mother and, at the same time, war profiteer. What Brecht demonstrates in the play is the impossibility of sustaining this dual role. One after another, Courage loses her children to the war which is also her source of livelihood, but, at the end of the play, worn and bent as she has become, she drags the wagon on her own, calling after the disappearing army, 'Take me with you!' (Brecht 1962: 81). *Mother Courage* presents an audience with an opportunity to learn a lesson that its protagonist never learns, a lesson summed up by the Sergeant at the end of the first scene in this way: 'When a war gives you all you earn / One day it may claim something in return!' (ibid.: 13).

Like *Mother Courage, Pinchdice and Co.* begins with a selling song, but in this case the song is sung by three out of the play's four characters. Together, they list the food they have for sale, then, individually, Pinchdice, Cleverlegs and Kisspenny introduce themselves to the audience. Each character will go on to present important differences from, as well as similarities to, her counterpart in Brecht's play. Kisspenny becomes Cleverlegs's 'sister', and lover. Unlike Courage, Pinchdice does learn, albeit only in the final moments of the play, and Cleverlegs extends dumb Kattrin's act of altruism in a way that gives form to her own desires as well as the needs of others. Despite her disability, Kattrin manages to raise a hue and cry and so to warn the sleeping townspeople of Halle of impending attack – 'The stone', Brecht writes, 'begins to speak' (ibid.: 74). But Kattrin is killed in the process, while Cleverlegs survives, and, though she finally accepts the need to shoulder (literally) the burden of the nurturance of another, she defines the terms according to which she will take on this responsibility.

Cleverlegs is named after her chief attribute. She is an acrobat and tumbler whose clever legs can also shin up a high siege tower to survey the surrounding landscape. Near the beginning of the play she speaks to the audience from this vantage point and paints for them a picture of what she can see from there: 'Outremer, the outlands; fierce and foreign . . . like the country the devil offered Jesus. A great dusty plain', and, at its 'hub . . . tracks like spokes leading off into the desert, in all directions' (Wilkinson 1991: 74). Cleverlegs's description of Outremer – the first in the play – presents this imagined offstage world from two seemingly contradictory perspectives. It is at once an alien space, the wilderness where Satan (the dark Other) tempted Christ, and a place that is given shape and meaning by the white city at its heart. Outremer is eventually renamed, and claimed, by Kisspenny as Syria. The white city is Damascus, her home as a young girl until terror of the crusaders transformed Christian families (including her own) into a source of hatred and fear. Through her naming and appropriation of the outlands, Kisspenny domesticates the alien Other. The city at its heart becomes for her, and eventually also for Cleverlegs, the lost and beloved home-place to which she yearns to return. In contrast to the privation, hunger and filth experienced by the crusading army outside the vast and hugely thick city walls, inside the city, she tells Cleverlegs, there are 'orchards full of fruit . . . oranges, pears, pomegranates' (ibid.: 80) and a hospital with large 'cool rooms, running water . . . a bed to yourself'. It is on the hospital that Kisspenny's dreams of return are primarily fixed. Here, the body she exchanges night after night for the bare necessities of survival could be soothed and made to 'smell sweet again' (ibid.: 81).

Kisspenny's body, the sign of her trade, is for Pinchdice, and for Eleanor of Aquitaine – the play's fourth, and only upper-class, character – a sign also of the Otherness they repudiate. Initially a business colleague, Kisspenny becomes for Pinchdice, after the latter wrongly suspects her of stealing from her, a 'squamy saracen', whose whoring is an 'abomination' before God. For Eleanor, Kisspenny is a reminder of St Augustine's likening of the debased, but necessary, prostitute to the sewers of a palace: 'If you take away the sewers the whole palace will stink' (ibid.: 91). Sewers in *Pinchdice and Co.*, however, have a dual function. The means of evacuating the city's waste, they are also a source of entry into the place the play represents as a focus of yearning. Through the concealed entrance that leads into the sewers, and thence into the city, Kisspenny regularly communicates with her sister, whose Muslim husband protected her when the remaining members of her family fled, and warns her of the crusaders' movements.

The secret entrance to the city provides Cleverlegs with the means by which, like Brecht's Kattrin, she alerts the unsuspecting citizens to the danger of an attack. One night, when she is in the vicinity of the hidden way into the sewer, she sees a woman emerge from below ground, to be then furtively embraced by Kisspenny. Not knowing that this is Kisspenny's sister, she is overcome with jealousy and reveals the secret entrance to Pinchdice, who, in turn, divulges it to Eleanor. At Pinchdice's instigation, Eleanor plans a surprise attack on the city. A small group of soldiers will enter through the sewers, and, under cover of darkness, open the gates to the awaiting army. When the horrified Cleverlegs hears of this plot, she insists on going into the city to give warning in Kisspenny's place, as her legs are quicker than those of her friend. On her return, she narrates the story of what happened: her journey through the 'mouth of hell', the 'devil's den'; her delivery of the message, despite the fact that she was effectively silenced through not knowing the people's language; and her return through a nightmarish underworld. The citizens had caught, and killed, the soldiers as they emerged from the sewer, but one wasn't completely dead. To Cleverlegs's horror, as she navigated her way along the filthy tunnel, 'God the Father roared . . . blew out [her] candle, and left [her] in the dark'. Then, out of the oozing blackness, a man's hand grabbed hold of her, 'a sticky, bloody hand', which grasped her ankle, and wouldn't let go until she kicked hard in the man's face (ibid.: 134).

Cleverlegs's return from her underworld journey links her with a character from a tale far older than *Mother Courage*. In the city Kisspenny's sister makes her a gift of a pomegranate, and, though Cleverlegs doesn't know what it is, she manages to bring it back with her into the other world, covered in blood and filth, but still whole. In *Metamorphoses* Ovid tells the story of Persephone who was ravished by Pluto and carried off by him into the Underworld. Ceres, Persephone's mother, was able to arrange her daughter's freedom, but only on condition that no food had passed her lips during her stay in the Underworld. Because she had eaten the seeds of the pomegranate, Persephone was obliged to spend a portion of every year in Pluto's kingdom. Cleverlegs's survival of her Underworld journey, bringing with her a pomegranate, transforms her into a modern Persephone. Unlike Persephone, she has not eaten of the pomegranate, and so is not obliged to remain in the Underworld. More importantly, she has entered the Underworld of her own volition, and returned from it as a result of her own ability and determination. Though the Plutoesque forces of the Underworld – the bloody hand of the soldier and the roaring of the patriarchal God in the darkness – pitted themselves against her, she struggled through to freedom. From hell, she emerged into the light.

In a somewhat similar way to her description of the outlands at the beginning of the play, Cleverlegs's narration of her journeys, first into and then back from the city, presents the Underworld as interpretable in clearly distinguishable ways. The first journey reimagines the sewer (the site of female deviance) as the means by which Cleverlegs, as heroine, saves the inhabitants of the city, whereas the second journey acts as a reminder of the misogyny that seeks to eradicate women's capacity for revolt. The sewer/Underworld is both a place to be revisioned and one to escape from. The city into which Cleverlegs journeys is itself implicated in the imprisoning function of the Underworld. Through her gift of the pomegranate, Kisspenny's sister becomes, like Cleverlegs, a Persephone figure: a correspondence is established between the two women. When Cleverlegs leaves, however, the sister remains behind, and the fact that Kisspenny has earlier given Cleverlegs a scarf that belonged to her sister – azure-coloured, signifier of sky and freedom – further identifies Cleverlegs with escape, while the sister (the giver/loser of the scarf) remains in a

101

form of confinement. At least briefly, therefore, the fair city is refigured as a site of deprivation.

In the fifth of her 1994 Reith Lectures, *Cannibal Tales: The Hunger for Conquest* (published in *Managing Monsters*), Marina Warner writes of the centre's need 'to draw outlines to give itself definition. The city', she continues, 'has need of the barbarians to know what it is' (Warner 1994: 74). From the beginning of *Pinchdice and Co.*, however, centrality is a matter of perspective. The city is at once the heart that gives definition to the outlands (outlines) and a further manifestation of Otherness for the crusaders who temporarily inhabit those outlands. In addition, the city means something different to each of the play's characters. To Pinchdice it is a source of further loot, to Eleanor a magnet that draws everyone to it 'like a poultice drawing pus' (Wilkinson 1991: 131). To Kisspenny it is the location of desire and loss, and to Cleverlegs a memory of heroic achievement and struggle for freedom. The place which assumes so many layers of significance is, however, never shown on stage. It is enacted only through the characters' stories and their perceptions of it. The play is set outside the city walls, among the women who straggle after the crusading armies. Likewise, the 'activities of men on the battlefields' – the catalyst from which the play's action springs – are, as Gabriele Griffin and Elaine Aston explain in their introduction to the play in *Herstory: Volume One*, 'not mimetically represented. [The men's] world is reported and established as an offstage space' (Griffin and Aston 1991: 13). Their unseen offstage presence constitutes the defining factor that leads to the existence of the female characters in this location, but the play's focus is on the women and on Otherness. The setting foregrounds a space that a patriarchal culture has defined as peripheral, both because it is woman-linked and because it is Other. As the many ways of seeing the city demonstrate, however, Otherness is a matter of perception. It depends what one defines as central; depends, in other words, on who does the defining.

Kisspenny, who reimagines the outlands through her renaming of this terrain, also redefines the crusaders – again through the process of naming. She terms them Franj, alien barbarians, thus allocating them to the position of the Other. Eleanor, by far the most powerful character in the play, momentarily glimpses her own future marginalisation. Though she is powerful, her power is circumscribed by the fact that she is a woman. 'History', she tells Pinchdice, 'is slipping out of [her] grasp.' She has a vision of what will in fact be her eventual fate, confined within the traditional woman's place: 'I see myself shut away in a room, in a tower, in a fortress ... imprisoned in my own home' (Wilkinson 1991: 133).

The play's two most clearsighted characters, Kisspenny and Cleverlegs, are alike in certain ways, and yet also display differences that are mutually supportive. Both have memories of childhoods spent trudging dusty roads, both yearn for a home-place, both were played in the two original productions by black actresses, a decision that stressed the similarity between them and their difference from Pinchdice and Eleanor. Though she longs to return to the city, Kisspenny knows, and Cleverlegs eventually comes to accept, that they must make their place in the outlands. It is not their blackness that bars them from the white city – there are people of their colour inside the walls – but their connection with the crusaders, and, in addition, Kisspenny's trade. You're 'either inside the city walls with the wives and virgins', she tells Cleverlegs, 'or you're outside in the whores' ghettoes' (ibid.: 103). Kisspenny is referring to European cities, but the same holds good for the city at the heart of the outlands. It too has its Other, that which it excludes. Unable to live in the city, Kisspenny and Cleverlegs establish the topography of the outlands, mapping it as a space where it may be possible to make themselves a home. Cleverlegs's love for Kisspenny has taken her, emotionally, as she explains, to the summit of a hill where a view she 'never expected' revealed itself spread out below her (ibid.: 105). She knows, despite its initial strangeness, that this is the place where she will remain. Though she partly longs (like Shanny Pinns in *Ironmistress*) to gallop away on a fast horse that will take her to the edge of the world, she accommodates her pace to that of Kisspenny who has become slow and ill. Kisspenny, in turn, helps Cleverlegs to learn the skills she will need in order to survive in the outlands. She unpicks Cleverlegs's distinguishing red cross and warns her that she must pretend to be dumb until she has learned the language. Unlike Kattrin in *Mother Courage* therefore, whose dumbness results from something a soldier stuffed into her mouth when she was a child, Cleverlegs's silence is a strategy deliberately adopted in the pursuit of survival.

The relationship between Kisspenny and Cleverlegs is a sym-
biotic one, but Cleverlegs also accepts a responsibility that will
almost certainly entail giving in excess of what she receives.
When the surprise attack on the city fails, Eleanor turns on
Pinchdice, imprisoning her in 'a wooden yoke, which rests on
her shoulders, and has holes for her neck and hands' (ibid.:
136), and making her dance like a baited bear. Eleanor does not
kill Pinchdice because she doesn't need to. 'Poverty will be thy
executioner', she tells her prisoner. 'You're bankrupt, Pinchdice, you've crashed' (ibid.: 138). Eleanor exits and Cleverlegs
and Kisspenny enter, preparing for their journey. Pinchdice asks
her daughter for help, promising to give her something in
return. 'Give me what? . . . What've you got?' Cleverlegs asks her,
prompting Pinchdice's realisation that she has nothing to offer
except her need. 'At last', Cleverlegs replies, 'Something you
can't pay for. Something you can't buy. Me. You can't buy me. Do
you hear?' (ibid.: 141). Then, acting on the lesson she has
learned from Kisspenny, Cleverlegs takes off her mother's crusaders' cross and warns her against 'talking English'. The three of
them must somehow merge into the landscape if they hope to
stay alive.

As they prepare to leave, Cleverlegs carries her mother 'on her
back, thus visually encoding', as Griffin and Aston note, 'the
burden Pinchdice represents in her life' (Griffin and Aston 1991:
14). Their final words are in the form of a song, 'War Games'. The
reality of war, which, like the army, has been largely relegated to
offstage space throughout the play, now reveals itself as the
crucial presence that defines everything else as Other. Shifting
and conflicting images of the city, and of Otherness, are replaced
by the stark antithesis of life and death. The hope is that the
characters have learned enough to survive. The terrain into
which they must silently merge is also the place for which they
have gained some skills of map-reading and, for Kisspenny and
Cleverlegs, the landscape of their desire.

Pinchdice's attempt to bargain with Cleverlegs prior to her
acceptance of the fact that her only claim on her daughter is that
of naked need provides a link with the play from which *Lear's
Daughters* draws its inspiration. In the first scene of Shakespeare's *King Lear*, Lear attempts to strike a bargain with his
daughters, and specifically with the youngest, Cordelia. He will

give up his kingdom and, in return, will 'set [his] rest' on Cordelia's 'kind nursery' (I. i: 123-4). This desire for 'nursery', for Cordelia as all-loving 'mother/daughter', forms the basis of Janet Adelman's analysis of *King Lear* in *Suffocating Mothers*. A text which is at first glance 'overwhelmingly about fathers and their paternity', on close acquaintance, Adelman writes, 'insistently returns to mothers' (Adelman 1992: 104). In contrast to Cordelia, the longed-for good mother/daughter, Goneril and Regan are the two 'monstrous mother/daughters', 'in part Cordelia's psychic progeny, generated out of [Lear's] terrible need for her' (ibid.: 116). Temporarily at least, Lear gains the mother he seeks, for Cordelia who, in act one, refused to 'love [her] father all' (I. i: 104), returns in act four minus her husband, or other signs of a self distinct from Lear's needs, and devotes herself to her father as though he were a little child. The final composite image of Lear and Cordelia – the old, grief-stricken father holding in his arms his dead daughter – can be read in a variety of ways, but Adelman points out that all interpretations 'play across – and require – Cordelia's dead body', which functions as 'a prop for Lear's anguish'. Having previously erased Cordelia's separateness, her individual voice, 'the play takes even her death from her' (Adelman 1992: 126–7). The very manner of Cordelia's death is crucial for she 'is choked', her voice which, at the beginning of the play, Lear found so 'troublesome' eternally silenced.

Lear's Daughters, by The Women's Theatre Group and Elaine Feinstein, ends where *King Lear* begins, with expectations of a tripartite division of a kingdom. In the final moments of *Lear's Daughters* a crown is thrown up into the air and three sisters, Goneril, Regan and Cordelia, reach up and catch it. The remainder of the play charts the separate, yet related, journeys that lead them to this point. The sisters' guide on these journeys is the Nanny, a surrogate mother figure and a storyteller, whose eventual retellings of childhood narratives point to the possibility of different ways of perceiving the past and present. The final character, the androgynous Fool, acts as the play's 'mistress/master of ceremonies' (Griffin and Aston 1991: 13), commenting directly to the audience on the progress of the action. Played in the original production by an actress in a costume, the back of which represented a man's dinner suit, and the front a woman's gown with artificial breasts attached, the

Fool's fluidity of gender arises from a need to be all things to all people in order to earn a living. 'Are you a man or a woman?' Cordelia asks, to which the Fool replies that this depends on 'who's asking'. 'How can you be so . . . accommodating?' Goneril counters (WTG and Feinstein: 32 and 33), and the Fool answers that this is what s/he is paid for. The Fool also acts the part of Lear – who therefore never appears as a distinct and separate figure – and of the Queen, faded and ghostlike even before she dies in childbed, victim of Lear's fanatical determination to have a son. Mediated always through the bizarre ambivalent presence of the Fool, both Lear and his queen are pervasive, yet distanced, figures.

The play begins with the Fool, who, with nursery-tale simplicity, proceeds to define the basic elements of what the audience is about to see. She/he/it holds up three fingers, representative of three princesses; then two more fingers, designating servants; a further finger, one offstage king, and yet another finger, 'One Queen dead'. The Fool stops, thinks, then repeats the 'finger business'. This time it identifies three daughters, two mothers, a father and a fool. Alternatively, the components of the evening's entertainment consist of: 'Six parts / Four actors . . . The Fool . . . One stage / One audience / One castle' (ibid.: 21 and 22). So, from the start, *Lear's Daughters* stresses analysis and restructuring. This is what the play will consist of, the Fool demonstrates, but its components can be taken apart and reassembled. Its meaning depends on the connections one makes. The Fool produces a blindfold, 'One prop', puts it on, and begins a game of blind-man's buff, catching in turn each daughter, who then directly addresses the audience.

Cordelia speaks first, of her delight in the shape and solidity of words, every one of them distinct and different. Reading was the first thing she ever did on her own, her first expression of self, and now she reads all summer long in a secret and hidden place among the raspberry canes and blackberries. When she looks up into the sky, 'it's full of words' (ibid.: 23). Regan speaks next, and her favoured form of expression is not words but the wood which she carves to release the shapes that she knows already lie within it. She loves the varied textures of wood that has been exposed to the elements: 'bark cracked and mutilated by lightning . . . curves smooth and worn by wind and rain' (ibid.). Goneril speaks last. She is a painter who sees a world that constantly 'breaks into colours'. She describes a self-portrait 'on a throne . . . scarlet, gold, black'. The eldest sister, she remembers both Regan's lightning-marked trees and Cordelia's secret den among the blackberries and raspberry canes. Like Cordelia, she looks upwards, and for Goneril the sky is 'full of stars' (ibid.).

In the original production the three daughters were distinguished by the colours they wore (Goneril in blue, Regan in red and Cordelia in yellow). The setting, designed by Jane Linz Roberts, 'a partial representation of a phallic fairy-tale-type tower . . . cast an imprisoning shadow over the three princesses' (Griffin and Aston 1991: 11). Gradually the play maps this fairy-tale tower, first the nursery, then the downstairs rooms: kitchen, storeroom, Counting House, parlour. The reference in the last two of these places to the nursery rhyme 'Sing a Song of Sixpence' is deliberate, but this is a strange, jumbled-up version. Instead of sitting decorously in the parlour, eating her bread and honey, the Queen has begun to spread honey on the flowerbeds. She has ordered all the hair to be removed from her body, and the pegs with which the maid should be hanging out the clothes are attached to her fingers. In place of the maid in the garden there is the Nanny in the nursery telling her stories that subtly probe the weak points of Lear's power.

The first story the Nanny tells is of the daughters' births. Goneril, she explains, shot out from her mother 'like a dart', all scarlet with blood (WTG and Feinstein 1991: 24). The Queen's crown fell off and, when it landed, it made a circle around Goneril's entire body. It was midnight when Regan was born. The Queen was sitting on her velvet throne and Regan 'dropped out like a ruby' (ibid.). When Cordelia was born, the Queen was outdoors and Cordelia 'grew like a red rose out of her legs' (ibid.: 26). A portent signalled each birth: a comet with a red trail rushing through the sky for Goneril, a volcano erupting for Regan, and a hurricane for Cordelia. A more important factor distinguished Cordelia's birth, however, for, in contrast to the births of her sisters, Lear was present.

Lear's response to each of his daughters has determined the course of her development and her relationship with her siblings. To begin with, Lear's interest focused on Goneril, but later he rejected her in favour of Cordelia. Regan is the unnoticed one, piggy in the middle, until Cordelia becomes Lear's favourite, and then Regan and Goneril form an alliance. Cordelia, whose first independent achievement was to learn to read, and who joyed in words, no longer uses her own language when she is chosen by Lear, but instead babbles baby-talk to please him. The sisters' individual destinies are already evident in their memories of their first, separate forays into the complex world of 'downstairs'. Cordelia recalls being lifted up high in the arms of a giant, so that her feet touched the sky, and also turning round and round, holding her skirts and crying, 'Look, Daddy, look, Daddy, look' (ibid.: 29). To Regan, Lear is not Daddy but 'my Father', a remote figure. In her memory he sits at a table, banging his fist and singing, slightly out of tune, his hands inside the dress of a woman, holding her breast. Not tenderly, just holding it, and the woman's face – which might, or might not, have been her mother's – is expressionless as wax. The first time Goneril went downstairs she sat on Lear's throne to see how it felt. When Lear came in, he was angry because he knew that Goneril was thinking of the day when she would displace him, and Goneril smiled because she was pleased that he knew.

Goneril's memory of going downstairs is overlaid with other memories in which longing for Lear, and rejection by him, are paramount. Scene five recalls a day in the sisters' childhood when they waited excitedly for Lear to return from a sporting tournament. When he eventually arrived, he pushed Goneril aside and, lifting Cordelia high into the air, he kissed her on each cheek. A story that Nanny tells in scene seven, cast in the timeless and apparently incontestable form of fairy tale, also involves waiting for Lear and then his sudden, brief incursion into his daughters' lives. 'Once, Lear had not been there', Nanny begins, 'and then suddenly he was.' Before he arrived, there had been rain for 'forty days and nights' (ibid.: 41), but, when Lear came, walking, Christlike, 'over the water' that divided him from the Queen and his daughters, the sun began to shine. Goneril is older in this scene, however, and she is no longer willing to accept unquestioningly a fairy-tale version of events. Cordelia is also puzzled. 'Over the water?' she queries, but, when Goneril supplies an imaginary bridge to link Lear and his daughters, Cordelia is happy to accept this, and Nanny incorporates a bridge into her story. The Queen crossed over the bridge to Lear 'and everybody had to cheer'. Goneril alights on the problematic words 'Had to?' (ibid.). Smoothly, Nanny finds an explanation –

that it was important the Queen should be seen at Lear's side –
but, though Cordelia and Regan happily concentrate on their
imagined memories of a reunited happy family in Nanny's fairy-
tale version of the past, Goneril remembers what she actually did
on the day of Lear's return. Instead of crossing the bridge to Lear,
she remained with Nanny. Lear's rejection of Goneril was
echoed by her separation of herself from him.

Goneril's search for an understanding of herself in relation to
her father leads to her exploration of the tower-castle that is an
extension of Lear, and especially of the cellars that underlie the
downstairs rooms. Once before, she has visited these cellars, in
that instance with Lear, who pushed her into a room filled with
gold, and, closing the door, whispered to her that one day
everything would be hers. Then, telling her that this must remain
a secret between them, 'he put his hand' – Goneril is silent for a
moment or two, and then continues – 'on my shoulder' (ibid.:
57). The night that Lear returns from the sporting tournament
and pushes her away in favour of Cordelia, Goneril returns by
herself to the cellars, but this time, instead of a room filled with
gold, there are bars, through which hands come clawing and
scratching. The treasure-cave of the all-powerful king of gold has
become a demon's lair in which human beings are left to rot.
Goneril can't piece the different images together, the cheering
crowds above ground and, below, the place which is both a
prison and a golden room in which she received the mark of the
King's favour. For the audience, her telling silence before the
words 'on my shoulder' reveals this mark, the placing of the
King's hand, as almost certainly a form of sexual abuse, and,
though Goneril is unable to make the connection between Lear's
abuse of herself and his wider abuse of power signified by the
hands that attempt to claw their way through the bars, a version
of the Pied Piper story that Nanny has earlier told the Fool relates
the clawing hands to forces that will scratch away at the basis of
Lear's power.

In Nanny's Pied Piper story there is a terrible famine in the
countryside, and the rats move therefore to the one remaining
place of plenty – the king's castle. As in the original story, the
Piper gets rid of the rats, and, when he is denied payment for his
services, lures away the children. Nanny's story, however, adds a
new twist, for, as the king looks down from his castle window, he
sees, in the shadows, a 'dark army' of children and, as he stares

at the glint of the children's teeth in 'the moonlight [and their] long fingers scratching at the doors', he is no longer sure whether he is looking at children or rats (ibid: 49 and 50). The children/rats, kin to both Lear's own misused children and to the prisoners in his cellars, scrabble their way up the castle walls and through slits in the windows. They chew through floors and walls, and then they gnaw the flesh from the king, leaving only bones behind them.

Like the king in Nanny's story, Goneril watches from *her* window, which is high up in Lear's tower, and, from this point of vantage, spies on her father. Immediately after describing the hands reaching through the bars, she looks out of the window and there is Lear, far below, preparing to go riding. He looks small and toylike, no longer invincible: 'A wooden man on a wooden horse' (ibid.: 58). Though Goneril is able to cut Lear down to size by looking down on him in this way, the apparent sense of distance from him that the experience additionally gives her proves illusory. At an earlier point in the play, Regan, the most marginalised and neglected of the daughters, also watched Lear from the window. Similarly to her first memory of down-stairs, what Regan saw was her father pressing his sexual attentions on one of the castle women. Though his wife had just died, Lear had his hand up the woman's skirt and was unbuttoning himself in full view of anyone who cared to watch. Regan's rebellion against Lear has taken the form of claiming her own right to sensual and sexual experience. Her response to never being the favoured daughter has been to grasp every experience available to her, and eventually she takes a lover, and becomes pregnant. When Goneril hears of this, she insists that Regan should get rid of the baby. After the Queen's death, Lear made Goneril take over her mother's task of keeping the account books, and her experience of adding up columns of figures has taught her to make an astute assessment of her own and Regan's worth to Lear. He will marry them, respectively, to the Duke of Albany and the Duke of Cornwall, and in this way will gain powerful allies. Regan with an illegitimate child is valueless. As Goneril makes this fact known to Regan, she underlines her words by tearing a page from an account book, crumpling it and throwing it to the floor. Regan stares into a mirror, in which she can see Goneril reflected, and tells her sister that her features have disappeared. Goneril's face has become Lear's.

In the following, and penultimate, scene, Goneril and Regan are married to their bridegrooms. Neither Albany nor Cornwall is represented on stage, and the Fool speaks the lines of the officiating clergyman and also Lear's lines. The sisters and Nanny frequently speak at the same time, and the words of the marriage service are intercut with dialogue from the preceding scenes. Increasingly, it is Nanny's lines that are heard most clearly through the melée and, with growing intensity, these goad Goneril into hitting out at Lear. One line, 'Cordelia the favourite', insistently reminds of Lear's betrayal. 'And you mustn't tell' evokes his molestation of Goneril. 'Cut the cake' and 'A knife for slicing' (ibid.: 63) refer to the present scene, with its wedding cake, and also hark back to the cake and a knife ('for slicing') which, along with lace, honey and the account books, the Queen used to keep in the parlour. On Nanny's final, loud 'A knife for slicing' Goneril attacks Lear's (the Fool's) eyes with a knife, but she is unable to carry through the action, and, after a few moments, the knife drops from her hands. In *Daughters and Fathers* Lynda E. Boose notes the infrequency with which daughters kill fathers, both in mythology and in actuality. Even Goneril and Regan, she writes, 'stop short of patricide'. A powerful taboo appears to exist 'at the boundary of a daughter's violence against the father'. It is this boundary that prevents Lady Macbeth from killing Duncan 'because he "resembled / My father as he slept" ' (Boose and Flowers 1989: 38). In *Lear's Daughters* Goneril, too, reaches this boundary, but is unable to cross it.

Whilst Lear's eyes escape Goneril's knife, Goneril is herself 'blinded' by the lace of her bridal veil, which cuts into her eyes (and, by implication, also the lace that her mother, aspects of whose role she has been forced to take on, kept in her parlour along with a cake and knife). In her last speech of the play, which disturbingly rewrites her first, Goneril looks up, as she looked up at the beginning, but now she can no longer see the sky. In place of the multicoloured world her painterly eye once saw, there is only the red of blood, in her eyes and on her hands. Though her hands touch and feel, she doesn't recognise them, for they are, in fact, not hers but Lear's. Her 'father's daughter . . . still he gives [her] stop and start. Controlling by [her] hatred, the order of [her] life' (WTG and Feinstein 1991: 68). In Shakespeare's play, Lear asks, 'Is there any cause in nature that makes these hard hearts?' (III. vi: 76–7). *Lear's Daughters* answers the question. The motivating force is Lear himself. Goneril is what he has made her, and Regan, whom Shakespeare's Lear wants to 'anatomize', in order to 'see what breeds about her heart' (III. vi: 75–6), is what Goneril, Lear's well-trained daughter, made *her* when she told her to destroy the child. Get rid of it, Regan recalls her saying, and, at that moment, she understands what Lear has done to them both. At the end of the play, Goneril sees only blood, but Regan is more clearsighted. Her vision of Goneril's face as Lear's has shown her also the knife that will cause the blood. The daughter who once used a knife to release the shapes she intuitively knew existed within pieces of wood will gouge out the eyes of Gloucester. Though, like Goneril, she will be unable directly to destroy Lear, she will mutilate the play's other father, destroying, with his eyes, the memory of the sister/father. The two sisters (the monster daughters of *King Lear*) will, however, remain bound together by their herstories until their deaths. On leaving the castle, Regan will set her 'face to a new game', which, though not beautiful, will be passionate, and she will stay with it until her end, 'carved out' at Goneril's hands. She 'would not have it any other way' (WTG and Feinstein 1991: 69).

When Goneril and Regan leave the castle, Cordelia moves to the window and watches them go. Her mother is dead and Nanny, the surrogate mother – the only mother Cordelia has ever really known – has been ordered to leave by Lear. Now that Cordelia will soon be married, she is expendable. Before Nanny goes, Cordelia, who has never been close to her, struggles to make contact. Earlier in the play, Cordelia tried to reject the little girl's voice she had developed for Lear. 'Spin for Daddy', Lear cajoled her, and, as Cordelia picked up her skirt, he told the men in attendance on him to gather round and watch his 'baby'. Momentarily, Cordelia refused to perform for the men's delecta-tion, but, when Lear sharply rounded on her, she resumed her baby talk and spun round and round in front of the leering crowd, finally collapsing on the floor, and gasping out 'Cordelia not want to be Daddy's girl' (ibid.: 53). As Nanny prepares to leave, Cordelia mentally journeys further back in time to the point in her childhood when she first went downstairs and Lear marked her as his new favourite by lifting her into the air. That was when she began to use the voice Lear likes so much, but, before that, she had had another voice. When she was very young, words were her chief means of expression. Reading was the first thing she ever did for herself. Since she first went downstairs, Lear has fashioned Cordelia's voice and language, but hidden in the recesses of memory is another voice and there are words in her head she has never spoken to anyone. She is unable to articulate the crucial words for which she is searching before Nanny goes, but in her final speech she finds what she has been looking for. As in her first speech of the play, she joys in the solidity and individuality of words. Now, she 'hold[s] two in [her] hands, testing their weight. "Yes", to please, "no", to please' herself: 'yes', she will and 'no', she will not (ibid.: 69). Through her 'no', her 'nothing', which is almost her first word in *King Lear*, Cordelia will, at least to begin with in Shakespeare's play, assert herself as a separate person, and voice, from the person and voice of her father.

Both *Pinchdice and Co.* and *Lear's Daughters* are fundamentally concerned with women's relationship to language. Kisspenny is empowered by her skill in naming. In contrast to Kattrin in *Mother Courage*, Cleverlegs deliberately adopts dumbness as a (temporary) strategy of survival. Cordelia in *Lear's Daughters*, whose own voice has previously been silenced by Lear, at the end of the play learns to speak out against him. Through her denial of Lear's will, Cordelia asserts her own. In *Metamorphoses* Ovid tells the story of the double mutilation of Philomela. It is a text, Elissa Marder writes in 'Disarticulated Voices: Feminism and Philomela', that 'invites a feminist reading not only because it recounts the story of a woman's rape, but also because it establishes a relationship between the experience of violation and access to language' (Marder 1992: 157).

Ovid's version of the tale of Philomela can be summarised as follows. The Athenian king gives his daughter Procne in marriage to Tereus, king of Thrace, in gratitude for Tereus's help in defeating the enemy forces that have been besieging Athens. After five years, Procne begs her husband to return to Athens and to bring her sister, Philomela, to stay with her in Thrace. Overcome with desire for his sister-in-law, Tereus rapes her, and, when she threatens to tell the world her story, cuts out her tongue and imprisons her in a remote place. Unable to speak her violation, Philomela weaves the story, using a scarlet design on a white background, and sends it, via a servant, to Procne. When

Procne 'reads' the message of the cloth, she first disguises herself
as a celebrant of the Bacchic rites that are in progress, then
makes her way to Philomela's prison, where she releases her
sister and takes her back with her to the palace. Whilst she is
deciding what revenge she should take on her husband, her
young son, Itys, comes up to her and, realising how closely he
resembles his father, she kills him with a sword. The two sisters
then tear the body apart and cook it. Procne invites her husband
to a sacred feast, and, when Tereus asks for his son, explains that
he is already here – inside Tereus. Still covered in blood, Philomela appears with Itys's head, which she thrusts in Tereus's
face. Tereus prepares to kill the two women, but, before he can
do so, all three of them are transformed into birds. Procne
becomes a swallow, Philomela a nightingale and Tereus himself
a hoopoe.

The sisters' terrible act of vengeance in Ovid's story arises out
of a dual silencing. Marder writes that the 'text appears to stage
two "rapes": one "literal" and the other "symbolic" ' (ibid.:
158), the latter violation being a 'stripping of a language of
violation'. Philomela's experience is of 'disarticulation', and the
only language through which she can recount what has happened to her (i.e. weaving), is one 'that is no longer bound to the
body' (ibid.: 160). At the end of Ovid's story Philomela, through
her transformation into a bird, effectively regains a voice of a
kind. Silence, Graham Huggan writes, in 'Philomela's Retold
Story: Silence, Music and the Post-Colonial Text', is converted
'into song'. Huggan, who notes that 'Philomela's story has become a paradigm for the reenactment of colonial encounter'
(Huggan 1990.: 12), contrasts the 'crucial role' played by 'the
word' in the 'maintenance of colonial hierarchies of power' with
music which, through its affiliation with silence in several post-
colonial texts 'can be seen . . . as providing alternative, [and
subversive] non-verbal codes' that destabilise 'over-determined
narratives of colonial encounter' (ibid.: 13). Timberlake Wertenbaker's retelling of the Philomela story, *The Love of the Nightingale*, both in its form and in its content, foregrounds spoken
language, its evasion and also its confrontative power. Deprived
of words, Philomele (as she is called in the play) finds, however,
a different language within which to express her violation – not
music, but another subversive non-verbal sign system. In addition, her rape is linked, as in Huggan's article, with the violent

invasion of countries, her brutal mutilation with wider instances of violation and dispossession.

The Love of the Nightingale was first performed by the Royal Shakespeare Company at The (original) Other Place, Stratford-upon-Avon in October 1988. About ninety minutes in length, and consisting of twenty-one short scenes, it was played without an interval. Wertenbaker has added a male and female chorus to Ovid's dramatis personae. Other new characters include a Captain, with whom Philomele falls in love on the way to Thrace, and whom, as a result of this, Tereus kills; Niobe, Philomele's chaperone/servant; and a group of actors who perform a Hippolytus play. It is while watching their portrayal of Phaedra's guilty and hopeless passion for her stepson Hippolytus, a play-within-a-play that has no equivalent in Ovid's story, that Tereus first realises that he desires Philomele. Instead of weaving her story, Philomele acts it out with the aid of three large dolls that she has made, representative of herself, her sister and Tereus. Philomele – not Procne – kills Itys, and there is no dismemberment or cooking of the body. The play ends with a conversation between Philomele and Itys in which the aunt tries to get the little boy to ask questions about what happened and, in this way, to see it anew. *The Love of the Nightingale* is an interrogative play. It ends with a question and, throughout, questions are asked, frequently about the nature and continuing relevance of the Philomele myth.

The chief asker of the questions in the play is Philomele. She is the character who most clearly delights in words, and, though Tereus tears out the tongue that articulates what he cannot bear to hear, the final scene restores Philomele's voice to her. When the audience first see Philomele, she is a young girl questioning her slightly older sister, Procne, about adulthood and, specifically, men and sex. Procne responds by asking a question of Philomele – 'If I went far away, would you still want to come and visit me?' (Wertenbaker 1989: 3) – that reveals her greater understanding of the limited choices, and questions, that are likely to be available to herself and Philomele as women. At the beginning of the Faber and Faber text of *The Love of the Nightingale*, Wertenbaker places two fragments from a lost play by Sophocles entitled *Tereus*. Both are in the first person. In the first, the female speaker laments the difference between a child's happy life in her father's house, and her fate when she comes to sexual maturity: 'thrust out and marketed abroad / Far from our parents and ancestral gods'. The second, and very brief, quotation hauntingly evokes the anguish and silence of exile: the 'envy' the speaker feels of those who have 'never had experience / Of a strange land' (ibid.: xi). For Procne, married life with Tereus is experienced as exile. Scene four begins with her asking the female chorus where 'all the words' have gone. The language of Athens, which gave to everything a clear and decipherable meaning, has been replaced in her new home by an alien, largely incomprehensible tongue in which the relationship between words and the entities to which they refer is slippery and elusive. Surrounded by what she perceives as silence, Procne longs for the sister with whom she used to toss words to and fro as in a game.

It is in order to fill the silence with her sister's words that Procne begs her husband to bring Philomele to Thrace. In the course of that journey Tereus silences Philomele in a dreadful way because of her skill with words. When she insists that sex must be preceded by consent, Tereus replies that fear implies consent and rapes her. When, despite her pain and loathing, she mocks his cowardice and threatens to reveal him to his subjects as a 'scarecrow dribbling embarrassed lust' (ibid.: 35), a puny, pathetic being empty of everything but violence, he cuts out her tongue. Her enforced silence makes her even more beautiful to him. 'Let me kiss those bruised lips', he says. 'You are mine. My sweet, my songless, my caged bird.' He kisses her, and, finally, after he has twice mutilated her, twice taken from her her voice – first her consent and then her anger – 'She is still' (ibid.: 37).

The language in which Philomele eventually gives form to her rage and agony is a physical theatre language. Like Ovid's Philomela, she employs a traditional woman's skill, sewing, but she uses it in order to create for herself an alter ego, a huge doll puppet through which she can enter and control the public space of performance. Whereas Philomela expresses her violation in a language that, as Marder writes, 'is no longer bound to the body', Philomele communicates her story through a figure that is separate from her body and yet, at the same time, replicates it and, because of the doubleness of the Philomele doll and Philomele as manipulator, also reinforces it. In place of her dual silencing by Tereus, she substitutes a larger-than-life doll-self,

116

and a puppeteer-self that together vividly articulate Tereus's guilt.

The speaking silence of Philomele's performance also provides the context for the reunion of the sisters who once played so lightheartedly with words. At the point when the Procne doll enters the action, the real Procne also appears and watches Philomele's performance. After years of refusing to join her women in their Bacchic rites, Procne has finally elected to take part in the mysteries she had earlier defined as barbarian. Believing Philomele to be dead, and herself therefore to be deprived for ever of her Athenian words with their clear and demonstrable relationship to meaning, she has allied herself to an alien and violent physical language. At first, nevertheless, she refuses to accept what Philomele's physical performance shows her, but when she sees her sister's mutilation engraved on her body, she believes. If 'it is true. My sister', Procne says, 'Open your mouth', and, when, slowly, Philomele does so, Procne asks, 'Is this what the world looks like?' (ibid.: 41). Bereft of its tongue, the mutilated mouth becomes a wound that, through its silent scream, articulates the horror of violation.

The tongueless mouth, signifier of the loss even of a verbal language to express violation and erasure, is the central potent image in a play fundamentally concerned both with the meanings and function of words and with the power of theatre to depict and interrogate a particular set of violent events. The stark horror of Tereus's rape of Philomele and his cutting out of her tongue, along with Philomele's appropriation of a speechless public language to make known her story, are incorporated within a play that is discursive, contemplative and often coolly ironic. Certain clues to an understanding of the differing moods of *The Love of the Nightingale* are provided by the Hippolytus play that is performed for Pandion (the father of Philomele and Procne), his queen, Philomele and Tereus before the latter two characters journey to Thrace. Initially, the action of this play is presented as a series of distanced events that both the actual and onstage audiences watch with detachment. The fact that (as Paul Arnott noted in his review of the production in the *Independent*, 23 Aug. 1989) the onstage spectators are 'themselves creatures of myth', and that, in addition, they provide a running commentary both on the Hippolytus/Phaedra story itself and the nature of theatre, prevents an empathetic involvement with the characters in the play-within-the play. At the tragic denouement of these characters' stories, however, Philomele weeps, thus inviting the real audience to question their detachment. Her tears also point to the fact that the summing up of the play-within-the-play's events by the male and female choruses, in which they stress the inevitability of what has occurred, should be viewed critically. King Pandion's subsequent comment, 'And now we must applaud the actors' (Wertenbaker 1989: 13), by drawing attention to the fictive nature of what has just taken place, invites a dual response: at once involved and critically distanced.

As a paradigm for the play as a whole, the Hippolytus play reveals *The Love of the Nightingale* as eliciting a variety of audience responses, sometimes empathetic and immediate, sometimes more dispassionate and analytic. The nature of myth is itself subjected to scrutiny. Myth, the Male Chorus tell us, is simultaneously 'an unlikely story', 'a remote tale', 'public speech', 'counsel, command' and 'The oblique image of an unwanted truth, reverberating through time' (ibid.: 19). The Philomele story is both that which cannot be rephrased (otherwise why would the play take the trouble to enact the myth?), and a means of examining the resonances of its 'unwanted truth' in the present-day world. Along with the nurse figure, Niobe, the male and female choruses offer further differing ways of situating oneself in relation to the myth. Niobe extends the rape of Philomele to the rape of countries. Her birthplace, she explains, was a little island that the Athenians coveted even though its only resources were 'a few lemon trees' (ibid.: 31). Her people fought the invaders, and the results were dead men, violated women and a silent, barren landscape. The male and female choruses, in contrast to their counterparts in the Hippolytus play, adopt increasingly opposed attitudes to events. At first the Male Chorus define their function as observers, 'journalists of an antique world' (ibid.: 14), who record because they lack the power to intervene, but, as Tereus's designs on Philomele become more evident, they determine to know nothing of what is happening. Refusing 'the pain of responsibility', they no longer ask questions, and, in order to sleep soundly at night, they do 'not see' (ibid.: 24). The Female Chorus, on the other hand, grope their way towards an interrogation of the violence from which they are geographically distanced, yet which they intuitively apprehend. Even before the rape of Philomele, whilst the Thrace-

118

bound ship is still at sea, they scent the approach of disaster, though they find it difficult to articulate their fears. The killing of Itys, which they do witness, creates an urgency as the result of which they find a clarity of language that enables them to present the myth, not as 'a remote tale', but as 'counsel command', 'public speech'. In their newly-found words, they attest to the importance of words, for 'Without the words to demand . . . ask. Plead. Beg for . . . accuse . . . forgive' (ibid.: 45), without the questioning and comprehending mind, there is only the terrible relentless logic of violence, atrocity heaped upon, yet never cancelling, atrocity.

The murder of Itys by Philomele is followed by a confrontation between Procne and Tereus in which Tereus, Philomele's violator and silencer, denies the existence of a language in which to explain his actions. These were, he claims, 'Beyond words'. His desire for Philomele was so compelling that neither words nor existing rules had any validity. Then Procne, who has 'obeyed all rules', of parents, marriage, loneliness, who has gone as a stranger to a strange land where words have become meaningless, tells her husband that she will help him to find the words to confront what he has done. Revealing to him the body of his son, she tells Tereus that it is he who has 'bloodied the future', and, in despair at what he sees, Tereus at last tries to explain his actions. They were caused by his love of Philomele, he tells Procne, but Philomele didn't want his love. Instead, she mocked and rebelled against him. This made her 'dangerous'. Wanting something and taking it is not love, Procne informs Tereus, and, when Tereus retorts that there was no-one to tell him what love was, Procne points out the fundamental flaw in his self-defence with the words: 'Did you ask?' (ibid.: 46 and 47). Face to face with the knowledge of what he has done, Tereus attempts to blot it out for ever by killing Procne and Philomele, but, as in Ovid's tale, this ultimate violent act is averted by the magical transformation of the three chief protagonists into birds. As Philomele explains in the final scene, they were all so angry that, without this intervention, the bloodshed would never have ended.

In the last scene of *The Love of the Nightingale* Philomele regains a human voice. The other important alteration to Ovid's story is the fate of Itys. In the Greek version Itys, literally eaten by the father, has no separate existence, or identity, from Tereus. In Wertenbaker's play, the child whom one of the Female Chorus refers to as 'the future', is guided by Philomele into an interrogation of his father's actions. The little boy wants to hear the nightingale sing, but Philomele insists that first he must ask her questions about what has happened. Does he understand why Tereus's cutting out of her tongue was wrong? Itys initially considers this task boring but, at the end of the play, he finds, and asks, the crucial questions: 'What does wrong mean?' and (following Philomele's explanation that 'It is what isn't right') 'What is right?' At this, the nightingale finally sings and Itys, who has now become interested in searching for answers, asks, in some surprise, 'Didn't you want me to ask questions?' (ibid.: 49). The play's ending therefore completes the original story – the transformation of silence into song – and acts as the culmination point for Wertenbaker's interrogation of its contemporary relevance. The myth exists both as that which cannot be rephrased and in an investigative remaking. As Catherine Wearing expressed it in *What's On* (30 Aug. 1989), 'Living alongside the apocryphal tale is a complex debate about the nature of myth, the life of language and what this modern moment is to make of its stories, its myths and its lies'.

Reviewers who expressed reservations about (and, occasionally, outright condemnation of) the play were less happy about this focus on debate, Michael Coveney in the *Financial Times* (10 Nov. 1988) finding the choruses 'awkwardly dispassionate', and Paul Taylor in the next day's *Independent* dismissing them as 'rather glib' and 'editorialising'. Wertenbaker's suppression of some of the horrifying events in the original also led to adverse comments. Both Michael Coveney and Charles Spencer, for example, were unhappy with her rewriting of Itys's death, the former commenting, 'The sisters kill Tereus's son, but surprisingly depart from the myth (and the *Titus Andronicus* connection) by not baking the boy in a pie for dad's dinner', while Charles Spencer in the *Daily Telegraph* (25 Aug. 1989) criticised Wertenbaker because 'she ducks the issue of the female characters' culpability . . . censor[ing] the more hideous details of the legend and distract[ing] attention from the crimes of Procne and Philomele with a disconcertingly sentimental coda'. Spencer's response is, in fact, based on a misreading of a text, which, far from ducking the issue, lays the blame firmly at Tereus's feet, whilst the 'coda' provides the explanation for the alteration of Itys's fate. A particularly hostile reaction to the play came from

Kenneth Hurren in the *Mail on Sunday* (13 Nov. 1988), who commented sardonically on Wertenbaker's 'feminist' retelling of the story. Of a reference in the play to 'the incidence of rape in car parks', he wrote, *'It's sad when you want to be meaningful and it sounds so frivolous'* (original emphasis). Given that the car-park reference is to the rape and murder of little girls, this is a particularly insensitive and distressing remark.

In her analysis of reviewers' responses to *The Love of the Nightingale* in *New Theatre Quarterly* (1993), Susan Carlson valuably contrasts the reception of Wertenbaker's play with that afforded to Deborah Warner's production of Sophocles' *Electra*, which opened at The Pit (Barbican Theatre) London shortly after the opening night of *The Love of the Nightingale*. Warner's *Electra*, she writes, was praised because it presented its audience with elements that 'for 2500 years have been equated with great drama: violence, action, big characters' (Carlson 1993: 271–2), and the element that Michael Billington especially valued, 'moral ambiguity'. By comparison, reviewers tended to be less happy with Wertenbaker's stylisation and coolness, often missing therefore her radical transformation of 'conventional theatrical narrative, character, and thought' (ibid.: 272). Wertenbaker's reworking of Ovid's story was a source of unease partly because of its didacticism – 'this seemed to be a code for "too feminist"' (ibid.: 271) – and also because of the form within which the playwright told *her* tale.

From a play that provides a commentary on an ancient story written by a man, I move to two dramatic explorations of a woman's text. On the evidence of lines from Book Ten of Milton's *Paradise Lost* that she quoted at the front of the first edition of *Frankenstein* – 'Did I request thee, Maker, from my clay / To mould me Man?' (743–4) – Mary Shelley herself viewed *Frankenstein* as, in a sense, a retelling. It is this aspect of *Frankenstein* – its debt to a seminal English text – that forms the starting point for Sandra M. Gilbert's and Susan Gubar's examination of Shelley's story in *The Madwoman in the Attic*. Mary Shelley, they comment, takes 'the male culture myth of *Paradise Lost . . . and rewrite*[s] *it so as to clarify its meaning*' (Gilbert and Gubar 1979: 220, original emphasis). In *Mary Shelley: Her Life, Her Fiction, Her Monsters*, however, Anne K. Mellor notes the startling originality of *Frankenstein*, a story which, she writes, has achieved mythic status, so 'profoundly resonant' has it become 'in its implications for our comprehension of our selves and our place in the world'. Shelley's myth, moreover, she continues, is 'unique, both in content and in origin. *Franken-stein* invents the story of a man's single-handed creation of a living being from dead matter. All other creation myths . . . depend on female participation or some form of divine intervention' (Mellor 1989: 38). Whatever debt Shelley may have believed that her story owed to *Paradise Lost*, therefore, her remaking, in Mellor's terms, is so substantial that what characterises it chiefly is its differentness from all earlier narratives.

In her introduction to the 1831 edition of *Frankenstein* Mary Shelley offered a genesis for her novel based on the circumstances of her own life at the time of writing. She explains in the introduction that she has set herself the task of answering the question she has frequently been asked: how, as a nineteen-year-old girl, she 'came to think of and dilate upon so very hideous an idea' (Shelley 1985: 51). She describes the rainy Switzerland summer of 1816 which led Byron, Percy Bysshe Shelley and herself to turn to the indoor activity of reading aloud ghost stories to keep themselves entertained. She notes Byron's proposition that each of them should write a ghost story and her own, initially unfruitful, search for an idea that would make the reader afraid to turn round, would 'curdle the blood and quicken the beatings of the heart' (ibid.: 53–4). It was her role as 'a devout but nearly silent listener' (ibid.: 54) to conversations between Byron and Shelley on the possibility of discovering the principle of life, and the relevance of this to recent experiments aimed at vivifying inanimate matter, that led, she writes, to a fearsome waking dream. With 'shut eyes, but acute mental vision', Mary Shelley saw 'the pale student of unhallowed arts kneeling beside the thing he had put together'. Then 'the hideous phantasm of a man' began to 'stir with an uneasy, half-vital motion' (ibid.: 55).

In its vision of death as the birthplace of life Shelley's waking dream embodies much that is powerful about *Frankenstein*, whilst at the same time providing disturbing echoes of Mary Shelley's own life. On 22 February 1815 she had given birth to a premature baby daughter, who died a few days later. Her journal for 6 March 1815 reads 'Find my baby dead . . . a miserable day'. Over the next few days there are a number of references to the dead baby, and then, on 19 March 'Dream that my little baby came to life again; that it had only been cold, and that we rubbed it before the fire, and it lived. Awake and find no baby. I think about the little thing all day' (Shelley 1947: 39-41). In her waking dream a little over a year later, dead matter *was* reborn. As Mellor explains, she was again 'dreaming of reanimating a corpse by warming it with a "spark of life"' (Mellor 1989: 40). Mary Shelley's own birth had been followed by death, as was that of her first, and subsequently her second and third, child, but in the case of her own birth it was the mother who died. Though Mary Wollstonecraft gave birth successfully to her daughter on 30 August 1797, the placenta did not follow, and on the advice of the midwife a male physician was called in who removed it, surgically, piece by piece. Possibly as a result of this process, infection and fever developed and, on 10 September, Mary Wollstonecraft died.

Mary Shelley's birth from the soon-to-be dead body of her mother and her subsequent motherlessness (for, though her father, William Godwin, later remarried, Mary never formed an affectionate relationship with her stepmother) has led commentators on *Frankenstein* to remark on the similarities between Mary's own life and that of the monstrous being she created. Mellor writes that 'Mary Shelley shared the creature's powerful sense of being born without an identity, without role-models to emulate, without a history' (ibid.: 45), and she quotes the creature's '*cri de coeur*' that was also Mary Shelley's: 'Who was I? What was I? Whence did I come? What was my destination?' (Shelley 1985: 170). In search of her identity, her herstory, Mary Shelley developed the habit of visiting her mother's grave in St Pancras Churchyard and reading there the books that were such an important part of her life, and which included the writings of the dead woman whose bones lay in the earth beneath her. When, at the age of sixteen, she fell in love with the married Percy Shelley, it was at her mother's grave, with its screening willow trees, that the two stole their secret meetings. On 26 June 1814 Mary told Percy of her love. A month later, in the company of Mary's stepsister Jane (later known as Claire), they ran away together. For the young Mary Shelley, therefore, love, her sense of self, and her engagement with language were all integrally bound up with her mother's grave. Her practice of studying Mary Wollstonecraft's writings on her grave, Gilbert and Gubar note, demonstrates Mary's awareness of the existence 'of a strangely intimate relationship between her feelings towards her dead mother, her romance with a living poet, and her own sense of vocation as a reader and writer' (Gilbert and Gubar 1979: 223).

The interface between Mary Shelley's life and the strange and deeply compelling story she wrote forms the subject matter for the two theatre pieces I discuss finally in this chapter: Liz Lochhead's *Blood and Ice* and Foursight Theatre's *Frankenstein's Mothers*. Both explore the nature, responsibility and pain of creativity. One of the three characters in *Frankenstein's Mothers* is Mary Shelley's Creative Voice. The other two are Mary Shelley herself and Mary Wollstonecraft. Two versions of *Blood and Ice* have been published, the first in Methuen's *Plays by Women: Volume Four*, which was published in 1985, the second in a revised edition of the same volume published in 1988. The former version, which was first performed at New Merlin's Cave, London, in February 1984, is the one I have chosen to concentrate on because of my fascination with the presentation of the servant, Elise, who becomes, among other things, a female Frankenstein. Apart from Elise, the other characters in the 1984 *Blood and Ice* are Mary, her stepsister Claire, Percy Shelley and Lord Byron. The action is presented as a reanimation of the past that takes place within Mary's mind. The play begins, and ends, in a 'ghostly nursery', a place of shadows in which 'bleached-out', 'nightmare toys' are scattered about (Lochhead 1985: 83).

At the start of *Blood and Ice* Mary sits alone in a cold circle of candlelight reading *Frankenstein*. Around her are packing cases and the weird, distorted toys. She sings the first verse of Byron's poem, 'So we'll go no more a-roving', but on the fourth line, 'Though the moon be still as bright', she breaks off from her song and speaks the final word then adds 'and cold. And lonely'. She opens a shutter and moonlight strikes her. Its cold loneliness is her element. Here, she dreams of what once was: her lover/husband now drowned, her first little dead baby that, in another, long-ago dream, she tried to revive by rubbing it near the fire. Now, when Mary wakes alone in the dead of night, she feels that she is a corpse, like her little baby, and she has to slowly rub herself to life again. In her attempts to turn her thoughts away from the past, she picks up a pen and begins to write, but the words too seem dead to her. Then, from the shadows, first

Percy Shelley's then Byron's voice calls her name, and, after a few moments, another, giggly, voice joins in. This is Claire, Byron's and possibly also Percy's, lover. Firmly, Mary shuts out Claire's voice, asserting that there were only three of them: Shelley, Byron and herself. She snuffs the candle out and takes off her dark-coloured shawl, revealing underneath a young woman's 'filmy white dress' (ibid.). The lights come up, the rich sunlight of late afternoon, and, as they do so, Percy Shelley comes bursting in, wearing nothing but a lace tablecloth. He has been trying to learn to swim, and, as he later walked back, naked, to the house, he saw that Mary had visitors and snatched up the tablecloth to spare their blushes. His hair is damp and he is laughing.

With Percy's entrance, the gloomy shadows are temporarily dispelled. In Byron's words, Percy is 'Light and Grace . . . Ariel, a pure spirit' (ibid.: 91) and Mary's passionate love for him leads her to move into his light-filled space. At the edges of the light the shadows always wait, however. Here Mary's anxieties about the wellbeing of her children, little William and Clara, have their home, as do her fears of Percy's infidelity. It is from the menacing yet fertile world of shadows that her monstrous story will take its life. The ghostly nursery, which is the play's first and recurring setting, is the nurturer of the tale of the creator who fashioned a being out of dead parts. It acts therefore as a dramatic representation of Mary's mother's grave. Here, too, birth, death, erotic love and creativity – the making of children and the making of words – are rooted together. Connecting, flowing through them all is the blood of the play's title.

The blood-link that exists between Mary Wollstonecraft's death, Mary Shelley's birth and her capacity to bear children of her own is expressed in act one through Mary's and Claire's momentary regression to childhood. In order to win a dispute, and get one up on her stepsister, Claire mocks her motherless state, informing Mary that she has overheard one of the servants describing her mother's death in childbed: 'Rivers of blood', she said. Mary turns away in distress, and Claire notices with horror that there are blood stains on Mary's shift. She is convinced that Mary is dying, but Mary realises that what has happened is simply that she has begun to menstruate. Far from dying, she has become 'a woman'. Tellingly, however, what the 'thin dark, red line' reminds her of is the written word, 'as if a quill was dipped in blood and scribbled' (ibid.: 88). Towards the end of the play, after she has almost haemorrhaged to death as a result of a miscarriage, Mary attempts to reject childbirth as a valid metaphor for literary creativity. When Percy criticises her for concentrating too exclusively on her own pain and loss, claiming his right to a part in these experiences, Mary retorts: 'You bleed on paper, I bled through every bit of bedlinen in this house' (ibid.: 112). But though she denies a rhetorical equivalence between blood and ink, Mary's experience of the 'dark river' of pain and of the 'rivers of blood' that almost killed her, as they did her mother, leads her back to the story she wrote of a monstrous form of creativity. In the guise of a dream, she retells her story and, in this retelling, Elise, the play's most marginalised character, moves centre stage, becoming in the process a kind of double simultaneously of Victor Frankenstein (the monster maker), of Justine (the Frankensteins' servant and one of the monster's victims), and of Mary herself.

In *The Love of the Nightingale*, Philomele begins the process of freeing herself from the silence Tereus has enforced on her through her construction of the doll that functions as her double. In *Blood and Ice*, by contrast, where Mary's dream narrative also concerns the making of a doll, doubleness takes on a nightmarish quality that arises out of the same disturbing element both in *Frankenstein* and in the Shelleys' own lives in the weeks prior to Percy's death by drowning. During this time, while Mary was still convalescing from her miscarriage, Percy was the victim of terrifying waking dreams and nightmares. One day, he saw a little girl, who resembled Allegra, the recently dead daughter of Claire and Byron, rise up out of the sea, clapping her hands. On another occasion, he met his double walking on the terrace, who asked him how long he meant to be content. In a hideous nightmare, he was visited by Jane and Edward Williams (friends of his and Mary's) who came into his room, all torn and bloody, and told him that the house was collapsing. When he rushed into Mary's room to warn her, he saw himself in the process of strangling her. Jane Williams, whose husband would also drown, saw Percy and his double on the terrace, though at the time he was out in the bay, sailing his boat. In *Frankenstein*, doubleness is located primarily in the frequently noted correspondence between Victor Frankenstein and the fearsome thing he makes. Though Frankenstein is the creator, the Creature at one point tells him that he is the master whom Frankenstein must obey. Additionally, Frankenstein describes *himself* as the murderer of the Creature's victims, in little William's case before he even knows that the Creature is definitely responsible. He comes to look on the Creature as a vampiric form of self, his own 'spirit let loose from the grave' (Shelley 1985: 120). In the final pages of the book the roles of the two beings are reversed, for, instead of being followed by the Creature, as was previously the case, Frankenstein attempts to track him down, eventually reaching the icy arctic regions to which the Creature has journeyed. The pursued has become the pursuer.

Doubleness in *Blood and Ice* is presented initially through a correspondence between Mary and Claire. Near the beginning of the play, these two very young women, dressed in filmy petticoats and chemises, are contained in an area of fire and candlelight. Between them is a mirror, and rhythmically, and in unison, they brush their long hair, each the other's image. Though they are not sisters, Claire claims that they resemble each other, in their bearing and in the circumstances of their lives. Like Mary, Claire has become 'a scarlet woman': she, too, has found herself a poet for a lover. In the shadows that fringe Claire's and Mary's light, the servant, Elise, waits resentfully and unnoticed, her arms full of the same delicate garments they are wearing. Elise is still there as a silent, contemptuous onlooker shortly afterwards when Percy and Claire blindfold Mary and inveigle her into playing a game of blind-man's buff. As Percy and Claire dodge round her, giggling and calling her name in a variety of voices, Mary stumbles into Elise, and, after feeling her face, shoulders and breasts, tentatively suggests that the person she has found is Claire. It is only when she discovers the petticoats in Elise's arms that she realises her mistake. That's 'only the maid', Claire informs her, 'and she's not *in* our game!' (Lochhead 1985: 89). Mary's feeling of Elise's face and body, her naming of the woman she has touched as Claire and her instant recognition of Elise's servile status on discovering the petticoats reveal her ambivalence towards Elise. Her initial discovery of Elise as a fellow woman, another 'Claire' who has just claimed kinship with her, is negated by her own, and more forcibly Claire's, exclusion of Elise from their charmed circle.

Unlike Claire, and also Byron, who respond to Elise as someone of no account, Mary does defend Elise's right to be treated with respect. In scene four of act two, however, Mary herself decisively rejects Elise. Her children, Clara and William, have died, and unable to bear the sight of the woman who was the Other presence at their deathbeds, Mary tells Elise that, when she looks at her face, she sees, in its place, first the face of little William and then an image of Elise bending over William, 'smoothing him with death's hands' (ibid.: 106). Hands act here as a sign of similarity between the two women. Mary's hands that earlier felt the contours of Elise's, a potential 'sister's', body have transformed themselves into death's hands that are both her double's and her own. Together, Mary and Elise held William as, in his fever, he twisted his sheets into 'a hangman's rope'. Elise's face mirrored Mary's knowledge that her child was about to die and, in her anguish, it seemed to Mary that the knowledge killed the child as surely as if Elise's 'fingers were round his throat' (ibid.).

Elise, Mary's other self at little William's deathbed, is kin also to Mary in another way, because, though the fact is never clearly stated between the two women, Elise is pregnant with Percy's child. When Mary calls Elise 'a wicked girl', Elise claims yet another form of kinship. Literate as a result of Mary's teaching, she has read Wollstonecraft's *A Vindication of the Rights of Woman*. Are the rights of which Mary Shelley's mother spoke only for rich women, she asks, and not also for the maid-servant? In a deliberate echo of the Claire/Mary mirror scene in act one, the two women look at each other and Elise asks, as Claire did then, 'Don't you think we are sisters? Are we not somewhat alike?' (ibid.: 107). Mary's response, which is to order Elise to leave with the husband Percy has provided as a father for her child, is made in the light of Elise's clear articulation of the connection between them.

Elise, the rejected Other and mirror-image, assumes, in Mary's mind, monster proportions near the end of the play, her death's hands enabling an act of creation that refashions the making of the Creature in *Frankenstein*. Throughout the play, the various characters have offered differing interpretations of monstrosity. Byron defines it as the product of frustrated love. Mary claims that it consists in children dying before their mothers. Claire notes that incest produces monsters, and Percy Shelley imagines a poor working man from 'the new hells' of the cities, a mechanic who has been transformed into a machine, his body a construction of 'wood and wires' (ibid.: 96). In act two, scene six, Mary calls Byron a monster and, in retaliation, he asks, if he is a monster, what is she? At his insistence, she returns to the story she created, readers of which, as she has just explained, 'scramble together Frankenstein and the creature he brought to life' (ibid.: 111). Turning to the part of the book in which Frankenstein begins, half-heartedly, to make the female the Creature has begged as a companion to alleviate his loneliness, she relocates Frankenstein's workshop from a remote island in the Orkneys to an amalgam of a hellish factory and the ghostly nursery. The original description in *Frankenstein* of the creator 'trembling with passion', as he tears to pieces the thing he has been making, is superseded in *Blood and Ice* by an image composed partly of Percy's monster/mechanic and partly of a nightmarish toy. In this new version, Frankenstein smashes his machine and tramples 'its intricacies underfoot', then flings 'the ragdoll-sack of organs' at the Creature, who keens over it as he cradles it in his arms (ibid.).

In the monstrous dream that Mary suffers and subsequently narrates, the ragdoll image takes on a new formulation. Immediately prior to the telling of her dream, Mary holds in her hand a doll with a face like her own, that Elise made to entertain little William and Clara, while ruminating on the fact that Elise's class and gender have meant that she was doubly born to servitude. In place of Percy's mechanic as machine, Mary sees in Elise 'a slave's slave – and that's a jumbled up collection of wood and wires' (ibid.: 114). Then, flipping the doll inside out, Mary reveals, underneath its skirts, a different kind of doubleness – an upper body, head and face modelled on Elise's own. In the dream Mary then recounts, she spies on Elise – the doll-maker and her own doll double – in the nursery, sewing a monster version of the reversible doll. With her hands that Mary has earlier defined as death-related, Elise stitches a 'life-size puppet', its 'long pale limbs, cadaver-loins gleaming whitely'. The head and top part of the body are invisible because they are covered by its skirts, and Elise is stitching the lower body with 'Long secret sutures'. She has learned these 'Hints on the stitching up and finishing of ladies', she explains, from 'Mary Wollstonecraft's Pattern Book'. Between the puppet's thighs she makes a good 'strong knot', so that it can't 'unravel' – during childbirth or sex? Then Percy comes in, naked and wet from the sea, as at the beginning of the play, and Elise, now no longer the creator, asks, 'Will you deny your spark of life to your female fellow creature?' (ibid.). Percy, who has, in his turn, become the double of Frankenstein, the monster-maker, lies on top of the monster doll to impregnate it with life. He names it Claire but, when he drags the skirts back from its upper body, he reveals, not Claire's or Elise's head, but, instead, Mary's belly, loins, thighs and 'screaming vulva', tangled up with his own head, and pulling him down to the depths of the sea where he is soon to drown.

In her dream of the making of monstrosity, which rewrites Mary Shelley's waking dream of the genesis of *Frankenstein*, Liz Lochhead's Mary extends the play's exploration of doubleness, so that, as in Gilbert's and Gubar's analysis of *Frankenstein* in *The Madwoman in the Attic*, all the characters appear to have the same face (see Gilbert and Gubar 1979: 229). Elise, as monster, becomes Elise, the maker of monsters. The monster doll is Elise, Claire, and, finally, Percy's face entangled with Mary's genitals, which have been transformed into a screaming mouth. Sex, birth and death cannot be unscrambled in the dream. Nor can the making of children be separated from the making of Mary's story. The hands that wrote it are also the hands that, in their replicated image, rested on William as a death portent, and sewed the monstrous doll/Creature. At the end of the final scene, however, Mary expresses remorse for sending Elise away, thus recognising Elise as a person in her own right and not as a nightmare double of herself. Then, in the final scene, in which, as in the first, she is alone (Percy, William and Clara dead, Claire far away in Moscow), Mary sorts out the various characters of her story one from another. Which of them is she? she asks herself: Frankenstein, the monster, or – worst of all – the female monster, worst because it is not only more hideous than the male, but also mutilated, only half-born, 'tied to the monster bed for ever' (ibid.: 115). The monster bed, an extension of the ghostly nursery with its blood-filled shadows, is, likewise, a source of dreadful creativity. Blood is not ink, to bleed on paper is not the same as to bleed through all the bedlinen in the house, but the relationship between creativity and birth/death has been the story Mary has lived as well as the one she wrote.

Finally, though, she rejects Frankenstein and the monsters as her fictional counterparts. At last, she sees who she is: 'Captain

Walton . . . Survivor. [Her] own cool narrator' (ibid.). Captain Walton's letters, telling the story of Frankenstein and his Creature, are written, first, as he sails towards the North Pole and, later, when his ship becomes becalmed in a sea of ice. As well as death and birth, *Frankenstein* is a tale of the nightmare of loneliness. Apart from blood, another of its essential components is ice. Ice has also played a crucial part in Mary's story. When she almost bled to death after the miscarriage, Percy saved her by plunging her into a bath of ice. In the final moments of the play, memories of the dead assail her: the first little baby that she tried to rub back to life, her mother, Percy and *his* dream of the sea invading the house. Now, she feels that ice is invading both her house and her life. Ice saved her once. Will it do so again? She hears Frankenstein calling to Walton from her story, telling him to persuade the mariners to continue on in search of the Creature over the treacherous ice-floes: 'The ice cannot stop you if your hot hearts say it shall not!' (ibid.: 116). Then, 'Mary sits down at her writing table. Quietly, but resignedly', she goes on, with life and with the creation of stories. Briefly, she evokes the memory of her dead lover, and then she 'Begins to write' (ibid.).

Along with blood and ice, a third element of Mary's life story, or, more precisely, of the lives – and crucially the deaths – of those intimately connected with her, was water. Both Percy Shelley and his first wife, Harriet, died of drowning. A little over a year after the birth of her first child, Fanny, Mary Wollstonecraft tried to commit suicide by soaking her clothes in rainwater to make herself more likely to sink, and then plunging into the Thames. In each of these water-related incidents a child was involved. Had Mary Wollstonecraft succeeded in her suicide bid, Mary Shelley would not have been born. When Harriet Shelley was taken from the Serpentine river on 10 December 1816, she was heavily pregnant. Her body was therefore her unborn child's grave, as the water was hers. Percy Shelley's vision shortly before his death, of Claire's and Byron's daughter rising from the sea and clapping her hands – in anticipation, perhaps, of his approaching fate – ghoulishly replays this water/birth/death scenario, little Allegra acting as a re-embodiment of Harriet's unborn child.

Water, blood and ice figured prominently in Foursight Theatre's *Frankenstein's Mothers* (1994), 'a romantic tragedy of
monstrous proportions', as a publicity handout termed it, created by three performers: Sue Pendlebury (Mary Shelley), Jill
Dowse (Mary's Creative Voice and, at times, Victor Frankenstein), Lisa Harrison (Mary Wollstonecraft); director, Ruth Ben-
Tovim; writer, Cath Kilcoyne; composer, Laura Forrest-Hay; and
designer, Dave Boechler. Visually, blood and ice were represented symbolically, through the costumes worn by Mary Shelley
and her Creative Voice, the latter being dressed in a red tunic,
evocative of the blood-linked sources of *Frankenstein*, and the
former in a glacially white costume that allied her with the blank
loneliness of ice. Water was physically present on stage. The
setting for the production consisted of three tall, skeletal, cage-
like structures, one for each performer – her base to which she
constantly returned. Each cage contained a small box that doubled as a seat and as a repository for the books the characters
were engaged in writing or reading. Downstage, in a line parallel
to the audience, were three small, transparent tanks, partially
filled with water, During the creation of the monster, lights
shining beneath these turned them into laboratory equipment.
Meanwhile, as Victor Frankenstein, Jill Dowse crouched over the
box in her 'cage', and a light shining up on to her demoniacally
exultant face and blood-red tunic transformed her into the
student of unhallowed arts of Mary Shelley's waking dream.
Mary's children were represented at one point by her washing of
a little baby's dress in one of the tanks, their deaths by the water
turning red. When Percy set out on his fatal journey to Leghorn,
a paper boat, a visual reminder of one of his favourite pastimes
before he graduated to sailing real boats, was placed in another
tank. A flower floating on the water of the third signified his
death. Percy himself floated now 'in the waters of his beginning'.
His birthplace was also his grave.

The birth waters of Mary Shelley's beginning led to the 'rivers
of blood' that occasioned her mother's death. In this she resembled her Creature/monster who was born out of the dead.
Like Victor Frankenstein, the monster-maker, she experienced,
in a short space of time, the death of almost everyone she loved.
As she came fearfully to understand, *Frankenstein* was disturbingly prophetic of her own life. In *Frankenstein's Mothers*,
Mary's Creative Voice expressed it this way: 'Imagine if . . .

Everything you ever wrote on paper came true . . . Any decision you ever made had already been made for you . . . One creative act haunted you for the rest of your life' (Kilcoyne *et al.* 1994: 23 and 24). Foursight Theatre depicted this creative act as the result of Mary's search for identity, for an understanding of what was pre-ordained, but hidden – the 'secrets' written in her 'blood'. *Blood and Ice* ends with Mary's conjuration of the arctic wastes she created in *Frankenstein*. In *Frankenstein's Mothers*, the Arctic was Mary's inner terrain from the beginning, and it was here – not in a shadowy nursery – that she created her story. Bereft of a mother, exiled (like Margaret in her memories of childhood in Charlotte Keatley's *My Mother Said I Never Should*) to a 'cold, white' place, where nothing existed to guide her, she wrote the book as a map, a template, by which she might perhaps be able to understand her life. Motherless herself, she grew – mothered – her own creature, and, in its beginning, her own took shape. As the Creature developed, Mary examined it to discover whether it would reveal the 'secrets of her blood'. Victor Frankenstein's rejoicing, in her novel, at his discovery of the power placed in his hands 'to give life to an animal as complex and wonderful as man' became for her a grotesque mirroring of the doctor's hands 'ferreting' in her mother's body 'searching for the afterbirth' (ibid.: 5). The monster's birth showed her her own. Together, the monster and Mary searched for an understanding of the place in which, guideless, they found themselves. 'Who is he?' the Creative Voice asked of the monster: 'A man – and not a man . . . [an] unman . . . lost and wandering / Seized by a multiplicity of sensations' that assail him 'from all quarters' (ibid.: 9).

Gradually, words identified themselves as signposts in the wilderness: 'Da da da' and 'Ma ma ma' for Mary, though she had no mother and her father was too busy to pay her much attention. The accumulation and structuring of words became her key to survival. She learned the words of others, and attempted to write her own. The man unman also learned the sounds and meanings of language. He found books and studied them, in order to try to discover who he was. Through the mastery of language, he believed that he would be able to blind the people he met 'To the horror of his deformities' (ibid.: 11).

But the monster in *Frankenstein* discovers that he has misunderstood the operation of language. He is able to tell Victor

Frankenstein his story, but this does not win him the affection or acceptance he craves. In *Frankenstein's Mothers*, Mary tried first to reach her dead mother through the latter's writings, but she found herself clambering over 'rocks of . . . grammar and syntax, cutting [her] knees, sliding along the most eloquent and passionate statements'. Mary Wollstonecraft's words did not 'paint the cadence of [her] voice or lay [her] scent' in Mary's nose (ibid.: 12). Initially, it seemed that the writing of her story would give her the closeness with her mother she yearned for. Through the act of writing, she would hear her mother's voice. The feel and scent of that mother's body would be written in the text the daughter created. But, though the writing of *Franken-stein* gave Mary an understanding of her origins, it revealed to her also her own loneliness replicated in the monster.

This loneliness was demonstrated in performance visually as well as through words. In an echo of the monster in Mary Shelley's story staring in at his maker through a moonlit case-ment window, a 'ghastly grin wrinkl[ing] his lips' (Shelley 1985: 207), Mary in *Frankenstein's Mothers* tried to reach her mother through the bars of her 'cage'. Perched on one of the struts of the cage, her body and head twisted to one side in her anguished attempt to make contact, her face wiped clear of all emotion except a simple childlike need, she transformed the monster's malevolence into a helpless and all-encompassing desire. When she had first discovered the genesis of her story in her waking dream of the 'pale student of unhallowed arts' and the thing he was manufacturing out of dead matter, Mary had felt joy at her discovery, but this had been followed immediately by the horrify-ing sense that she could never rid herself of the Creature's face. Her look of desperate longing as she attempted to contact her mother through the cage-bars revealed the face by which she was haunted as in fact her own.

Mary's story – the tale of the monster which was her means of understanding her own origins – itself became monstrous, spreading its ghastly tentacles into all the recesses of her life. The text through which she was to learn 'the secrets of [her] blood' (Kilcoyne *et al.* 1994: 13) revealed itself as being 'written in . . . blood' (ibid.: 36). Torn between her desire to write and her love for her child, for example, Mary tried to persuade her little boy to go and play so that she could get on with her story. When he insisted on staying with her instead, her Creative Voice spoke, over Mary's attempt to cajole him, the words of the passage from *Frankenstein* in which the monster kills his first victim – a little boy also named William. Appalled, Mary tried to deny these 'monstrous thoughts' and to separate her daily life from the Voice that seemed able to articulate nothing but 'monsters and dead children' (ibid.: 16). However hard she struggled to keep them apart, the two insisted on merging, with the result that the book that was meant to provide her with a map of her past laid out the tracks of her future.

The most dreadful – the most monstrous – correlation between Mary's book and her life was the one between Frankenstein's destruction of his half-completed female monster, the companion for whom the monster in his loneliness had begged, and Mary's own miscarriage. Mary's washing of the little baby's dress in the tank of water, and its staining of the water red, was followed by Jill Dowse as the Creative Voice also going over to the dress and rubbing it hard so that the water became still redder. As she did so, she evoked Victor Frankenstein's anxieties about 'the filthy process' of creation in which he was engaged. He 'was about to give life to a female'. Together the two monsters 'would thirst for children. A race of devils would be propagated on the earth that might threaten the very existence of man' (ibid.: 27). Immediately after the Creative Voice's words, Mary described the agony of her miscarriage, the 'little life . . . Clinging, tearing' at her womb (ibid.: 28), ripping her to pieces, as Frankenstein ripped apart the female he was engaged in making. Mary's tortured body, mutilated by the foetus that strove desperately to hang on to the possibility of life, and the foetus itself, became, together, a metaphor for the destruction of the second monster. The little life struggling for existence was both that potential monster, and Victor Frankenstein destroying a female body. Mary herself was the first monster seeking in anguish for the Other, related, life she had been promised. After killing three out of four of her other children subsequently to their births, her ghostly text had now scored its deathly marks on the baby in the womb.

The horrifying experience of her miscarriage turned Mary's forebodings into 'a disease' which infected 'the minds of those around her' (ibid.). Then, despite his premonitory dreams and Mary's warnings, Percy sailed to his death and, in her quest for solace, Mary remembered her grandmother's dying words which had haunted her daughter, Mary Wollstonecraft, all *her* life, and which she had prophetically echoed in a letter written on the day she gave birth to the baby who would become Mary Shelley – shortly therefore before she, too, died: 'a little patience and all will be over'. Perhaps these were the words most indelibly 'written' in Mary's 'blood'. Maybe endurance was the most that was possible.

In both *Frankenstein's Mothers* and *Blood and Ice*, words are written in blood. In the former, the search for words is simultaneously a search for blood-secrets. In the latter, words are an emanation of the bloody nursery: blood *is* distressingly similar to ink. But, though words tie Mary into death and loss, they are also the agents of what freedom she manages to achieve. Her text may have made its mark on her, but, through it, Mary Shelley made her mark upon the world. Alongside its horrifying evocation of Mary's words in *Frankenstein* prophetically writing her own life story, *Frankenstein's Mothers* depicted her quest for an individual authorial voice. When she angrily commanded her Creative Voice to 'leave [her] life alone' because it had 'sapped [her] dry', the Voice replied, 'I thought you wanted to be an author' (ibid.: 22). Authorship, the authority of her own voice, was hard to achieve because, though Mary perceived herself personally as lacking a herstory, when it came to writing she was overwhelmed with models: her mother, her father, Percy Shelley, Coleridge's *Rime of the Ancient Mariner* which, as a young girl, she heard its author recite in her own home, and lines from which she included in *Frankenstein*. When Mary sought inspiration for her ghost story, her Creative Voice could at first only quote from pre-existing texts. Reviled by Mary for its lack of originality, it threatened to desert her, and, in anguish, she implored it to stay. Her imagination was her closest friend and solace. Without it she would die. The finding of the genesis of her story, the growing of the monster, was therefore also the nurturing of the feared, yet beloved, Creative Voice. In the *Rime of the Ancient Mariner*, the speaker is terrified to turn round 'Because he knows a frightful fiend / Doth close behind him tread'. These are two of the lines quoted in *Frankenstein* (Shelley 1985: 103), and 'fiend', Coleridge's word, is also Mary's alternative epithet for 'creature' or 'monster' in her novel. 'Fiend', however, requires only the addition of one letter to transform it into 'friend'.

136

At the end of *Frankenstein's Mothers*, Mary acknowledged her separation from her monster/her voice. 'It is out there', she explained, 'wandering in the world alone, without me'. The final words were spoken by her Creative Voice. A 'creature without precedent . . . an idea / A thought / An obsession', it existed 'alone', on its 'own terms' (Kilcoyne *et al.* 1994: 37). Not only had Mary Shelley's voice found its individual and distinctive cadence, her 'unique' (Mellor 1989), unprecedented Creature had, as Marina Warner writes in *Managing Monsters*, also 'leaped the boundaries of the novel' (Warner 1994: 20). Untrammelled, it began its own quest for an understanding of who and what it was.

Foursight Theatre's monster, the man unman, existing on its own terms, suggests potential other, as yet unformulated, interpretations. Unnamed by Mary Shelley, its possible names are multiple. Given the fact that the manifestations of monstrosity in *Frankenstein's Mothers* were depicted by women, and that Foursight Theatre focused largely on the monster's genesis in/by means of motherhood, one possible name for the man unman seems to me to be woman. In this reading, Frankenstein's mothers gave birth to a daughter, a creature once despised, considered monstrous, who became free and wandered on her 'own terms', seeking maps of her present and future, as Mary Shelley had sought them in her book for her past. This interpretation of the monster, as a sign of the unman/woman in search of reliable maps for an unchartered terrain, evokes one of the characters discussed in the next chapter, Pam Gems's Queen Christina, a woman who was reared as a man and, as a result, found herself lost in a wilderness, unable to construct a sense of self.

In all the plays examined in chapter five, characters are in quest of maps of self, and, in three of the four plays, also of a different kind of map-reading that links to Mary Shelley's novel. In *Managing Monsters* Marina Warner comments that *Frankenstein* has become '*the* contemporary parable of perverted science' (ibid.: 20). In his attempt to create life Victor Frankenstein penetrated 'into the recesses of nature [to] show how she works in her hiding places' (Shelley 1985: 92). His gendering of science as masculine, penetrative, dominant, and of nature as the passive, feminine Other, along with his abandonment of, his refusal

5

QUESTS FOR MAPS

Sheila Yeger's *Variations* is a dream-play in which all the female
characters are split-off aspects of the central figure, Louise. The
action is structured around Louise's train journey to Berlin to
collect information for a biography on Clara Schumann (child
prodigy, composer, wife of Robert Schumann and mother of his
children and, possibly, also lover of Brahms). Prior to the start of
the journey, there is a prelude, which consists chiefly of Louise
recounting a sequence of dreams to Richard Last, her psychotherapist, and watching Marilyn Monroe in *Some Like it Hot* on a
television screen. The two subsequent acts and the final coda are
set chiefly on station platforms, in train compartments, hotel
rooms and the reading room of a library. Act one begins on a
station platform in Germany. It is night time. The sound of a train
pulling out of the station is heard, and a young, blond-haired
guard notes its time of departure in a log book. Louise enters.
Aged thirty-nine, she is neatly and sensibly dressed. She has
booked a sleeper on the 21.49 from Aachen to Berlin and, having
arrived at Aachen with forty-nine minutes to spare, has been for
a cup of coffee. At least, she planned to order coffee, but
somehow found herself asking for chocolate instead. It was
'surprisingly good . . . comforting' (Yeger 1991: 178). Neither
she nor the Young Guard can speak each other's language, but,
by pointing to her timetable, he manages to explain to her that,
on Sundays, the Berlin train departs ten minutes earlier. Louise's
careful itinerary has gone wrong.

There is a blackout and, when the lights come up again, it
is several hours later. Louise sits on a luggage trolley, dozing.
Rhea enters. She is 'relaxed, easy', about twenty years old,
and is carrying 'a large, shabby back-pack' (ibid.: 179). Though

she is waiting for the Berlin train, she may, she tells Louise, go instead to Zürich – in the opposite direction. She is broke, and, after cadging some money from a disapproving Louise, goes off to get a cup of tea and a sandwich. One by one, the remaining three passengers enter, plus a fourth character, the Polythene Woman. The passengers are figures from train-linked movies: Laura from *Brief Encounter*, Anna from *Anna Karenina* and Marilyn Monroe from *Some Like it Hot*. Laura, who wears a 1940s suit, a hat and high-heeled shoes, enters first. She is nervous and from time to time consults her watch. She looks at Laura and then away. The Polythene Woman, so named because she is dressed almost entirely in polythene, enters next. Her feet, in their wrappings, look like parcels and she rustles as she shuffles along. She disconcerts Louise by standing and staring at her, then crosses to a large waste bin, rummages in it and takes out a newspaper. Anna enters, a dark, elegant woman in her thirties, wearing a fur-edged cloak that partly obscures her face. She walks along the platform to Louise and then stops. Briefly, her eyes meet Louise's, and then she hurries on. Marilyn is the last to enter. A look-alike from *Some Like it Hot*, she walks 'with a definite wiggle . . . is improbably blonde, undeniably glamorous . . . wears a straight black coat, with fur around the bottom, a little cloche hat and carries a ukelele in a case and a small bag' (ibid.). As she comes on to the platform, a train whistle is heard in the distance and there is a whirl of smoke. Marilyn walks past Louise and disappears into the smoke, but then reappears at the other end of the platform. The women stand surrounded by swirling smoke, and waiting for the train which can now be heard approaching.

Louise's encounter with the Polythene Woman and the movie-screen characters on the smoky platform establishes the play's dreamlike quality, its sense that one character is potentially transformable into another. The costumes of each character, Sheila Yeger explains, though individual and distinctive, should also echo what Louise is wearing, 'to the extent that . . . given different circumstances, any of them could be Louise' (ibid.: 174). The fact that Anna, Laura and the Polythene Woman make a point of looking at Louise as they enter also suggests some unexplained connection. Marilyn does not look at Louise, but her, possibly key, function within the play is hinted at by Louise's viewing of *Some Like it Hot* in the prelude. Marilyn is differentiated from Laura and Anna (her movie-screen counterparts) because she is named, not after the movie role, but after the actress who played the role. The possibly greater authenticity this might accord her is queried, however, by the publicness of Monroe's 'private' life, and the attendant difficulty of disassociating the actress from the role. Marilyn in *Variations* consists of a variety of largely interchangeable roles. When she enters the train compartment, she appears younger than she did on the platform, and, when she speaks, it is 'with just a hint of acquired American laid over the Midlands' (ibid.: 180). Marilyn is simply a stage name, she explains. She is on her way to a gig in Hamburg. When she cleans her face for the night – removes the mask of one role – she looks even younger, and she falls asleep sucking her thumb like a child. Later in the play, however, she wears 'the pleated white dress of the classic photograph of Monroe' (ibid.: 198) and speaks with an American accent. Here she is vintage Monroe. Elusive, transformable as the smoke with which she first enters, Marilyn is part icon, part child, part elemental force. As the different parts of her merge and reassemble themselves, so the play's characters jumble and re-form, revealing themselves as potential selves of Louise.

The fact that parts can, and in some cases have to, be doubled in performance adds to the sense of similarity and the feeling that everything is somehow known, yet not understood, from the beginning. When Louise falls asleep on the train, she dreams of the young Clara Schumann, 'grave, wooden, unchildlike, almost grotesque' (ibid.: 184), played by the same actress who plays Marilyn. The actor who plays Richard Last, Louise's psychotherapist, appears in her dream as Fredrick Wieck, Clara's father, and is then retranslated into Last. When Louise wakes up, he, Clara and her fellow passengers have disappeared and, instead, Rhea (who also plays Anna) sits where Marilyn sat. The train approaches Berlin station, and, whilst Rhea calmly and casually reaches for her back-pack, Louise anxiously organises herself and her belongings. In this strange and disturbing world, where faces have an alarming tendency to dissolve into one another, she struggles to maintain order, to keep to her 'tight schedule' of academic research.

The symbol, and focus, of this 'tight schedule' is the Berlin reference library that is the destination of Louise's train journey. From the beginning of the play, however, this library, which is the focus of order and clear, analytical method, is also associated with anxiety and disorder. In the prelude Louise recounts a dream which begins with her first working in a library and then going out to her car, where she discovers the dead body of a little girl partially hidden under a blanket. An elderly, tramp-like woman (a forerunner of the Polythene Woman) appears and shouts to Louise that this is the place where she lives. Louise drives quickly away, looking for somewhere to bury the body – to hide it more successfully – but her intention is frustrated by one of the child's arms, which she suddenly realises is sticking out from under the blanket, and by a face looking in through the car window. The fact that Louise comes to the realisation that *she* put the body in the car, and the angry woman's insistence that she lives there (i.e. where Louise is) reveal the child and the woman as disowned aspects of Louise herself. Though she tries to hide away the little girl (the 'dead' childhood self that insists on making its presence felt by sticking out an arm), and to hide *from* the angry, disorderly woman that is another feared self, the protruding arm and the face at the window indicate that hiddenness will ultimately be unsustainable.

This dream and a further dream that Louise describes a little later also establish a link between journeys and the disturbingly unexpected. In the second dream, Louise is on a railway station with a vast amount of luggage, far more than she can cope with. The train is leaving but Louise is unable to get on it because she hasn't got a ticket. Somehow, all her luggage has been put on to the train and, as the train pulls out of the station, she runs along beside it calling for this luggage. Two bags, one a briefcase (presumably containing her research notes), are thrown out to her. She goes to pick up the briefcase, but the strap, which had already been hanging off, becomes a snake that clings to her and won't let go. Though she does not yet understand this, the library-related briefcase is an object of fear. The designated means of control (the library) is likewise something she will need to escape from.

The snake that grasps Louise so determinedly has another, phallic, connotation. Later in the play it is established, first that the briefcase was a twenty-first birthday present from her father, and second, that the father sexually abused Louise when she was a child. It is the father who is the real controlling agent in Louise's life. Her 'teacher' as well as her abuser, a clergyman who believed (as did Clara Schumann's father) that work and duty were more important than happiness or self-expression, he refused Louise's childhood requests to learn the piano, or for what he defined as costly luxuries: a doll that said 'Mama', candy floss, a Knickerbocker Glory.

The desired, but unobtainable, doll is able to speak the affectionate word that Louise herself has never been able to utter. Between Louise and her mother, Vera, there is an emotional chasm that it is almost impossible to bridge and that is symbolised in the prelude by Louise's description of a dream in which Vera is talking to a group of Japanese students, 'rabbiting on the way she does and nobody can understand a word she's saying' (ibid.: 175). To Vera, Louise has always been emphatically the father's child, a cold little creature whom Vera had to teach herself to love as she would learn a foreign language. To Louise, her mother has remained alien, her thoughts and feelings incomprehensible as a foreign language. Vera is the uncaring betrayer, who failed to protect her from the father's abuse, but also a hated, and feared, aspect of self that, at times, Louise feels is physically invading her (like an alien), entering her 'body by stealth', occupying her 'under cover of darkness' (ibid.: 177).

In Louise's Japanese-student dream, her mother's words that cannot be understood are followed by a sound representative of her father, the church bell ringing for Evensong. The prelude ends with an echo of this bell. First, the voices of small children are heard singing 'All Things Bright and Beautiful' in a blackout. Though 'ragged', their singing is also 'spontaneous', but then the voice of Louise's psychotherapist (a father figure) is heard telling the children that he wants to understand every word: 'No mumbling, no bumbling . . . clear as a bell' (ibid.). The children comply with his instructions, but their spontaneity has been replaced by self-consciousness. Later in the play, the words of the hymn become for Louise a talismanic guarantor of safety and control. Other songs and brief snatches of instrumental music that are woven into the play's action point, however, to the existence of possibilities that disturb and threaten the maintenance of control. The German language, which is spoken at times to an uncomprehending Louise (who is therefore placed in a position similar to the Japanese students in her dream), similarly evokes a set of potential meanings and a form of communication hidden from Louise. Like the faces that dissolve, one into another, sounds jumble and then make themselves anew no matter how much she tries to hold on to the bell-like clarity of 'All Things Bright and Beautiful' – brightly beautiful, she learned from her father, precisely because God 'made them all', willed them into being exactly as they are.

A major recurring musical motif in the play is a fugue by Clara Schumann, her Opus 16 in G minor. In an introductory note, Sheila Yeger refers to two meanings of fugue, both of which are relevant to *Variations*. *Variations* is a fugue, in both a musical and a psychiatric sense. Musically, it is fugue-like in that different voices (and possibilities) are placed in counterpoint to each other, and, psychiatrically, because the whole piece takes the form of an attempted flight, supposedly towards order and analysis but in reality away from childhood-induced fears and anxieties.

A few notes from Clara Schumann's fugue 'played rather suddenly on the piano' (ibid.: 186), followed by the noise of the train arriving at the station, serve as a bridge from the first to the second part (movement) of the first act. The lights fade on the train compartment, and when they come up again Louise is in a small hotel room. Here, she tries to organise the next stage of her research project by telephoning the library to check the availability of the Clara Schumann material. Her inner anxiety is betrayed, however, by her (abortive) attempt to speak to Richard Last, her psychotherapist, on the telephone (a control-linked object), and her subconscious awareness of the existence of possibilities outside of her rigid schedule by the way in which her hands, seemingly of their own volition, pick up the elastic band that has held together her index cards, on one of which is the library telephone number, and twist it around a bunch of her hair. As she is looking in surprise at this new image of herself in the mirror, a porter, who closely resembles the Young Guard Louise met on the station platform, enters. He is carrying a silver jug of hot chocolate – the drink that Louise bought on the platform instead of the coffee she had meant to order. The Porter with his gift of chocolate represents the possibility of a sensual fulfilment Louise both desires and fears. Embarrassed at being caught playing with her hair, she pulls off the elastic band, but the Porter leads her gently to the mirror and, finding a couple of rubber bands, makes two bunches of her hair. 'See', he says. For a moment or two, they stand motionless, his hands on her shoulders, Louise staring at their reflection. Then 'quite viciously' she pulls her hair out of the bands. 'Hot chocolate', she tells the Porter, is a children's drink. She 'didn't order hot chocolate . . . or tea . . . or coffee [or] anything' (ibid: 188).

Louise's denial of the responsibility of having ordered anything leads to the setting being immediately transformed from the hotel room to the reference library with its promise that order, and ordering, will have already been established within safe parameters. Louise is sitting, surrounded by books and manuscripts (protected from the possibilities suggested by the Porter and his chocolate), and, as she makes notes, she reads aloud from one of the books in 'a clipped, precise tone' (ibid.). A man sitting opposite her switches on his reading light and is revealed as Richard Last. Louise tells him that her research is going well, but then, after a pause, begins to speak of a long-ago visit to the London Planetarium with her father, returning therefore to the childhood that she had rejected as irrelevant in the previous scene. She was eight or nine, and the time of year must have been spring because she remembers seeing tulips. When they arrived at the Planetarium it was closed until two o'clock and Louise cried because, as she explains to Last, 'he wouldn't let me in'. '*He?*' Last queries, and quickly Louise amends 'he' to 'they' (ibid.). She and her father walked the entire length of Baker Street, she remembers. Her mother had made her wrap up warmly and she was hot. When she saw a picture of a Knickerbocker Glory, she longed for one, but her father told her it was 'astronomically expensive' (ibid.). Louise repeats 'astronomically' and then laughs, connecting 'astronomically' with 'astronomy' and the closed Planetarium. She did eventually get into the Planetarium, but found it 'Frightening . . . Too many stars . . . Too many possibilities' (ibid.: 189). What she wanted was safety. When Last asks her where she would be safe, she is unable to deal with the implications of the question, and she replies that she doesn't know. Last responds by beginning to write something which Louise is unable to see and, when she asks *what* he is writing, he replies in German, and as though he were a complete stranger, that he doesn't speak English. Louise's inability to face the implications of what safety – and its opposite – would consist of have transformed Last from a possible guide on an inner journey of discovery into a producer of indecipherable hieroglyphics.

145

Though she is unable to undertake the inner journey Last proposes, Louise finds in Clara Schumann a model for self-knowledge with which she is more at ease. When her husband was dying, Clara destroyed a large proportion of the correspondence between Brahms and herself, and Louise is convinced that the reason for this must be that it consisted of love letters. She takes up a notepad and begins to write her own love letter, confiding to the unnamed recipient her loneliness, her desire to hold him and her memories of his 'long, pale back', his 'mouth hot and open' against hers (ibid.). Where earlier, therefore, she had tried unsuccessfully to decipher what Last was writing, now she constructs her own text. Additionally, she echoes, and refocuses, her words from her Planetarium memory. 'Let me in Clara', she begs. 'Please. Why won't you let me in?' (ibid). In the following scene, Clara and Brahms (played by the same actor who was also the Young Guard and the Porter) act out a further version of this request. This time it is the man who begs to be let in, while Clara refuses because she is afraid she will be lost – will 'drown' in the blueness of his eyes (ibid.: 191). When Louise next appears, in a bathrobe and with wet hair, she is a water-linked figure, a Lorelei as the Porter later calls her when she prepares to drown in the blueness of *his* eyes.

When the Porter reappears, he is again carrying hot chocolate, but, prior to this, Louise partially relives the childhood incident with which chocolate has become linked for her. She recounts this memory to Vera, while lying curled up like a child, her thumb in her mouth and a rag-doll clutched close to her face. In a childlike voice, she recalls the day when she was eight or nine (the same age, though she doesn't make this connection, as she was in her memory of the Planetarium). It had been raining all week and, after school, she went to the river bank, 'squatted down and picked up great big lumps' of mud, which she smeared on her face so that some of it found its way into her mouth. It tasted strange – rather like chocolate. She plastered the 'sticky, warm, lovely, dirty mud' all over her school uniform. 'And then' she continues, 'and then . . .' (ibid.: 192). A light comes on revealing Last sitting at Louise's desk, and Louise, speaking now as an adult, describes her father coming to find her, and locking her in her room just as she was, all covered in mud. Again, she repeats 'and then', but, instead of explaining what happened, she looks at Vera for a long time, then says, 'Nothing. And then nothing' (ibid.).

When the Porter enters with the hot chocolate, Louise first tells him, as she did before, that she didn't order anything, but then she drinks the chocolate and, as he takes the empty cup back from her, their hands meet. He takes both her hands gently in his and the two of them hold each other's gaze. Her discovery that his name is Johannes (John, her father's name) alarms her, but she allows him to kiss her. Then, she does something she always wanted to do when she was little, but was prevented from doing because her father disapproved. She dips her fingers into the empty cup, and sucks them. Then, she dips them in again and holds them out to the Porter. When he hesitates, she pushes her fingers into his mouth. Laughing delightedly, she smears chocolate on to her breast, pulls him to her and kisses him deliberately and passionately as the lights fade.

When the lights slowly come up again the bed is dishevelled and Louise, covered only with a sheet, is naked and grubby. Her memory of what happened floods her first with a luxuriant feeling of sensuous fulfilment, plus a sense that she is about to give birth to a long-desired 'child', but gradually she is overcome with anxiety. Desperately, she attempts to disclaim responsibility for what took place, asserting that she 'didn't order chocolate . . . didn't order anything' (ibid.: 195). In a last, frantic attempt to return to the ordered world of her research, she puts on her raincoat over her bathrobe, saying that she must get into the museum (i.e. the library transformed into a receptacle for dead objects, and therefore clearly linked to the dream she recounted in the prelude) before it closes. The lights change to a surreal night-time street. There is a sudden blare of music from a juke box and Louise enters 'running, wild-eyed, barefoot' (ibid.), a distorted image of Marilyn's 'Running Wild' song from *Some Like It Hot* which has been sung earlier. Strange, nightmarish versions of Anna and Marilyn appear. Anna (a character haunted by her desire to be reunited with the child she gave up to be with her lover) enters with an empty push-chair and calls, not for her own child, but for Clara who, she fears, has starved to death. She exits and a light comes up to reveal 'Marilyn' standing with her back to Louise. Louise asks 'her' the way to the museum and, when 'she' turns round, it is not Marilyn but 'a man in drag, grotesque but alluring' (ibid.), who propositions her. A light shows Laura at a bus-stop, reading a letter. She turns to Louise. 'Unimaginable bliss . . . unimaginable despair', she says (ibid: 196), then turns away. As Louise stands, lost, lights reveal the Polythene Woman sitting on the ground, surrounded by her bundles. The more sex you get, the more you want, she tells Louise. Once, the Polythene Woman was beautiful. Men desired her, she was 'in charge'. Now, she's old, drying up, even 'in here', her genitals.

Richard Last appears and, though he wears an 'indeterminate uniform' (a sign that he no longer represents certainty), Louise is still convinced that he must act as a promise of order and control. Rapidly, she recites details of her research into the life of Clara Schumann and the opening words of the 'Our Father', then sings, in a child's voice, 'All Things Bright and Beautiful'. These words are meant to act as a mantra to protect her, but they can no longer guarantee her safety. The museum is closed, Richard Last tells her in German. Convinced that this can't be true, Louise continues the words of the hymn. 'The Lord God made them all', so everything must be all right (ibid.). Daddy said so, he promised. Nothing is her fault. She has been 'commissioned' (sanctioned) to carry out her research, she never ordered chocolate, it was all a dream. She beats violently on the wall with her fists, and the act ends with her calling to Clara to tell them to open the museum, to tell them it's not her fault.

In the second half of the play, the various female characters increasingly reveal their interconnection and their function as aspects of Louise. Anna's desire for her child (translated in Louise's nightmare vision into a desperate longing for the dead Clara) and Marilyn's sadness because she hasn't had a little girl are seen to be related fragments of Louise's unacknowledged, grieving childhood self and her half-understood yearning to give birth to a 'child' that would be an expression of a more integrated, adult self. Anna, Laura and Marilyn are linked by their experience of sexual passion, Marilyn and Anna by their suicides (the latter by throwing herself under a train). Laura, similarly, considers death under the wheels of a train, as does Louise. Like Clara, Louise experiences passionate sexual love with a younger man, and her academic research is fuelled by the desire to know whether Clara 'let [Brahms] in' (ibid.: 203). If she can find the love letters she seeks, these will constitute a map that, in contrast to the timetable of trains between Aachen and Berlin that she misread, or Richard Last's incomprehensible writing in German, will provide her with a reliable means of orientating herself.

Vera, one of Louise's most estranged selves, has links with Laura and the Polythene Woman. Laura sacrificed herself by returning to her husband. Vera's developing love for a young curate was sacrificed when, even though he himself felt no affection for her, her husband sent the curate away. The Poly-thene Woman has had extensive sexual experience, but she is now dry and papery and her journeys, like Vera's, are ended. In addition to Laura and the Polythene Woman, Vera is connected with Marilyn, although the two women seem so different. Mari-lyn, the adored 'Golden body' in its 'pleated white dress' was, as she herself explains, 'Sacrificed' (ibid.: 198 and 199).

Immediately after Marilyn makes this comment, a few notes of the fugue are heard played on the piano and Vera is seen in an area of light. Visually a contrasting figure with Marilyn in her white dress, Vera is wearing 'deep mourning' and, in her hand, she holds 'a bunch of wilting tulips' (ibid.: 199). Tulips, the flowers Louise remembered in the context of the Planetarium, have previously been revealed as associated with Vera. When we first see her, Vera is arranging tulips in a vase, and this is also what she is doing in a memory she recounts of the young curate watching her. When the mourning figure of Vera appears, Louise draws her attention to the fact that the flowers are dying, but Vera answers that everything is dying, and goes on to describe her hatred for her husband. Once, she was red-haired, vibrant as red, living tulips, but he drained her of colour. Now, she mourns what can never be, and her memory of her husband's sexual nature reveals him as the recipient of the love letter Louise began to write in the library: 'Large, cold hands when he wanted, long cold back when he didn't' (ibid.). There is something more, Vera indicates to her daughter, that she must say to her, but, in the event, it is not Vera, but Anna and Marilyn (the two women most connected in the play with death, but also with sexuality), who speak the message Louise needs to hear. 'Tear life open, Louise', they say. 'Run . . . from calmness, compassionate endurance, silence. Scream, Louise, Scream' (ibid.).

At the end of act two, Louise does finally scream. She has been talking, for the first time, to the older Clara Schumann, who is played by the same actress who plays the Polythene Woman. Louise insists that, though she refuses to admit it, Clara did 'let

[Brahms] in'. 'I *know* you', she tells Clara. 'I *know* who you are' (ibid.: 203, original emphasis), but Clara rejects Louise's inter- pretation of her life. Though Louise believes that she is looking everywhere for Clara, she will not find her because, like the museum, her eyes are closed. In German, Clara tells Louise to look to herself for the answers she seeks and, when Louise fails to understand, reminds her that they don't even have a language in common.

There is, however, another, non-verbal language that Louise has partially understood, and that is the fugue. Clara elucidates it more fully, explaining its characteristic structure and its possibly autobiographical nature, and, in response, Louise recalls her encounter with the Porter, where the lack of a common verbal language was no barrier, and instead of hiding and holding back, everything became 'wet and flowing' (ibid.). Within her mind, the floodgates that have held the past in check break open and she understands that all the selves, feared or desired, are her self. She has travelled, but she has failed to get anywhere because that wasn't the answer. Crouching on all fours, she articulates the real answer: 'Louise . . . all of me . . . all of these . . . Louise is I . . . I . . . I' and, in a scream of liberation, she releases the hidden, disowned aspects of self (ibid.: 204).

The play ends with a coda, set on a railway platform. In contrast to the night-time station scene at the beginning of act one, it is now early morning, a time of new possibilities. Rhea sits on a luggage wagon, eating an apple. A guard enters, an older man than the guard in act one. Louise follows. Her clothes are creased, she is shoeless, untidy, dirty and hungry. Rhea hands over the apple and, for the first time in her life, Louise bites into an apple that someone else has been eating. She opens her briefcase, takes out all her papers, stuffs them into the waste bin and puts the briefcase in after them. The only things she has retained are her passport, wallet and the rag-doll she clutched as she described her memory of smearing herself with mud. The Polythene Woman comes in, rummages in the bin and extracts a piece of newspaper. 'That's me', she tells Louise, showing her a picture in the paper. 'Little Clara. Men ate me like chocolate . . . In, out. In, out' (ibid.: 205). Her eyes on the Polythene Woman, who is at once Clara, Louise's unloved, abused childhood self, and a feared, used-up, similarly unloved, potential older self, Louise, for the first time, describes what her father did to her. It began the time when she had been playing in the mud. He bathed her, scrubbed her clean, then pushed his thumb inside her as far as it would go. She thought it was a punishment, and, later, she let him continue to abuse her because she was afraid that otherwise he wouldn't love her. But she sacrificed herself pointlessly, because he didn't love her anyway. She let him in, but his heart was closed against her.

Laura enters and Louise wants to ask if she knew her mother, but is unable to do so. Earlier, Louise and Vera have almost made loving contact through the touching of hands, but, at the last moment, their hands failed to meet. Again, this time with Laura (a Vera substitute), there is almost a coming together, but it doesn't quite happen. In addition to her role as an aspect of Louise, Vera is also the mother who, for whatever reason, did not manage to protect her child, and the breach between them cannot be completely healed. Instead, a healing of a kind is enacted between Louise and Rhea in which Louise, the older woman, is nevertheless the daughter – in that she is fed (with the apple) and then comforted when Rhea puts her arms around her. It is Rhea who offered, in act one, guidance as to the nature of the journey that Louise was really trying to make, and, though Louise ignored the guidance then, she accepts it now. Laughingly, the two women tell the Guard that they might go to Ostend, or, possibly in the opposite direction, to Lucerne.

It is to the Guard that Louise confides the unhappiness that led her to make her initial journey. Her father's lack of love, she tells him, broke her 'inside and out' (ibid.: 206) and she had to find a safe place to hide. With this articulation of the mainspring of her need for hiddenness and safety, Louise finds the means of translating the indecipherable script that the psychotherapist turned foreign stranger wrote in the library, and, simultaneously, all the male figures in the play reveal themselves as interrelated. 'Goodbye Richard', she says to the Guard (ibid.), and, when he tells her that his name is not Richard, she replies that she knows his real name. It is Johannes. Alongside the abusive, cold father (John), there is also Johannes/Richard (a caring father-figure) and Johannes/Brahms/the Porter (passionate lover). Louise has experience of them all, and though the past cannot be altered, it is laid to rest.

Louise's selves – Anna, Laura, the Polythene Woman – are around Louise and the music of Rhea's pipe is heard. The

Polythene Woman has lit the paper in the waste bin to make a fire to warm her hands. Louise kisses the rag-doll, then throws it on to the flames. Alone now, 'in time to Rhea's music', she dances slowly and with great pleasure. Previously, when she spoke of dancing, it was in the context of her controlling father; 'Dance for Daddy', she said. Anna, and later Marilyn, have provided her with other models of dancing. Each has danced for her own sensuous enjoyment. At the end of *Variations*, Louise also 'dances for herself'. As she performs this intensely pleasurable 'private ritual' (ibid.), the lights slowly fade around her.

Louise dancing for her own pleasure rather than for Daddy at the end of *Variations* brings to mind Cordelia in the final moments of *Lear's Daughters*. Earlier, Cordelia has danced for her abusive father, but eventually she resists his control, finding in her case an individual voice rather than a self-affirming pattern of movement. In addition to its own distinctive journey, *Variations* has echoes of moments in other dramatic journeys I have explored. Louise's rag-doll is reminiscent of Philomele's alter ego and the monster doll Elise makes in *Blood and Ice*. Vera's and Louise's hands that fail to touch recall both abortive moments of missed contact between mother and daughter in the plays examined in chapter two and also the link between Mary's and Elise's hands in *Blood and Ice*. Louise's search for a language of self finds its counterpart in a number of plays that form the subject matter of earlier chapters. The final three plays discussed in this chapter repeat some of these motifs. Dolls feature in both *Queen Christina* and *The Grace of Mary Traverse*. In each of the plays daughters' relationships with fathers, and, in *Pax*, also with mothers, are problematic. All depict a search for alternative ways of seeing and being, plus the difficulties attendant on creating new maps for old.

In Pam Gems's *Queen Christina*, which was first performed at The Other Place, Stratford-upon-Avon, in 1977, the protagonist is in search of just such a map. As I suggested at the end of chapter four, her quest has some similarities to that of the monster in *Frankenstein's Mothers* in that Foursight Theatre's 'man unman' (in my reading, woman) could serve as an apt description of Christina. The sole surviving heir to the Swedish throne, the seventeenth-century Christina was brought up as a boy and trained in 'manly' skills so that she could assume her father's crown on his death. Unlike Garbo's movie image of Christina, a 'shining, pale, intellectual beauty' who gives up her throne for love, Gems's character is, in her author's words, 'a dark, plain woman with a crippled shoulder, daughter of a beautiful mother whose health . . . ha[s] been ruined by yearly pregnancies in the effort to provide a male heir' (Gems 1986: 47). Constructed by her upbringing as a man, Christina's 'maleness' provides her with a yardstick by which to measure what has value. She despises femininity – although she finds it sexually desirable in women when it is allied to beauty. Her own ungainly body, with its 'bloody periods', seems to her a monstrous joke. In contrast to Garbo's Christina, she gives up her crown because she discovers that, in addition to the manly attributes she has developed, she is expected to perform the traditional woman's function of breeding in order to secure the succession. Faced with the prospect of marriage and childbearing, she prefers to abdicate. Her transformation into a man has been too successful. The 'only truth' she knows is a man's and she will not 'pollute' it. (ibid.: 30).

The construction of Christina as a man, and her own affirmation of maleness as a sign of self, is expressed in act one through a sequence of visual images. In the first scene, Christina is a little girl, crouching fearfully in the dim glow of firelight as she listens to the screams of her mother giving birth to another stillborn child. Her father's promise that she will herself be a queen distresses her and, quickly, he alters 'queen' to 'king'. Christina will be like himself, not like her mother. When he exits towards the sound of the Queen's sobbing, Christina begins to follow him, but then stops and hugs her doll, the sign of the traditional little girl that she will soon cease to be.

The second scene, 'Betrothal', opens with a suitor awaiting the adult Christina's arrival. As his only experience of her is a flattering portrait that bears little resemblance to its original, when a lovely, exquisitely dressed young woman enters he not surprisingly assumes that this is Christina. The arrival a few moments later of what the script describes as a man, a battered, crooked-looking figure who proceeds to fondle the young woman, first bewilders and then outrages him. When he grasps the truth, he is too appalled to protest. The 'man' (Christina) takes his 'nerveless arm' (ibid.: 19) and mockingly stands by his side in the semblance of a wife. Wordlessly, the suitor exits, never to return.

In the final scene of act one, 'Abdication', Christina puts off her man's clothes and wears instead a white dress, like a bride. Left alone at the end of the scene, after she has been divested of her crown, she performs another, and private, ceremony. She rips away the masquerade, the false womanly 'skin' of the bride she will never be, to reveal, underneath, her riding clothes and boots. Ecstatically, she whirls round with arms extended and then runs offstage leaving behind the dress that is an absurd irrelevance to the only self she knows.

Christina's 'maleness' provides her with a map, a way of operating in the world. She has chosen the life of a 'free rover' and, in this guise, she travels first to France and then to Italy, taking, or more precisely, buying, her sexual pleasures from both women and men as she goes. She is searching, however, for another, intellectual and metaphysical, map which will enable her to orientate herself in the world of ideas and of the spirit. Whilst still in Sweden, she was already in quest of this map. Sometimes it seemed to her that such a thing must exist, and that, if she could discover it, she would become a cartographer of meaning. 'Why are we given life?' she speculated. 'In order to suffer . . . to be stoic? If so, why the larch tree?' (ibid.: 20). Then, overcome by horror of the kind of God that could deliberately construct the world with all its brutality and pain, her hope was that no map existed. 'Pestilence . . . the murder of children – by design? Better no meaning at all' (ibid.: 21). Contemporary ideas about the physical world, however, indicated to her new ways of charting the universe and the world of ideas. The concept of the earth as a ball hanging in space delighted her with its imaginativeness.

In her journey across western Europe in the second half of the play Christina is initially attracted to, and then rejects, two opposed sets of ideas (two map readings), first those of two famous Bluestockings in Paris, and then of the Pope in Rome. When she meets the Frenchwomen, she is surprised by the elegance of their clothes, which seems at odds with what she has heard of the iconoclastic nature of their beliefs. She is particularly disappointed, when she lifts up one of the women's skirts, to discover that the famous blue stockings don't exist in reality. When she learns of the radically separatist nature of the women's lives, and, particularly, of their hatred of men, whom they define as the enemy, she begins to feel like an 'impostor'. After all, she only gave up her old existence because she wanted 'to live'. She honours the women's 'courage' but is unable to accept their solutions and, instead, journeys on to Rome to continue her researches into life's meaning 'at the feet of the Holy Father' (ibid.: 35).

At the beginning of act two, scene two, which is set in the Vatican and is entitled 'Papa', Christina, the 'free rover', is momentarily eclipsed by Christina, the loving daughter, looking to the all-knowing father who will unscramble the twisted and muddied contours of her spiritual world and render them comprehensible. The Pope's map, however, offers Christina no better understanding of the inner landscape of her life than did that of the Bluestockings. Instead of women with individual characteristics and needs, the Pope sees 'woman', and, for him, woman has 'a sacred destiny', which is to procreate within a marriage sanctioned by the Church, and, so, to become the basis of an ordered and orderly society. Copulation outside of marriage, and the avoidance of conception within it, are equally sinful. Nature's laws must not be violated. The destruction, in the womb, of a potential child is murder. 'Woman is creation!' the Pope asserts, 'Would you turn her into an assassin?' 'And what of a woman's flow? A child a month, deceased', Christina counters. What too of 'a man's ejaculation? . . . whole populations denied breath. Nature is wasteful, Pope' (ibid.: 37).

Christina's rejection of the Pope's concept of nature leads, at the end of the play, to her articulation of her own understanding of the relationship between nature and women. The emotional journey by means of which she reaches her conclusions takes her through a variety of ideological terrains. At the end of act two, scene two, the Pope exits, having promised to pray for her soul, and Christina responds by pressing her hands to her body and vowing that *its* needs will be satisfied. In the shadows, she perceives the dim shape of a man, Monaldescho, who will be the means of that satisfaction, and bids him come forward. Mutual need is the basis of their relationship, his for advancement, hers for sexual fulfilment. When Monaldescho pretends love for her, Christina turns on him with anger, but when he qualifies his love as arising from the fact that she is a queen, she applauds his honesty. Monaldescho betrays Christina, however. At the prompting of Cardinal Azzolino, an emissary from the Pope, Christina agrees to assume the crown of Naples, if it can be wrested from its Spanish conquerors, whereupon Monaldescho informs the enemy of her military plans. His treachery arouses contempt in Christina, but it is his desperate babbling of 'Madonna, madonna . . . I love you' as he frenziedly clings to her skirt and pleads for mercy, that arouses in her a murderous fury, and, in a moment of blinding anger, she seizes a dagger and strikes him in the throat, killing him. When Cardinal Azzolino, who has been present throughout the incident, expresses horror at its barbarity, she rejoins, 'Are we all to be like you . . . hiding from life in a woman's skirts?' (ibid.: 42)

Christina's castigation of Azzolino's response, the 'weakness' which she defines as the product of his feminine clothes, is followed by a revulsion against the murder she has committed, which expresses itself through a rejection of the male garments that have previously signified her identity. In the scene after the killing, act two, scene six, which is entitled 'Dolls', she sits (at first completely motionless), wearing a dressing-gown and a cap. She has stopped eating and one of her women, Lucia, tries to tempt her with some of her favourite sweets. Lucia puts the sweets on Christina's lap, but there is no response and, not knowing what else to do, she exits. After a few moments, Angelica, Lucia's little daughter, enters. Of a similar age to Christina in the first scene of the play, and like her, at that point, carrying a doll, Angelica serves as an echo of the child that existed prior to the construction of Christina as man. Angelica feeds sweets to her doll and then puts one into Christina's mouth. When Christina makes no move to swallow it, Angelica gives her a little slap and tells her to eat it and to stop being naughty. As if the nursery language reminds her of the long-ago child that was herself, Christina responds for the first time in the scene. Silently, she begins to cry, and, when Angelica leaves, she turns her head in order to watch her go. Slowly, Christina begins to eat the sweet.

The following, and final, scene opens with Lucia entering with flowers and wine preparatory to the arrival of Cardinal Azzolino. She is accompanied by Angelica who has ribbons in her hair. Christina is wearing a pink overgarment, 'festively decorated', as though to emphasise her regression to her childhood self. She resembles a doll, and the room she is in has become her doll's

house. The killing of Monaldescho, executed out of 'mere tem-
per', has made her a prisoner in this room which is now her
'whole world'. To go even as far as the door fills her 'with terror'
(ibid.: 43). The person who rescues her from the room is
Angelica, the child who, in the previous scene, managed to
engage her attention despite her misery. When Lucia runs in, in
terror because Angelica is choking (offstage), Christina forgets
her own fears and rushes out to help. It is only when she returns,
having saved the child by giving her 'a fine blow in the stomach'
(ibid.: 44), that she grasps the fact that she left the room.

Christina's exit from her doll's house is a distant echo of
Ibsen's Nora's, but, just as her way into this ideological space has
been different from her predecessor's, so too is her leaving of it.
Prior to her final exit, Nora's entire life has been lived within the
doll's house, and the only choice that is finally available to her is
whether to remain within the doll's house, with all its attendant
values, or to leave it, husband, children and former self behind.
By contrast, almost the entirety of Christina's life has been lived
despising not only the doll's house, but all facets of women's
lives. Her horror at the death of Monaldescho causes her to
retreat temporarily into the doll's-house room, but this is only a
staging post on her new journey, a quest for a different map of
being. Her saving of Angelica has taken her into the servants'
quarters with their warmth and their smell of ironed clothes,
baking and babies. This encounter with the serving-women's
world that is the necessary precondition for her imprisoning, yet
privileged, doll's house room, teaches Christina two things: her
desire for a child, and her previous misjudgment of what she has
termed woman's 'weakness'. Reared as a man, she now begins to
question whether this was a 'favour'. 'To be invited to join the
killing, why, where's the advantage?' (ibid.: 44). She doesn't
imagine that 'every man is a murdering brute', she tells Cardinal
Azzolino, 'far from it, or we'd not have survived this far', but it is
women, nevertheless, with their ability to share, rather than to
take (to share their very bodies with their children), who, she
now realises, 'have kept us alive!' (ibid.: 45).

Christina is unable to remain in the women's world of the
servants' quarters. Even if she wished to do so, her upbringing
and social position would make this impossible. She brings back,
however, from this meeting with the other world, the understanding that she is a woman, though 'What that is, heaven

knows . . . the philosophy is yet to be written' (ibid.). A misfit in her seventeenth-century world, Christina, the man who is now unman, searches for a map that might delineate the contours of self and of other, future women. Why must she choose between having a child and an active life? she asks Azzolino, and when he, like the Pope, cites nature as the source of gender stereotyping, she replies that nature 'is us! . . . It is we who change and create change!' (ibid.).

In her Afterword to the play, Pam Gems writes of Christina's relevance to our present-day world. It is possible for a woman now to have children and yet still lead a mentally active life, possible also to choose not to have children, or to have them outside marriage. What are needed, however, Gems suggests, are maps of the new terrain in which we find ourselves. The 'new breed' of women have to make their voices heard, and what those voices say needs to include an articulation of what Christina understood when she visited the servants' quarters – the interconnection of all human beings. Despite its title, *Queen Christina* is not only about one woman, but, rather, about that woman's eventual perception of the ways in which her life relates to other lives. Christina's quest for maps translates itself, in our world, into a search for a blueprint for a society that would bring into a more harmonious balance a variety of opportunities, needs and responsibilities, a society better suited to the needs of both women and men, 'and to the happiness of children' (ibid.: 48).

Christina's search for maps, for inner journeys towards an understanding of self, and of ways of being in – and of changing – the world, finds a new formulation in Timberlake Wertenbaker's 1985 play, *The Grace of Mary Traverse*. Similarly also to Pam Gems in *Queen Christina*, Timberlake Wertenbaker uses past landscapes partially, at least, to explore the present. *The Grace of Mary Traverse* is set in the eighteenth century, but, as Wertenbaker explains in her prefatory note to the Faber and Faber edition of the text, it is not a historical play. The characters are her 'own invention' and, where she has 'used historical events such as the Gordon Riots [she has] taken great freedom with reported fact' (Wertenbaker 1989: 57). The eighteenth century acts as a 'valid metaphor', a time of instability within which a number of the characters search for new paths forward that will have relevance to our world in addition to their own.

Along with her explanatory note, the author prefaces her play with two quotations. The first, from the writings of Sappho: 'If you are squeamish / Don't prod the beach rubble' (ibid.: 55), is repeated in act one, scene three. By means of a process that her name encodes, a character called Mrs Temptwell has persuaded Mary Traverse to leave the imprisoning security of her father's house, and to explore the forbidden London street outside, forbidden to Mary, that is, by her father. When Mary complains of the filth in the street, Mrs Temptwell replies that 'dirt runs out of great houses', like the one owned by Mr Traverse, and then goes on to quote Sappho's maxim, appropriating it, as she does so, as part of her own background. 'It's a saying we had in our family', she explains (ibid.: 67). Mary's incursion into the street leads to a desire to replicate the experience of men, to 'Run the world through [her] fingers as they do' (ibid.: 71), and, to this end, she makes a Faustian compact with Mrs Temptwell. She will be able to remain in this world, to live as men live, learn what they know, but the price is that she can never return to what she was. Experience once gained cannot be denied. Prod the beach rubble, and you will have to confront all the smelly detritus you find.

The second quotation, which is taken from George Steiner's *In Bluebeard's Castle*, questions the morality, and indeed the possibility, of debating a 'definition of culture' today given the barbarities perpetrated in the twentieth century, but concludes that we should not accept this eventuality as self-evident: 'The numb prodigality of our acquaintance with horror is a radical human defeat' (ibid.: 55). In Wertenbaker's play Mary's traversing of the world of men that she has appropriated as also her world brings her into close contact with a degree of brutality and horror that takes her to the brink of despair. Like Gems's Christina who decides that 'no meaning at all' would be preferable to 'the murder of children – by design', Mary fears that cruelty is endemic: that even God, should he exist, wouldn't be able to 'love this world'. For Christina, the possibility of another way of structuring experience is imaged by the larch tree. To Mary, grace, if this could only be achieved, suggests a similar possibility, and her journey in the play (her traversing of the world she has chosen) gradually defines itself as a quest for grace.

The play begins with Mary's attempt to acquire one form of grace: the elegant, decorous nullity of an 'agreeable' woman. Act one, scene one is set in the drawing room of her father's house, and here Mary practises the art of graceful conversation. Sitting facing an empty chair, she talks to it 'with animation' (ibid.: 59). Behind her stands her father, watching and correcting her. In order to be 'agreeable', he explains, 'a young woman must make the other person [the man to whom she is speaking] say inter-esting things', or, at least, believe that he has said interesting things. If one subject fails to engage him, she must 'glide' effortlessly into the next leaving 'no gap' (ibid.: 60). Mary's models of the perfect, graceful woman are the dolls she played with as a child: 'silk-limbed, satin-clothed, leaving no imprint' (ibid.: 62). Left alone in the drawing room in scene two, she walks to and fro, trying to leave no trace of her passage. Her father's 'brightest adornment' in the doll's house that is her allotted space, she aims to learn from her dolls how not to breathe. This is a skill, Mrs Temptwell tells her, when she enters, that Mary's mother grasped to perfection: 'She died of not breathing in the end'. Still, it hardly mattered. She'd been so quiet anyway that it was a week before her husband realised she was dead. Once he did understand what had happened, death simply added to her charms. She was 'so beautiful in her coffin' that he was unable to stop looking at her. 'Death suits women', Mrs Temptwell explains. Mary herself would 'look lovely in a coffin' (ibid.: 63). Once she has conquered the art of not breath-ing, she will be able to move from her doll's house to this even more paradigmatic women's space. When Mary protests that she doesn't need a coffin in order to look lovely, Mrs Temptwell ripostes that some women have all the graces of a corpse while they are still ostensibly alive. So quiet and dull are they that they seem 'dead already' (ibid.: 64).

Unsettled by this imputation of dullness and deadness, Mary is willing to listen to hints of the seductive possibilities of the world outside her father's house – possibilities, Mrs Temptwell tells her, of which a girl who lives in a neighbouring house (number fourteen) is only too well aware. This girl spends all her time staring out of the window at the street. Once, she even asked a servant to take her outside – on foot! This girl isn't dull: she

'Glitters with interest' (ibid.). To Mary's objection that she has driven through the streets in her carriage and never found anything to attract her there, Mrs Temptwell counters that this is because the streets are emptied first to make room for Mary's progress. Intrigued by the alluring prospect of the street, and determined not be outdone by the girl at number fourteen, Mary decides to disguise herself and to venture out in the company of Mrs Temptwell. It can't do any harm, she reasons, and it would probably add to her skills as a conversationalist. She would 'glitter with knowledge' (ibid.: 65).

Once Mary has experienced the outside world, she rejects her previous existence in her father's house. Her entry into the London streets teaches her three things about this public world of men. It is a cruel place, a place she doesn't understand and a place the physical and ideological landscapes of which she is determined to master. Though she does not immediately understand the significance of what she sees, the first person she meets there, Lord Gordon, functions as Mary's initial guide to the mores of the street-world. Lord Gordon resembles Mary in that he too is looking for a way of making himself more interesting, for, despite his wealthy background, he has so far failed to make the smallest impact on society. Even his horse finds him so boring that it falls asleep when he rides in Hyde Park to display himself to the fashionable people there. At the beginning of act one, scene three, which is set in Cheapside, London, Lord Gordon speculates as to what he can do to get himself noticed. Maybe he should turn to politics – make a speech in the House advocating more draconian punishment for criminals – but stealing a handkerchief is already a capital offence, so there doesn't seem much mileage in this idea. Another possibility would be to make people laugh, but the problem here is that he would first have to think of something witty to say. He could become a rake, but unfortunately the ladies are 'demanding' and he fears that his 'manhood won't rise above middling' (ibid.: 66).

Through his encounter with Mary, and with another young woman called Sophie, Lord Gordon discovers a key to making himself interesting and, in the process, his 'manhood' rises to a degree that he finds eminently satisfactory. When he realises that, like everyone else, Mary is ignoring him, Lord Gordon responds by drawing his sword on her and, so, forcing her to look at him. Intoxicated by the fear that then rivets her attention on him, he determines to heighten her terror still further by raping her. At this point, however, Sophie enters and her protest at what is happening distracts his attention with the result that Mary escapes. Lord Gordon rapes Sophie in Mary's place and finds, as a consequence, that he has become 'a different man' (ibid.: 70). The agent that has transformed him is an intuition of the mechanics of power.

Throughout the rape of Sophie, Mary watches and tries to understand what she is seeing. When it is over, Sophie starts to leave, walking painfully. Momentarily, she comes face to face with Mary, and, when Mary looks at the ground after she has gone, she notices, with wonderment, that there is blood there. The rape and the blood are, to begin with, signs that Mary cannot fully interpret. In the following scene, she describes to Mrs Temptwell her bewilderment at the things she has witnessed in the streets: men walking abroad fearlessly, tearing 'into skin without hesitation and litter[ing] the streets with their discarded actions'. Mary has 'no map to this world', which she walks 'as a foreigner' and she senses 'only danger' (ibid.: 71). She is, however, determined to master its contours, and Lord Gordon and Sophie have presented her with two opposed poles of experience – that of the violator and that of the victim. Confronted by a choice between power and blood, Mary opts for the former.

Her identification with the power-seekers is nevertheless complicated by her need, not only to experience what they experience, but to understand also the hidden motive-springs of behaviour. One of her first actions is to pay a Mr Hardlong to initiate her into the mysteries of sex, but, though she eventually finds the act pleasurable, it presents her with a further piece of the map of experience that she doesn't yet possess, for Mr Hardlong forgoes part of his monetary payment in order to have sex with Sophie (whom Mary has taken into her employment). Mary is as young and as good-looking as Sophie. Why should Mr Hardlong go from herself to the other woman?

By the next scene (act two, scene four), which is set in a gambling den in Drury Lane, Mary has understood the secret of Sophie's attractiveness to men, which lies in her silence, her apparent imperviousness to desire and her consequent stirring of desire in others. Sophie is a blank, an empty sheet on which men write themselves, and Mary discovers in herself a desire to utilise Sophie in the same way. When Mr Hardlong asks Sophie to console him because he has lost a large sum of money to Mary, Mary points out to him that it is she who is in the position of buyer. Sophie must therefore service her needs, not his. Lifting her skirts, Mary commands Sophie to traverse the terrain of her sexuality: its richness and gentleness, its 'cool convexities' (ibid.: 89). In the process of providing Mary with a map of pleasure, Sophie reveals a further reason for her desirability. She is the bringer of tranquillity, the giver of the benison of sleep. Herself a negation, she leads others into sweet, dreamless nothingness.

Alongside her charting of the pleasure and power of sex, Mary attempts to study the operations of greed. Is this the chief source of cruelty, the 'dominant worm in the human heart' (ibid.: 94)? In the gambling-den scene, Mary wins money, from Lord Exrake at cards and from Mr Hardlong in a cock fight, and then wagers everything she has (four thousand pounds) on one last grotesque bet: a race between two old women, two 'hags', so weakened with age and want that they can move only infinitesimally slowly. The hag on whom Mary's opponent, the politician Mr Manners, has placed his bet inches to the finishing line marginally ahead of Mary's, and, after scooping up his four thousand pounds, Mr Manners gives his competitor a shilling for her pains. Mary's competitor asks her to be kind – to give her something in her turn – and, by reply, Mary questions the existence of kindness. Is it anywhere to be seen around them? she asks. When the old woman persists in asking for some return for running to the best of her ability, Mary whips her, to score into her flesh knowledge of a world barren of kindness. The old woman falls to the ground, and, bending over her, Mary is assailed by a memory of a previous occasion when she leaned over another old woman – or perhaps it was even this same woman. Mary was outside a church and her father had given her money to hand to the woman. She remembers people smiling as they watched her, remembers looking at the movement of her wrist and herself smiling 'at its grace' as she gave the woman the coin. 'Was that better?' she wonders (ibid.: 92). Could it be that that was better?

Grace gradually provides Mary with the only viable map for a more just world, but, for a long time, she has only occasional glimpses of the potentialities if offers. Penniless after her experiences in the gambling den, she enters the night-scape where prostitutes swarm, not to whore, she insists, but to learn more about cruelty and greed. Are their seeds always present in the human heart waiting for the right conditions in which to germinate? From the beginning of *The Grace of Mary Traverse*, Mary, like Philomele in Wertenbaker's *The Love of the Nightingale*, until her tongue is torn from its roots, is an asker of questions. It is this faculty that is in fact her saving grace, for her questions form themselves gradually into the latitudinal and longitudinal lines of the map she most deeply seeks. Fittingly, given that her ability to question is a by-product of his teaching her to talk (speech being inseparable from thought), Mary encounters her father in her guise as prostitute and turns her interrogative skills upon him. Her face is covered when Giles Traverse first meets her and he does not initially realise who she is. When he does recognise her, he denies her connection with him. The woman who stands before him is a whore: she cannot therefore be his daughter. Mary Traverse is dead.

In reply, Mary first unpicks the ideology that assigns women into separate, mutually exclusive categories (daughter and whore) and then identifies the pivotal problem as being located within the possessive case: she can be a daughter and a whore but she cannot, at the same time, be *his* daughter. Her analysis leads her to a disquisition on his misappropriation of grace. Giles Traverse has made 'fatherhood an act of grace, an honour [she] must buy with [her] graces' (ibid.: 98), and which he withdrew as soon as she disgraced him. Though he listens to Mary's words, Giles only partially understands what she is saying. His response is to offer to take her back – but only on condition that she becomes again his 'graceful daughter' (ibid.: 99). Instead, Mary suggests a different bargain: money with which to continue her researches into experience in return for the right to claim that his daughter is dead.

Immersed once again in the pleasure-seeking world she had left, Mary finds that it offers not experience but only another 'endless round of puny, private vice'. She has abandoned the cloistered seclusion of her father's house only to enter 'another bounded room' (ibid.: 106). Her quest for a new, unconfined terrain leads to her becoming interlinked with two other searchers: Lord Gordon and Sophie's lover, Jack. Lord Gordon has found that the power he experienced when he raped Sophie has later eluded him, but he is still in search of visibility. If he cannot be powerful, at least he can be noticed. Jack is a poor man, a radical who dreams of a 'new world', but lacks the oratorical skills to publicly communicate his vision. When Mary hears, via Sophie, about Jack's new world, it offers her the means of escape she is seeking from her 'bounded room'. Freedom, she decides, is the desire that sits in the inner recesses of the human heart. Jack has no words to articulate what he yearns for, so she will speak on his behalf.

It is at this point that Mr Manners, who, so far, has been on the periphery of the action, moves nearer to the centre-stage position he actually holds in the wider world of which Mary Traverse is a part. Mr Manners does not need to assert his power because he is truly powerful. In his own eyes, however, he is simply power's servant, for all his energies are focused on one goal – the continuation of the established order – and nothing is so productive of the maintenance of that order, he believes, as a little, carefully regulated, disorder. A taste of panic and bloodshed will ensure that the majority of people turn thankfully away from the possibility of revolutionary change towards the reaffirmation of what previously existed.

To this end, Mr Manners manipulates an uprising that he later quells by brute force. He first separates Mary off from the followers her eloquence has enlisted by inviting her into the Houses of Parliament – not the House itself, of course, but an adjoining room – supposedly so that the politicians there will have the benefit of hearing what she has to say. Mary's relationship to language, and particularly her interrogation of causality, undergoes a change in the Houses of Parliament. When she comes out, she continues to ask questions, but Mr Manners is now her mentor and he guides her tongue along a path he has marked out. In order to create a new world, it is necessary to identify what is wrong with this one, Mary declares. What is the enemy of liberty? Jack's answer – 'tyranny' – is gradually and subtly subverted by Mr Manners, who provides a scapegoat in place of the tyranny exercised by government. A bill that would give Catholics back the right to own property is about to go before the House and it is bound to prove unpopular. Through Mary, Mr Manners feeds the seekers after a new world with horrifying stories of barbarities practised by Catholics (drinking the blood of Protestant children, for example) and in this way, transforms them into a desperate mob bent on the destruction of the perceived enemy. His moment come at last, Lord Gordon offers himself as their leader. 'No Popery! Follow me', he cries (ibid.: 117), and the chant 'No Popery' is taken up until it becomes a tumult. Liberty and new beginnings are forgotten in the turmoil.

For a while Mr Manners allows the riot to run its course. The mob move, eventually, towards Holborn to attack the distilleries there that, so rumour has it, are owned by Catholics. Thousands of gallons of gin are loosed into the streets and, as the throng surges greedily towards them, torches carried by people at the front fall into the liquid and transform it into a sea of fire. Maddened by the looting and violence of which they have been part, people crouch like animals and lap up the burning gin. Exultantly, some of their number tear off their clothes and dance in the middle of the inferno. A man pushes a girl into the flames, pulling up her skirts as he does so, and falls on top of her. As he consummates his passion, a wall collapses on them and kills them.

It is only when the blackened remnants of the mob move towards the Bank of England that Mr Manners acts, ordering a detachment of soldiers in to fire on them. The resulting deaths will, he knows, act as a form of catharsis. The order that will be re-established will last for at least the next forty years. Act three ends with the offstage sounds of shooting and the screams of the victims. Onstage, the charred figure of Mrs Temptwell, who has witnessed the horrors of the riot at first hand, counts the cost in human bones, building them into a neat pile as she simultaneously assembles a casualty list that incorporates, in its highest numbers, pre-echoes of twentieth-century atrocities within those of the present: 'One, two . . . six million, twenty million . . . one, four, one' (ibid.: 123).

Confronted by the terrible logic of the arithmetic of destruction, Mary denies the possibility of a new world. The best that can be hoped for is the obliteration of the present one with all its hideous cruelties. Echoing Mrs Temptwell's evocation of the wholesale slaughters of the twentieth century, Mary envisages humanity's last act, the final curtain of which will be a white cloud that will cancel everything that has ever been. Given that destruction is the only reality, Mary plans to kill the daughter to whom she has recently given birth, but she is prevented from doing this by Sophie. Throughout the majority of the play, Sophie, on the blank sheet of whose body men, and also Mary, have imprinted their desires, has herself been virtually silent. Like Mary, Sophie has questions – in her case, how she might feel less tired, why her belly hurts – but she can formulate them only with great difficulty. Through her relationship with Jack, however, Sophie begins to claim a fuller right to language. In her first encounter with Jack in Vauxhall Gardens (act three, scene two) she speaks only three, repeated, words – 'Yes', 'No' and 'Jack' – but these map her nascent sense of self. 'Yes' in its interrogative form, and 'No' reveal her understanding of, and agreement with, Jack's view that stealing food is not wrong given their hunger and the fact that so many of the well-fed do not earn the bread they eat. Her final 'Jack. Yes. Jack' (ibid.: 101), affirms her active desire for him, in contrast to her earlier mute compliance with the importunate demands of other men. When Mary speaks of her intention to kill the child, Sophie is able to use her new-found ability with words to insist that Mary is wrong in this, and in her interpretation of the world. Mary's method of thought is mistaken, she asserts, because it takes place always from a distance. What is vital is to look 'from near'. Close up, what comes into view is the first light of mornings, the suddenness of turning a corner and seeing something beautiful as if for the first time. These are the map-lines Mary should have studied.

Sophie's articulation of the importance of nearness leads to her singing of what Wertenbaker describes as 'an incredibly beautiful song' and, in the perfection of a 'gracenote', Mary glimpses a means of moving beyond her present despair. 'If I were God', she tells Sophie, 'your song would appease me and I would forgive the history of the world.' 'Touch a baby's skin. It's the same thing' (ibid.: 127), Sophie replies. The possibility of grace evoked by Sophie's song and words seems however, at first, to be raised only to be erased, for Sophie's advice to Mary is followed immediately by her sighting of Jack on his way to Tyburn where he is to be executed for his part in the riot. Sophie's terrible scream of despair when she understands what is about to happen to Jack temporarily obliterates her grace-notes, and, in the subsequent scene, which is set at Tyburn, Mrs Temptwell questions the attainability of grace, particularly on Mary's part. Mary is from a class that takes while others give. Giles Traverse's brother destroyed Mrs Temptwell's grandmother, by using his power as a magistrate to have the old woman hanged as a witch, and, in this way, gain control of the land on which her cottage stood. Mary herself has always acted selfishly despite her professed belief in a new world. Her quest for experience has been at the cost of others' lives. She will not therefore find grace: 'She hasn't the right' (ibid.: 129).

In the final three scenes of the play, Timberlake Wertenbaker traces the outline of a map of grace over the brutalities of the existing world, seeking, in this way, a new world of a different kind from the one the rioters were tricked into attempting to discover. In act four, scene one, after hearing Sophie's song, Mary learns to see nearness: the carved stone of the new houses, 'Soft grey lines sloping against the London sky' (ibid.: 127). In the next (Tyburn) scene, Mary attempts to refind grace. Can it exist despite what is happening to Jack? For Sophie, grace seems annihilated and, far from rescuing Mary's child, she now suggests that they should place her under the wheels of the cart that has brought Jack to the gallows. It is Jack, in this scene, who offers hope of the continuing availability of grace, through his rejection of a proposed debasement of language. Except in the privacy of his relationship with Sophie, telling words have always escaped Jack. In his final moments he is goaded towards public speech by two characters who plan to appropriate the perceived authenticity of a condemned man's last words for their own ends. Lord Exrake hopes that his own repetition of these words, last thing at night, will bring him the sleep he craves, and an unnamed man, who is employed by a firm that manufactures a beverage called Olvite, promises to look after any dependents of Jack's in return for his endorsement of the product at the foot of the gallows. Jack's choice, instead, of silence is an act of grace, its beneficence underlined by Mary's taking Sophie in her arms and turning her head away from the gallows, and by its leading into the musical articulation of beauty that ends the scene: Schubert's Adagio in E flat major Opus post. 148, 'Notturno'.

'Beauty', in the context of the evanescent play of light on the river, is the opening word of the final scene. Set in a garden, this scene brings together Mary, her father, Sophie and Mrs Temptwell, and affirms the continuing existence of grace. 'And now the light lifts itself', says Mary, 'streaks the chimneys. Gone' (ibid.: 129). But, though vanished for the moment, grace *is* reclaimable. Once experienced and understood, the process is there to build on. Despite its location apart from the bustle of the world through which Mary has journeyed, the last scene is not a removal from the world, but a coming together, of the characters and of their (particularly Mary's) knowledge of the world as it is. From this present knowledge it may be possible to remake the future. One day, Mary promises, it will be possible to love this world. 'Will you know how to make it just?' Mrs Temptwell responds (ibid.: 130), and, given the importance of questions in the play, her words cannot be set aside. They are immediately followed, however, by Giles's and Mary's evocation of Mary's little daughter – the new Mary Traverse who is imagined as being on the point of entering the scene. 'There she is', exclaims Mary, and her words have the effect of a promise (ibid.). Mary's words end the play. The audience do not see the child, whose fate (in the context of the quest for grace) has been the subject of debate in the two previous scenes, and who, as a consequence of this debate, is now representative of a deeper understanding of grace than was suggested by the 'graceful daughter' into whom Giles tried to construct Mary. Whether a just world is achievable remains unknown, but a map exists and the traversing of its contours might – perhaps – lead a traveller into this terrain.

The Grace of Mary Traverse opened at the Royal Court Theatre in October 1985. Deborah Levy's *Pax* was first performed at the Oval, London, by the Women's Theatre Group, in August of the same year. Like Mary Traverse, the characters in *Pax* struggle both to decipher existing maps and to fashion new ones. Though, unlike *The Grace of Mary Traverse*, *Pax* is set in the present, making sense of the past is a crucial project for the two younger characters. As its name suggests, it is also vitally concerned with peace, both now and in the future. Its exploration of the possibility of a better future world is, therefore, a further link with *The Grace of Mary Traverse*.

In her Afterword to *Pax*, in volume six of Methuen's *Plays by Women*, Deborah Levy describes being commissioned in 1984 by the Women's Theatre Group 'to write an "anti-nuclear play" ', her dislike of ' "last two minutes in a bunker"-type scenarios' and her consequent decision to create a piece instead 'about twentieth-century Europe' (Levy 1987: 112). The necessity of exploring past, present and future led to her discovery of four archetypes, four characters. The first, the Keeper, is 'the past . . .

169

Europe herself, burdened by the weight of history she carries always with her. The second, the Mourner, is the 'present'. Like Masha in Chekhov's *The Seagull* she is 'in mourning for her own life'. She is also 'stuck', unable to 'move on' (ibid.). The Keeper's Hidden Daughter is the future, who tries to make sense of the present using the evidence of sight, hearing, smell and touch. What she discovers fills her with dismay. The fourth character, the Domesticated Woman, is both past and present. Through her, Levy wanted to examine the 'contradictions of capitalism and patriarchy'. She began by disliking the Domesticated Woman, but when she discovered her 'frailties', the 'bargains' (ibid.), the character had had to make in order to survive, she felt a greater degree of sympathy for her.

In contrast to the other three plays discussed in this chapter, *Pax* does not take the form of a physical journey. Its setting throughout is the 'Wilderness', the offstage terrain therefore of *Rutherford and Son* and the ideological landscape from which Judith, in *Granite*, failed to free herself, though Jo (*Piper's Cave*) and Augustine (*Augustine, Big Hysteria*) succeeded. This time, however, the wilderness is not an ideological construct that confines women, but a desolate landscape that is the product of mass killings, devastation and potential ecological disaster. Specifically, the location is a large, isolated house, possibly called 'The Retreat', an ironic naming given the determination of past and future horrors to intrude on the house's apparent seclusion. In style, the play is a rich and inventive collage of textual, visual and aural elements. Its mood is sometimes tender, often bleakly humorous, the ending hopeful – though only just. Pax for peace: pax for fingers crossed.

Act one, scene one takes place at night time. Onstage are a number of apparently random objects, some covered with a cloth: a globe of the world, a Buddha, a vertical slab of marble, an oriental rug, oil lamps and modern lamps, wind chimes, and an old statue of the Madonna and Child. Offstage, the Keeper sings a lullaby in a European accent. Her voice is punctuated by the sound of bells ringing, first an old 'heavy' bell, then the 'piercing' ring of a modern bell and, finally, the two bells 'tentatively' ringing together. From offstage, the Keeper, who has stopped singing, can be heard saying that she wants to go back to Prague. Then she enters, wearing a kimono which is fastened with string at her waist. She has silver hair and diamanté earrings, carries a lighted candle and is sorting through a bunch of keys. As in the children's game of the same name, she is the Keeper of the Keys, in her case to past nightmares and griefs. As she later explains, she has witnessed countless acts of brutality: pogroms in eastern Europe, twenty million dead in Russia, human beings melting like plastic in Hiroshima and Nagasaki. Like Hannah Snell in Shirley Gee's *Warrior*, she knows that everywhere there are ghosts. While the Keeper is still sorting through her keys, the Mourner enters carrying 'a small, neat suitcase' (ibid.: 87). In her neatness and precision she resembles Louise in the early scenes of *Variations*, and, like Louise, she is engaged in a quest to decipher the past, though a far more distant past than that of Clara Schumann, for the Mourner is an archeologist who records and labels dinosaur remains in an attempt to understand why, after successfully roaming the earth for a hundred and fifty million years, these creatures became extinct. 'The clue', she tells the Keeper 'is in the eggs they left behind' (ibid.: 89), which gradually became thinner so that the embryo could no longer get sufficient calcium to form its skeleton properly. Since the recent death of her mother, however, the bones she arranges and reassembles remind her of her mother's bones and nothing makes sense to her anymore. Even the map that the Keeper sent her (of Albania) was apparently a mistake, and she is late because she got lost and there was no-one from whom she could ask directions.

The Hidden Daughter (H.D.) is similarly at a loss to understand the place in which she finds herself. Was it a cornfield she was in that morning, she wonders, or a missile base? Why are the plants eating themselves, and is the strange, sticky substance on the leaves nerve gas? Why, when she goes fishing, are the fish always dead? Who, or what, she is she doesn't know, though this seemed clear when she woke up in the morning. In order to provide herself with some sort of continuity, she marks a cross on the wall each day, another similarity to the Mourner who has recorded her existence by writing her name and address on the wall of her bedsit.

H.D. and the Mourner are also alike in that they search out the runes of folk beliefs and fairy stories to see if these can offer guidance. 'A quiver, a bow, a cauldron, a spindle, a spoon, a mirror, a wreath of string . . . bringing the soul's travel back to its place of origin' (ibid.: 95), H.D. recites. She wants to know where she originated, who she is. The Mourner peels an apple, trying to ease it off in one piece which will then form the first letter of her lover's name and entitle her to a wish. But she hasn't got a lover, doesn't want a wish, and the apple peel (like H.D.'s string) has assumed the shape of a wreath, which brings her thoughts back to her mother.

The recurrent sound of a piano also leads her to think of her mother, who was once a famous pianist. Perhaps what she is hearing is her mother's ghost playing. When the Mourner was little, her mother was too busy playing the piano to take much notice of her and, later, though she sensed her mother wanted to talk, her own attention was fully taken up with a dinosaur skeleton she was engaged in constructing. She dreams now of meeting her mother on a bridge (a connecting device between past and present). Once, long ago, she smashed a teapot belonging to her mother. On the bridge, she would hand her mother this teapot, lovingly mended. Her gift would signify her employment of her skills in reassembling the past in order to heal the fracture between her mother and herself.

While the Mourner has had only limited contact with her mother, H.D. knows nothing at all of her father, not even who he was. The Keeper refuses to enlighten her or (though she was the mother's cousin) to give the Mourner any information about her mother, and the two young women turn therefore to the Domesticated Woman for help. The Domesticated Woman, who, like the Mourner, is paying the Keeper a visit, is American, brightly dressed, has bleached hair and carries a cactus plant with three buds on it, a reminder of each of her three sons: Scott (the sensitive one), a policeman; Brem, a farmer; and Mark (the youngest) who is stationed somewhere nearby, close to a cornfield. The Domesticated Woman responds with sympathy to the Mourner and H.D., though she is unable to tell the Mourner very much about her mother. Rather than cataloguing dinosaur bones, it would be better, she suggests, if the Mourner used her intelligence to find herself a husband. To the delighted H.D., she reveals the fact that her father was a doctor, though she is chary of giving any more information. She does, however, assure H.D., who wants to be certain of the validity of this long-desired clue as to her genesis, that she never tells lies. Fascinated by the Domesticated Woman's difference from the few people she has previously seen, H.D. strokes her hair, only to discover that it is a wig that comes away in her hand. The first act ends with her astonished remonstrance that the Domesticated Woman has promised always to speak the truth.

H.D. attempts to sift truth from falsehood in the past and present in order to move forward into the future. The Mourner weeps over past and present and fears the future. She is afraid to eat an egg the Keeper cooks for her breakfast because she doesn't know what she might discover inside it. Experience of dinosaur eggs has not filled her with a sense of optimism. Despite the fact that H.D. finds it difficult to distinguish between what is and isn't true, she is the character who eventually acts as a guide to the Mourner into both the past and the future. Her relevance to the Mourner (and the possibility, therefore, that she may be able to help her to interpret clues correctly) is indicated by the fact that, like the Mourner's mother, she plays the piano and it transpires that it is the sound of H.D. playing, not her mother, that the Mourner has been hearing. H.D. leads the Mourner towards a more fruitful relationship with her past through an enactment of the mother's funeral, which she suggests as a way of remaking the event as the Mourner would have wanted it to be. H.D. plays the Mourner's mother at the funeral and, in this guise, tries to find a way of making contact with the Mourner. All forms of communication are problematic, she explains, even music, her chosen language. She had believed that she could 'control the breath . . . of a melody', but she discovered that 'a woman's breath . . . is broken' (ibid.: 104). Touch, too, is a language that she thought she understood, but she found that this was not the case. Eventually, however, H.D./ the Mother and the Mourner hug each other in a lengthy, healing embrace. Though the Mourner has not been able to give her actual mother the mended teapot, she has found a bridge into the past through the aid of this surrogate mother.

Following the first funeral, H.D. instigates another, this time for her own father. For this funeral, the vertical marble slab is brightly illuminated, a tribute to the 'hierarchical', 'Vertical . . . Facist Daddy' H.D. discovers (ibid.: 106 and 108). Dressed in a white coat, first the Mourner, then the Keeper, play the father, a seemingly gentle, cultured man, yet also a geneticist who tried to breed a blond master race. The Keeper, and the child he fathered on her, were part of his experimental programme. Speaking as the father, the Keeper predicts the imminence of nuclear dis-

173

aster. Every age, s/he tells H.D., 'gets the technology it deserves'. But H.D. rejects the 'false fathers', 'Auschwitz and Vietnam', and, at the same time, a fatalistic future scenario (ibid: 108). The Mourner has handed her a pea (the subject of the first experiment in genetics) which she found in the pocket of the white coat, and, taking as her model not a geneticist but a farmer, H.D. determines to be her own generator. She is a pea and she will plant herself. Her approval of farmers is also expressed in her response to the Domesticated Woman's cactus plant. When the Domesticated Woman's attention is elsewhere, H.D. creeps in and picks two of the buds (nips the plant, and the sons, in the bud). She spares one of them, however: the farmer, Brem.

Close to the end of the play, H.D. leaves the Wilderness, but she leaves also a message for the Mourner on a tape the latter has recorded about dinosaur eggs. When the Mourner plays the tape, she hears, along with her own exploration of the distant past, H.D.'s voice promising her a map that will help her to negotiate the future. The map is in the pocket of the white coat the Mourner wore as H.D.'s father and from which she took the pea that enabled H.D. to redefine her own future. On the map is a further message from H.D. If the Mourner wants to find her, it reads, she will be able to. The place where she is is 'cold, harassed, uncertain, but never lonely'. She will teach the Mourner survival and travelling skills, making 'a fire and walk[ing] long distances' (ibid.: 109–10).

Prior to *her* departure, the Mourner presents gifts to the Mourner and the Domesticated Woman. When she first arrived, she gave the Keeper some rare, fossilised animal bones, but the Keeper reacted angrily to these. She had seen too many more recent bones. As she prepares to leave, the Mourner gives the Keeper a suitcase, because the Keeper has never had one and has had to move from country to country with her belongings in brown paper parcels. To the Domesticated Woman, the Mourner gives an egg. There may, or there may not, be life inside it – this is uncertain – but the Domesticated Woman must keep it warm and safe, just in case. Despite her limitations, the Domesticated Woman is a nurturer, someone who, against the odds, manages to keep things going.

Like the Mourner, the Domesticated Woman brought the Keeper a gift when she arrived, in her case an electric carving knife, a sign of her culture and also perhaps of that culture's capacity for carving up the world in its own interests. The Keeper angrily rejected this gift, but, near the end of the play, the Domesticated Woman and the Keeper exchange 'gifts', not of objects, but of acts of kindness. After the Mourner's exit, the Domesticated Woman weeps, partly because she longs for a daughter of her own, and partly because her back aches. Though her husband has money, she has none of her own and she was obliged to scrub floors to earn money for her fare to visit the Keeper. 'What is a daughter?' the Keeper asks. Between them, they have two young women, 'Mad as nettles in a storm' (ibid.: 110). The Keeper also weeps, she tells the Domesticated Woman. Her pillows are always damp. She promises to ease the Domesticated Woman's back by rubbing it with eucalyptus and by warming a brick for her bed. First, however, the Domesticated Woman takes a hairbrush the Keeper is holding and gently brushes the latter's silver hair. This was a task H.D. used to do before she left, and the fact that the Domesticated Woman now performs it links her to H.D., while, at the same time, the tender brushing of the Keeper's hair evokes the embrace between H.D. and the Mourner.

In the final, brief, scene of the play the Keeper is alone. As she covers objects with a white cloth, she speaks of the places she has visited. She is glad that she saw Paris before its skyscrapers were built, Bologna before the river was turned into a gravel pit, Britain 'before it became nuclear' (ibid.: 111). Surrounded by whiteness that reminds her of leukaemia, she sits near to the lighted globe of the world. In the course of the play she has expressed a desire to return to Prague, Czechoslovakia, Yugoslavia, Romania, Essex, Vienna. The maps she sent the Mourner and the Domesticated Woman were of Albania and Moscow, the 'wrong' maps as they thought. But the Keeper, and her Wilderness, are all those places. 'There I am', she has told the Mourner at one point (indicating the globe), 'With dust in my bellybutton' (ibid.: 109). At the end of the play, she ponders the advice she used to give the young, not to be in too much of a hurry, and wonders if this is now such a good idea. It seems, however, somewhat ungracious to be dissatisfied with life when one is a hundred and ninety years old. As the lights fade, the globe still remains lit. The sound of 'wild hopeful music' is heard (ibid.: 111).

6

CORRESPONDENT WORLDS
Encounters with fairies and angels

Caryl Churchill's *The Skriker* opened in the Cottlesloe auditorium of the Royal National Theatre, London, in January 1994, and Anne Devlin's *After Easter* at The Other Place, Stratford-upon-Avon, in May of the same year. Though these two plays are very different in mood and, to a considerable degree also in subject matter, there are, it seems to me, sufficient points of contact between them to make a consideration of their similarities, and differences, a valuable exercise. At, or near, the beginning of each play, for example, a young woman is in a mental hospital after giving birth to a baby. Both plays stage a journey (in the case of *The Skriker*, a double journey) and a return. Both present the 'real' world as permeated by a spirit world, the denizens of which (angels and demons in *After Easter*, fairies in *The Skriker*) profoundly affect the lives of the human characters.

These points of similarity are, however, also crucial sites of difference. In *After Easter* Greta is reunited with her baby, whereas in *The Skriker* Josie has killed her child before the play begins. In both plays the point of departure from which the characters begin their journeys is late-twentieth-century England, but the places *to* which they journey – and, in a crucial instance, return – are very different. In *After Easter* Greta journeys to an actual geographical location, Northern Ireland, from which she returns to England. In *The Skriker*, first Josie and then Lily journey to the Underworld, a shadowy realm, forgotten and disowned by the 'real' world, to which it is both Other and disturbingly similar. Like Greta, Josie returns to the England she left behind but when Lily, in her turn, comes back, she finds herself transported a hundred years into the future and surrounded by evidence of ecological disaster. The interconnection of the human and spirit worlds is also differently represented in the two plays. In *After Easter* the majority of the supernatural happenings are mediated through Greta, who both experiences and recounts them, whereas in *The Skriker*, by contrast, the fairies are physically present. The eponymous character – hob-goblin, 'shapeshifter and death portent' (Churchill 1994: 1) – is itself a fairy, and other fairies and creatures from folklore burst through into the human world from the Underworld as the action progresses.

The two plays are further linked, and distinguished, by the narrative function of their central characters. Churchill's play begins with the Skriker in the role of storyteller and, apart from a short sequence of silent action, this is also how it ends. Greta is the major storyteller figure in *After Easter* and it is as a storyteller that she ends the play. Stories in *After Easter* centre, however, around family, Catholicism and Ireland, whereas the Skriker's stories relate encounters between human beings and fairies. Not only are the Skriker's stories different from Greta's, so, too, more importantly, is the language in which they are told. In the playwright's words, the Skriker is 'ancient and damaged' (ibid.). Though forgotten by human beings, the fairies continue to suffer the consequences of human actions, for they are being poisoned by the noxious substances that human beings have released into the earth and its atmosphere. One consequence of this is that the Skriker speaks a damaged language, reminiscent of someone who has had a stroke or who is suffering from schizophrenia. It constantly begins sentences that it has difficulty in finishing because its train of thought is interrupted by other meanings and possibilities, in the form of word clusters that are interrelated through associated meanings, puns or similarities of sound, and that attach themselves to the original idea.

The Skriker is, as I have noted, a tale-spinner and it is fitting therefore that the first tale it tells should be one in which spinning plays an important part. In the form of an encounter that once took place between itself and a human girl, the Skriker narrates the story that in the Brothers Grimm version is known as 'Rumplestiltskin' and in English folk tale as 'Tom Tit Tot'. 'Heard her [i.e. the girl's mother] boast', the Skriker begins, 'beast a roast beef eater, daughter could spin span spick and spun the lowest form of wheat straw into gold' (ibid.). The ways

178

in which related meanings or a sequence of similar sounds ('boast, beast . . . roast beef eater . . . spin span spick and spun', for example) constantly adhere to, and disrupt, the throughline of the narrative make following the story tantalisingly difficult – tantalising because it is just possible, on first acquaintance, to grasp the main ideas and yet one is also always conscious of other meanings slipping just out of reach.

At the point in the Tom Tit Tot story, for example, when the girl cries because her husband, the king, has ordered her to make good her mother's boast and spin the straw into gold, while she, of course, can do no such thing, the Skriker's language is as follows:

> Weeps seeps deeps her pretty puffy cream cake hole in the heart operation. Sees a little blackjack thingalingo with a long long tale awinding. May day, she cries, may pole axed me to help her. So I spin the sheaves shoves shivers into golden guild and geld and if she can't guessing game and safety match my name then I'll take her no mistake no mister no missed her no mist no miss no me no.

> (ibid.)

The basic story is that the girl weeps and, while she is weeping, sees a little black thing with a long tail. She cries to it to help her and the Skriker spins the sheaves into gold. If the girl is unable to guess its name, it will take her. An exposition of the Skriker's words that includes the various meanings contained within the portmanteau story would, however, go something like this: The girl weeps. The word 'weeps' suggests others of a similar sound, 'seeps deeps', that are suggestive also of a diffusion of moisture ('seeps') and depths of unhappiness ('deeps'). As a result of her weeping, the girl's face becomes puffy, which suggests cream puff, i.e. a cake, which, in turn, leads to 'cake hole' (mouth) and, from hole, to 'hole in the heart operation'. The girl sees a little black thing. Black becomes 'blackjack'. Thingaling is like dinga-ling and lingo, of course, is language. The little blackjack thing, the Skriker, speaks its own language and, in addition to its tail, for it is a beast as its opening line made clear: 'Heard her boast beast', (i.e. *to* the beast, me), it has a long tale to tell. The girl cries 'May day' (the international call for help). May makes the Skriker think of may pole, with its folkloric connotations, then poleaxed (axed = asked).

So the Skriker 'spin[s] the sheaves'. Sheaves suggests similar sounding words, 'shoves shivers', the latter perhaps with the added sense of the girl's fear – of the king and probably also of the Skriker – and 'golden' which leads to 'guild' (a pun on 'gild') and 'geld', referring perhaps to the German for money and prophetic also of the state of impotence to which the Skriker hopes to reduce the girl when she tries to guess its name. If she can't guess my name, the Skriker begins to say, but related words tumble from its mouth at the same time. Guess transforms itself into 'guessing game', i.e. the activity in which the girl must engage. Game suggests game and match, as in tennis. Match becomes 'safety match' because matches provide light, illumination (for the girl in her attempt to guess the name), and matching the name will ensure her safety. If she fails, the Skriker will take her. Make no mistake about that. Mistake is transformed into 'mister', which, punningly, becomes 'missed her', then, through an association of sounds, 'mist . . . miss . . . me'. There will be no mist, no obscurity. I will not miss her, warns the Skriker, not me.

In the event of course, as in 'Tom Tit Tot' and 'Rumplestiltskin', the Skriker's plans are foiled. The girl guesses its name correctly, at the last possible moment, and the Skriker goes off in a state of fury. In the remainder of its long opening speech the Skriker tells a sequence of other 'damaged' versions of stories of the relationships between mortals and fairies. Throughout these stories a number of motifs recur: time, for instance, and also dancing, trickery, fairy prohibitions on certain human actions and the sinister, magic nature that food can assume. The first two of these motifs come together in the Skriker's story of mortals dancing with fairies in a bluebell wood (an enchanted place) and, as a result, being transported to fairyland. The only way they can be rescued is if a friend returns to the bluebell wood a year and a day later. The dancers will then reappear and it will be possible to drag the mortals from their midst. They will be convinced, however, that no time at all has passed since they began dancing, and they will become listless and pale in their longing to return to the fairy dance.

Being caught by the fairies picking flowers, or eating fruit in an enchanted orchard, are other means by which people can find themselves in fairyland. 'Never eat a fruit or puck luck pluck a flower if you want to get back [to] . . . your own' the Skriker warns. People are told what not to do, but when did they ever do what they were told? They will 'eat the one forbidden fruit of the tree top' with the result that 'down comes cradle and baby' (ibid.: 3). Along with fairy food, human food can also be dangerous to mortals if they have been tricked by a fairy into entering a magic timewarp. In one of the Skriker's stories, it remembers how it tricked a human bridegroom by getting him to hold a candle until it went out, with the result that he arrived at his wedding only to find that a hundred years had passed. He was then foolish enough to eat something, and he crumbled 'to dust panic' (ibid.: 4).

Perhaps because it is so essential to life, the stories in which food plays an important role are among the most macabre. Disturbingly, human beings figure in some of the Skriker's narratives as fairy food. A Kelpie, for example, half man and half horse, eats people, as does a monstrous hobgoblin, Rawheadandbloodybones, that sits in a dark cupboard crouched on a pile of bloody bones, chewing the remains of its latest victims: 'Dollop, gollop fullup' (ibid.: 2). The very name 'goblin' sounds alarmingly like 'gobbling', as the Skriker punningly realises when it eventually resolves to go up into the human world and chase after people and gobble them up: 'gobbledegook de gook is after you' (ibid.: 5). It is not only goblins, however, who eat people. People devour their own kind. Near the end of its opening speech, the Skriker refers briefly to the words of an old song, 'The Juniper Tree'. Later in the play, a character called the Dead Child sings the complete story, which is of a mother who killed her child and baked her in a pie, whereupon her father ate her. Her brothers and sisters 'picked [her] bones / And they buried [her] under the marley stones'. This song is just one of the ways in which the main, connecting ideas within the Skriker's fragmented language are later developed more fully. Enchanted food and its relationship to the death of a child, fairy trickery, the disregarding of fairy prohibitions and the danger of timewarps – all these elements find greater coherence within the main body of the play, to which the Skriker's complex talespinning is prelude.

Towards the end of its opening speech the Skriker finds itself remembering occasional human acts of kindness to the fairies – leaving out a saucer of cream, for example, or giving a Brownie a pair of trousers. Just as people who have danced with the fairies long to return to them, so, too, fairies can become fascinated by, and yearn to be with people. Each set of beings is magic to the other. Nowadays, however, people have forgotten the fairies and they are being poisoned by the pollution that is destroying the land and the rivers. The Skriker tries to forget people, in its turn, but it can't. People have got into its head and it vows that it will get into theirs. Though it is afraid of human power, its desire for revenge is stronger than its fear, and it determines that, along with other fairies, it will go up once again to the human world, where it will catch people by giving them wishes. 'Ready or not', it warns, 'here we come quick or dead of night night sleep tightarse' (ibid.).

So, the Skriker enters the human world and the first person it latches on to is Josie who, being mentally disturbed, is, in a sense, damaged, as is the Skriker. Visiting Josie in the mental hospital is Lily (who is expecting a baby), and Lily becomes the Skriker's other victim. In the human world the Skriker assumes mostly human shapes, many of them characterised by vulnerability and neediness, for a sense of reciprocal need and attraction is one of the main elements the Skriker remembers from past relationships between fairies and human beings. It is Lily who responds sympathetically to the vulnerable manifestations of the Skriker – a derelict woman in the street, for example, who asks her for a hug and a kiss, or a child who wants a cuddle and a home – whereas Josie is always aware of what only gradually becomes evident to Lily, the malevolent presence in all these forms of the Skriker. The key experience that reveals to Lily the Skriker-nature of the various 'people' she has been meeting comes when the Skriker has transformed itself into a man, in which guise it asks for Lily's love. In order to demonstrate what the man really is, Josie stabs 'him' in the arm and chest. Apparently bleeding to death, the man asks Lily if she loves him and, when she says that she does, 'he' takes off 'his' bloodstained shirt and tie, only to reveal identical clean ones underneath. The horrified Lily then protests that she doesn't love 'him' (now, in fact, clearly 'it', as Lily's question 'What are you?' demonstrates). The Skriker, however, knows better. 'But you do [love me] you know', it says (ibid.: 46), and this analysis is correct, for both Lily and Josie – the latter despite, or perhaps because of, her greater awareness of the Skriker's nature – are unable to resist the fascination of the fairy world. Each of them later gives the fact that she has missed the Skriker as a reason for entering the Underworld.

In their longing for the Skriker, Josie and Lily resemble the human dancers in the Skriker's story who became pale and listless after they were pulled out of the fairy ring, and it is through dance that other human characters in the play reveal their seduction by the fairy world. A young girl, the Passerby, throws down a coin for a fairy called Yallery Brown who is playing music, and then begins to dance. Like the dancers in the fairy ring the girl wants to dance to the fairy music for ever. Another character, the Girl with the Telescope, is entranced when she spies, through her telescope, a Green Lady dancing with a Bogle. Afterwards, she constantly looks through the telescope in the hope of seeing them again – but she never does. The Man with the Bucket is enthralled by the Green Lady and gives her a cake he has made from a film of gold on the surface of the water in his bucket. He dances with her, but becomes gradually weaker and weaker and has, eventually, to propel himself along in a wheelchair. A woman meets a Kelpie in a bar and goes off with it, riding on its back. Later, they too dance together, but towards the end of the play the Kelpie enters with her body which it proceeds to cut up. The Telescope Girl pines away when the Green Lady and the Bogle fail to return and then, in despair, slashes her wrists. Attracted by her blood, the Kelpie begins to eat her. This last detail was added in performance and does not form part of the 1994 edition of the play. The vampiric aspect of the fairies' interest in human beings is already clear in the text, however, from the fact that the Skriker drinks Josie's blood when she is in the Underworld.

Human blood is desirable to the Skriker because, as they did in the past, fairies continue to find human beings magic. The Skriker is particularly fascinated by television and it tries to get a bewildered Lily to explain how it works. In their turn, Josie and Lily are drawn by the Skriker's magic. Before it entered the human world, the Skriker predicted that it would catch people by giving them wishes, and in the first human shape that it assumes (a middle-aged fellow patient of Josie's in the mental hospital) it offers Josie a wish if, in return, she will let it stay near her. Josie responds by wishing that the Skriker would have Lily rather than herself, and it is through this wish that the Skriker first gets its hooks into Lily – though Lily fails to grasp this fact for some time, seeing in the various manifestations of the Skriker only a sequence of defenceless, needy people.

After Josie's release from the hospital (by means of a wish of Lily's), the two of them play out a version of the fairy story that is usually known as 'The Kind and Unkind Girls' or 'Diamonds and Toads'. In this story, a young girl is on her way to draw water from a well when she meets an old woman who asks her for a drink. The girl fetches water from the well and the old woman rewards her by causing flowers and jewels to fall from her mouth every time she speaks. Another girl, in some versions an elder sister of the first, in others a stepsister, then goes to the well in her turn, but she is rude and selfish and refuses the old woman's request. Her 'reward' is that toads jump out of her mouth whenever she speaks. In Caryl Churchill's play, the Skriker, in the form of the Derelict Woman, is the fairy-tale old woman. Lily hugs and kisses her, as she is asked to do, and, to her delight, discovers that pound coins tumble from her mouth when she speaks. Josie angrily denies the old woman a kiss when her turn comes and the result is that she spews out toads along with her words. This division of Lily and Josie into the kind and unkind girls of the fairy story is complicated, however, by the fact that Josie recognises the Skriker for what it really is, her own damaged self enabling her to detect the damaged Skriker. Lily does not therefore represent a simple vindication of the value of kindness, or Josie a cautionary example of the effects of unkindness. Lily does not know what she is being kind to, whereas Josie has a pretty shrewd idea as to what the recipient of her unkindness is. In a sense, what she rejects is her own damaged self.

The ironic presentation of 'The Kind and Unkind Girls' story is a pre-echo of the narratives that Josie and Lily play out in the Underworld. In the Underworld, Josie finds a magic feast that has been prepared for her, and, though a lost girl, who is in fairyland because she ate an apple in an enchanted orchard, warns Josie that if she eats or drinks anything she will never get back home, Josie ignores her advice and, as a result, becomes, like the lost girl, a prisoner in fairyland. Many years pass and Josie begs the Skriker to allow her to visit the human world once again before everyone she knew there is dead. The Skriker refuses her request and, in addition, warns her against putting her hand in a nearby fountain. Despite this prohibition, Josie plunges her hand in the water, but, in place of the retribution threatened by the Skriker, she finds herself back in the human world where no time at all has passed since she left. Her understanding of the damaged nature of the Skriker, and of the Underworld, has enabled her, on some level, to grasp the fact that the Skriker has tried to prevent her from doing the one thing that would ensure her freedom.

Lily enters the Underworld as a kind girl. She misses the Skriker, but she also believes that, if she does what it wants her to do, this will be sufficient to stop it harming other people. In addition, she is confident, wrongly as it turns out, that her self-sacrifice will be of a strictly limited kind. While she is away, time will stand still in the human world, as it did for Josie. She is so certain of this that she leaves her baby behind in the upper world. Unfortunately, Lily finds herself acting another role in addition to the kind girl: that of the bridegroom in the story the Skriker told at the beginning of the play. The Skriker has tricked her as it did the bridegroom. It lights a candle and gives it to Lily to hold. 'Watch the lightyear', it tells her. 'Just hold this candle the scandal' and Lily stands 'still . . . till what?' as the lights darken (ibid.: 51).

When light returns, an old woman (Lily's granddaughter) and a deformed girl (Lily's great-great-granddaughter) are there with Lily and the Skriker. A hundred years have passed, though Lily has been conscious of none of them, 'a black whole hundred yearns', as the Skriker puts it. It is not simply another century, but 'another cemetery' (ibid.: 52), and the polluted planet is now destroying people (the deformed girl, for example) as people have destroyed it. Lily in her kind-girl guise has not been enough to save it. Something more far-reaching than that was needed. When the deformed girl understands that Lily is from the past, she is filled with horror and rage, but the old woman is sorry for Lily. People in the past couldn't help what they did, she tells the girl, 'they were stupid . . . not evil', and she offers Lily some food (ibid.). Like the tricked bridegroom, however, Lily finds this food from the future lethal. In the Skriker's words she 'bit off more than she could choose. And she was dustbin' (ibid.).

Both Lily and Josie are caught within timewarps, though timewarps of a different nature. To each of them food is danger-ous in the context of their magic journeys, but Josie is enchanted by eating fairy food, whereas Lily is poisoned by human food that is polluted as a result of human actions in the past. Josie escapes from fairyland. Lily is destroyed when she returns to the human world. Despite these differences between them, however, Lily and Josie, the kind and unkind girls, exhibit, eventually, one important similarity. Like Lily, Josie tries to protect the world from the Skriker's vengeance, but her way of doing this is to perform lesser acts of cruelty herself in the hope of preventing the Skriker's major ones. The problem is that Josie finds it increasingly difficult to know which of the horrors she hears about are the Skriker's doing and which are the nightmare result of human actions. So, she goes 'further and murther in the dark, trying to keep the Skriker sated', but the 'gobbling . . . and hating . . . and looting' (ibid.: 49) and the crises around the world grow daily more terrifying. Neither Josie in her murthering dark, nor Lily, voluntarily entering the Underworld in her self-styled role of saviour, is able to prevent the future chain of disasters. In the sense that babies represent the future, even Lily's care for her child has little more in the way of a beneficial result than has Josie's murder of hers. In its narration of Lily's return to the human world, the Skriker becomes momentarily once again Tom Tit Tot from the first tale it spun. Whirl 'whir wh wh', it begins, and then continues, 'what is this? Lily was solid flash. If she was back on earth where on earth where was the rockabye baby gone the treetop? Lost and gone' (ibid.: 51). The baby is lost, gone, because, in the hundred years that have elapsed since Lily determined to visit the Underworld, it has aged and died, and the future itself, as the deformed girl reveals, is also lost. *The Skriker* is, finally, not so much a fairy story as a warning against believing in fairy stories – at least the kind where everyone lives happily ever after.

Though the Skriker succeeds in taking revenge on human beings, the fairy world is still inextricably bound up with the human world, and the increasingly polluted planet will destroy the fairies along with human beings. Revenge is therefore bitter-sweet. The damage experienced first by the Skriker and Josie, and the poisoned parts of the world, has now developed so that it is irredeemable. In *The Fairies in Tradition and Literature*, one of Churchill's sources for the fairies and folkloric characters in her play, the author, K.M. Briggs, gives a variant name for the Skriker – Trash. This name is explained as deriving from 'the padding' of the creature's feet (Briggs 1967: 222). Trash is, however, also rubbish. Mortals and fairies, along with the earth they jointly inhabit, will all, as the Skriker succinctly puts it, shortly be 'dustbin'.

The front cover of the programme for the original production of *After Easter* and the front cover of the Faber and Faber edition of the play depict the same illustration: a picture of the Earth as a shining, transparent bubble within which floats a young woman. Her eyes are closed, her arms extended above her head, her body curved as is the Earth. In *The Skriker* the Earth is maimed, on the brink of destruction; in *After Easter* individual places (in Northern Ireland and England) are seen as disfigured by human violence and values, but the beauty of the Earth becomes a symbol for the inner world that Greta gradually constructs. The programme and book-cover design of the woman within the transparent bubble derives from Greta's description, in scene three, of a birth experience (or the reliving of a birth experience), when she saw a beautiful 'sphere lit up in space far below' her, and heard a voice telling her to 'Enjoy [her] fall through space and time' (Devlin 1994: 26). In the design, Greta is placed within the light-filled Earth. Herself a time- and space-traveller, she free-falls beyond the confines of established spatial and chronological dimensions. It is an image that physicalises the spiritual and emotional journeys Greta undertakes in the play.

In addition to these inner explorations Greta goes on an actual journey, or, rather, two journeys – from England to Northern Ireland and then back again to England. As Anne Devlin explained in her programme note, *After Easter* is a 'quest play'. Almost fifteen years before its first scene, Greta left home and family in the north of Ireland. Turning her back on all aspects of her identity, including her Catholicism, she journeyed 'resolutely away from Easter 1916, and the traditional routes of that familiar dark story'. As the play begins, the ghosts of her past, which she has excluded for so long, 'call her home'. 'Home' in *After Easter* is, however, a problematic concept. Though, unlike *The Skriker* (where the prevailing sense of damage renders 'home', in the sense of sanctuary, or nurture, unobtainable), *After Easter* reveals 'home' to be both a sustainable idea and a place that can be reached, the journey to that goal is nevertheless a painful one. The locus of the forces of dark as well as those of light, 'home' is the shadowy past that gave birth to, and haunts, the present.

The 'ghost' that most urgently calls Greta home is an apparition that she sees in scene two. She has been taken out of the mental hospital (in which she is seen at the beginning of the play), for Easter, by her sister Aoife who has come over from Belfast for this purpose. In scene two, Aoife and Greta are staying at the London flat of their younger sister, Helen. The scene begins with Helen and Aoife talking onstage while Greta is asleep offstage. Suddenly, 'a bloodcurdling wail' is heard (ibid.: 9) and a distraught Greta rushes in and describes an apparition she saw standing at the foot of her bed when she woke up. Pale and gaunt, dressed all in white and with long black hair, it was this 'ghost' that cried out, Greta insists, and not herself. Aoife defines the apparition as a banshee and Helen as a manifestation of Greta's suppressed anger, but though Greta partly goes along with both these explanations, her own names for the apparition are 'Mother' and 'Ireland' – the twin forces, in other words, that are drawing her back into her past. Though the audience only learns of this later in the play, Greta's mother (Rose Flynn) used to beat Greta, and the youngest child, Manus, in terrible drunken rages, and Greta's addressing of the apparition as Mother – and her admonishment of it not to harm her family – tacitly recognises in its perturbing contours this demonic aspect of her mother. The apparition becomes representative of Greta's homeland through its terrible wail, in which, Greta tells her sisters, she could hear the whole of Ireland crying out to her.

By reason of its appeal to her for succour, the apparition positions Greta as a kind of Virgin Mary (a figure known to Catholics in one of her guises as Our Lady of Perpetual Succour), and the fact that this role has some relevance to Greta is clear in the first scene of the play where the psychiatrist asks her if she still thinks she's the Virgin Mary. Greta's response to this question, however, 'Och, I think everyone is the Virgin Mary' (ibid.: 2) questions Catholicism's right to decide who and what is of value. If all women are the Virgin Mary, then all are special. It prefigures, too, Greta's revisioning of the Madonna and Child image at the end of the play. To begin with, separated as she is from her child, and deemed mad, Greta is a kind of mutilated madonna. In the final scene she holds her regained child in her arms and tells it a story of her own making. A human mother, not a religious icon, she rewrites the past – history – into her 'own story'.

In order to find the authoritative voice in which she speaks at the end of the play, Greta has to undertake the outward and inner journeys that enable her to reassemble the components of her past: home, family, faith, and Ireland. Part of this reassembly process consists in coming to terms with the dual aspects of experience: the realisation, for example, that her mother was both monster and nurturer. The unreserved love she always felt for her father is also revealed as having a dark and dangerous side. It is the news that her father has had a heart attack that causes Greta to listen to the apparition's promptings, and, along with her two sisters, to travel to Belfast. Shortly after the sisters' return, their father dies, and in scene six, as Greta 'is waking' and talking to the dead Michael Flynn, he sits up in his coffin. Father and daughter talk happily together, reliving shared memories, but later, when the corpse is again lying down in the coffin, and Greta asks what heaven is like, the dead man's hand comes up out of the coffin, without warning, and grabs her by the throat. What this stage moment demonstrates is the potential self-destructiveness of over-identification with the dead. As Helen tells Greta in the next, and penultimate, scene, she must let her father go. Otherwise, she will be dragged into the grave with him.

The doubleness of experience, the close relationship of light and dark, is something that Greta has partially understood from an early age, but, for a long time, she has been in retreat from this knowledge. She has wanted 'to be full of light' (ibid.: 20), and she has erected barriers to keep out the dark. In performance, the setting, which, apart from a few items of furniture, consisted of images partly suggestive of containment – doors, windows, cupboards, a fence, the wall of a bridge – paradoxically revealed the insubstantiality of barriers and boundaries. Doors, after all, open as well as close. Windows are barriers of a kind, but their function is to let in light. A bridge, by definition, serves primarily as an agent of unity rather than division. Boundaries, moreover, offer little protection against anyone determined to cross them. In scene five, the fence around Rose Flynn's back yard is no obstacle to the British soldiers who come after Manus for failing to stop at a roadblock. This insubstantiality of apparent boundaries is an extension of Greta's own permeability, her availability to other time-spaces and possibilities. Although she has attempted to block off this part of herself, both Aoife and her cousin Elish, a nun in Belfast, recognise Greta's potentiality as a spiritual voyager, Aoife describing her as 'clear' and 'transparent' and Elish as 'effortlessly and unconsciously almost always in a state of grace' (ibid.: 28). Both women see Greta as 'chosen' by God, though Elish fears that such distinction carries with it the danger of being 'chosen by evil as well. Nothing stands alone' (ibid.: 29).

The terms in which Greta experiences her spiritual journeys are those of her Catholic past. Though she has relinquished her faith, it is this that provides the iconographic reference points that enable her to begin to map the worlds in which she finds herself. In addition to her role as a version of the Virgin Mary, Greta becomes a shamanic Christ figure. Like Christ descending into Hell prior to his resurrection, Greta traverses spirit worlds where death and birth co-exist. In the course of the play, she tells four stories of other-worldly events that have occurred in her past, and her gradual understanding of these stories also helps her to piece together the map she needs. In chronological sequence, though not in the order in which she tells them, these stories consist of a birth narrative, two stories involving fire-related events (the first of which took place on the feast of the Purification of the Virgin Mary – also known as Candlemas – the second at Pentecost), and a death narrative. The birth event occurred, not surprisingly, on Greta's birthday, in November, 1981, a couple of years after she arrived in England. For three days before her birthday, she had been unable to sleep and she was, as a result, tired and delirious. Eventually she did sleep, on the floor of her room in a sleeping-bag, and it seemed to her that the sleeping-bag was the womb into which she had returned to be reborn. She 'felt very far down inside [her] own body' (ibid.: 25), and, looking around the room, she saw an old man in a corner watching her. He had a pointed beard and he was dressed like a priest in a long, black soutane. To Greta, it was as though he had always been there observing her. She felt very small and weak and she had the sense that she was looking round the edge of a wing chair, or possibly a pram hood. Suddenly, the figure of the old priest loomed above her and placed a pillow over her face in order to smother – to silence – her. As she struggled against the stifling blackness, she heard 'a kind warm voice' (ibid.: 26) in her ear telling her to turn around. She obeyed and found that she could breathe after all. It was then that she saw the beautiful globe beneath her and heard the voice, the same voice that had told her to turn around, advising her to enjoy her fall through space and time.

The Purification event took place three months later, on 2 February 1982, in the course of a dinner party Greta was giving. The candles on the table had gone out. As she relit them at the fire and began to return them to their stand, a flame leapt and lit up her hair, and, at the same moment, a strange cry came out of Greta's mouth. In her relation of the experience to her cousin Elish in her convent, Greta repeats the cry. It is, the stage directions note, 'a beautiful sound' which echoes the nuns' offstage singing of the early morning office for the dead at the beginning of the scene. A little over three months after the Purification experience, on Pentecost Sunday, though Greta didn't at first realise this, she was lying in bed in a house in the village of Porlock that she had borrowed from friends. It was five in the morning but Greta was not asleep. In the curtain facing her bed there appeared a flame which grew brighter as she watched it. When she turned away for a moment to switch on the light, the flame vanished and Greta was disappointed because she realised that if she had only kept still 'and simply watched the flame it would have remained and [she] might have learnt something' (ibid.: 23). As it was, her anxiety had caused the flame to disappear. Later that morning, when she listened to the radio, she discovered that it was Pentecost. What she had seen was a 'tongue of fire'.

Shortly afterwards, Greta's husband told her that he was having an affair and the two of them went to stay in a house in Exmoor to try and talk things through. It was while staying in the Exmoor house that Greta experienced her 'death'. She fell asleep one night, and when she awoke – and she is certain that she was awake and not dreaming – she found herself lying beneath the stars, and the constellation above her was as clear and close as if she were on a mountain top. She felt a terrible despair and, opening her mouth, she 'let out a huge cry until [her] voice filled the whole sky' (ibid.: 14). As her voice left her body and went up into the stars, Greta knew that she had died.

The map that the four stories reveal of Greta's life in England consists of a birth, symbolising an apparent escape from the stifling blackness of her Catholic past, followed by a purification of Greta's new self (death-linked, however, by the fact that the beautiful sound she made when her hair was aflame resembled the office for the dead) and by her apprehension of the possibility of giving birth to her own Pentecostal 'tongue of fire'. In these three stories, birth, voice and death are closely interconnected, but in the final story the birth motif is absent. When Greta 'dies', her voice is engulfed by the stars. She is, Devlin writes in her programme note, an 'exile', who has failed to make the necessary 'transition from the language of the hearth to the language of the heart', and the 'tongue' with which she speaks is therefore not her own.

Greta's response to her 'dying', and to the news of her husband's infidelity, was to deliberately become pregnant so that her husband would stay with her, but though she gave birth to twins, their doubleness has simply reinforced her sense that her deepest self had died. As she confides to Elish, she had 'no context' within which to interpret her other-worldly experiences. So she shut them 'in another room and . . . lived in the outer room of [her] life' (ibid.: 26). The birth of a third child eleven years later has returned her to the door of this inner room, but she fears to open it. It is the cry of the apparition, laden as it is with the old pains and griefs of Ireland and family, and sharp with the present danger to her father, that first opens up the possibility that the door may be yet another permeable boundary. After she hears the wail of the banshee, Greta experiences severe abdominal pains, for which two explanations are offered: first, that she is being punished because she is refusing to do what her inner voices tell her to do (for example, to 'Take the communion out of the churches and give it to the people in the bus queues', ibid.: 16), and second, that she is experiencing birth contractions which signal the return of her voice that disappeared into the stars on the night that she 'died'. In her quest to find her way into the hidden room of her life, Greta visits Elish in her convent, but though Elish is supportive and sympathetic, she filters the experiences that Greta relates to her through the mesh of Catholic orthodoxy so that they lose their particularity. Elish's advice to Greta is that she should return to her Catholic faith, for only in the lee of its rocklike security can someone of her very special abilities – and vulnerability – find the protection she needs, but though tempted by the sanctuary Elish proposes for her, Greta finally rejects it.

The following scene, scene four, is set in the Royal Victoria Hospital, Belfast, where Michael Flynn is lying in the heart ward. In this scene, Greta and Manus meet for the first time in the play. Unlike Greta, Manus still lives in Northern Ireland, but he, too, is in quest of 'home', home in his case being the Irish heritage that his anti-clerical, left-wing father tried to keep from his children in the belief that it would be harmful to them. As part of his search for his roots, Manus has taught himself to play traditional airs on the fiddle, and his rendition, in this scene, of 'The Harvest Home' evokes both a sense of Irishness and of 'home' – the place of return for which he and Greta yearn. Towards the end of the scene, however, 'home' becomes the site of violence and horror. Emergency alarm bells ring and policemen in bullet-proof jackets rush in to protect the wounded survivors of a sectarian killing who are being brought into the hospital for treatment. Nine people are dead, murdered in a pub on the Donegal Road in retaliation for an earlier attack on a betting shop. 'Is this the Harvest?' (ibid.: 43) Greta asks in distress, and her words echo both Manus's music and something Elish said in the previous scene. Elish believes that Greta's gifts would have been put to best use if she had become a nun, but, as her motherhood makes this impossible, she could think of herself instead as 'a nun in the community'. Mothers, Elish explains, 'are the real harvesters of souls' (ibid.: 28 and 29). This could be Greta's function.

Greta's response to the killings is to attempt to become a 'harvester', not of souls but of lives. In obedience to the commanding voice in her head, she steals a chalice full of communion wafers and distributes the wafers to people in the streets, believing that in this way she is helping to stop the killings. As in a dream, her actions give physical form to an idea: the relocation of 'communion' from the divided and divisive world of the churches into the community. In a statement that she issues, Greta insists on the importance of integrated schools, highlighting the Irish churches' hypocrisy in condemning violence while keeping the schools segregated. The local newspaper, however, misinterprets her motives, attributing her actions to a form of protest at the Catholic Church's refusal to ordain women priests. To Greta, it seems that the newspaper report demonstrates the pointlessness of her speaking out. If her words are simply transcribed into others her audience would prefer to hear, she might as well be silent.

It is at this point that Aoife enters with news of their father's death and Greta responds by repeating the scream of the 'banshee' that was heard offstage in scene two, but this time she experiences the sound as part of herself, not 'dissociated' from it. Through her recognition of the admonitory voices that have spoken in her ear as aspects of self, Greta reclaims the voice that disappeared into the stars on the night she 'died', the voice also that struggled to be reborn in Helen's flat after the banshee's earlier scream. What Greta still needs, however, is a language through which the voice can articulate itself. Her problem, as she explains to her father's corpse in the next scene, is that she is 'a copier' (ibid.: 59). In England, where she taught children and adults, who had previously failed to acquire this skill, to write, she had two students who were copiers, and in them she recognised herself. One was a man from Mayo who came to England in 1956, the other a young Hindu boy. The man from Mayo got a job on the railways, but, when he was promoted, he discovered that he had to keep a note of train times and numbers and of anything unusual that occurred. Not being able to write, he copied the notes and reports from previous years, but he was afraid that someone might notice and so he joined Greta's class. The Hindu boy came to England from Nairobi when he was nine. On his first day at school, not knowing how to write his own name, he copied the name of the child sitting next to him. For a surprisingly long time, no-one realised that the name he was writing was not his own. By the time that they did, he was hopelessly confused, and so he too was sent to Greta. But, though she has taught her students language, Greta knows that she is a fake. Like the man from Mayo and the Hindu boy, she has been an alien in a foreign land, speaking the words of those around her only in the sense that a parrot does, while their meanings have been hidden from her. Greta has also resembled the man from Mayo because, like him, her 'clock stopped' when she left Ireland (ibid.: 58). She has never really arrived in England, but has inhabited instead a limbo space characterised by dissociation between sounds and words, word and meaning.

While Greta has consciously lived in limbo, in the 'outer room' of her life, those parts of self from which she was cut off have, however, been space- and time-travelling, and these parts are intuitively aware of alternative possibilities. Another, and different, version of Greta from the man from Mayo and the Hindu boy is also suggested, in scene four, by a young, pregnant woman called Melda who dances as Manus plays 'The Harvest Home'. In one sense, Melda acts as a reminder of Greta's separation from her child. An escapee from the 'banana ward', Melda has been diagnosed as mad. She is pregnant for the third time in two years. Her previous two babies were taken from her, as she was considered incapable of taking care of them properly, and the same thing will happen again. In another sense, however, and in the same kind of dream language that Greta employs when she takes communion into the community, Melda's dancing suggests a different way of responding to experience, a dance of alternative possibilities which offers, as do Greta's other-worldly encounters, a potential escape route from a fixity of response. In her birth experience, when she obeyed the voice that told her to turn around, Greta was rescued from the blackness that threatened to engulf her and she floated instead towards the light-filled globe. Even Greta's loss of voice on the occasion of her 'death' can be understood differently. When her sisters ask her to describe the stars into which her voice disappeared, her response is that there were seven of them, 'in an arrangement'. To Aoife this is proof that what Greta saw was The Plough, 'symbol of the Irish Citizen Army' (ibid.: 15), and, to Greta therefore, a representation of the 'familiar dark story' from the pages of which she wishes to escape. To Helen, the stars are The Pleiades, The Seven Sisters. The 1994 programme gives The Weepers as an alternative name for The Pleiades and notes that their rising is associated with spring, while 'their setting marks the time of harvest'. Though weeping and harvest suggest the grieving Ireland to which Greta is drawn, but also fears, other harvests *are* possible. In addition, spring carries with it the sense of new beginnings. The Plough and The Pleiades are simply names, after all, that other people have given these stars. What Greta sees is an arrangement of seven stars. The voice that left her to enter the stars on the night she 'died' may have done so to enact its own process of naming.

The names that caused Greta to start out on her journey were 'Mother', 'Ireland' and 'family'. These are the words that have called her back into her past. Near the end of scene six Rose,

Greta, Aoife, Helen, Manus and the dead Michael Flynn (in his coffin) are all present on stage. The setting is the dining room of the Flynn house. From the street outside, the sound of guns being fired and of shells exploding can be heard. As a protection against the danger of flying glass, Rose hides under the table and, after a brief hesitation, her children join her. This retreat under the table is preceded by a terrible raking over of the past, and a release of present angers and jealousies, that centre chiefly around a battle as to which member of the family Michael Flynn loved most. Rose and Aoife fight over which of them has the best right to give Michael a last kiss. Aoife turns savagely on Helen when she enters wearing one of their father's sweaters over her nightdress. Greta remembers Rose's jealousy of herself, the way in which Rose would storm into a room in search of the husband whose love she believed Greta had stolen. It was the sense of guilt she felt because of her father's love that caused Greta to accept the batterings her mother gave her – the belief that she deserved them – and the realisation she comes to that, despite these beatings, her father loved her mother more than he loved herself, causes her great distress. The family group under the table is emblematic of the personal and cultural history that has created it, the table demonstrative of the flimsiness of the family's means of protection against the continuing effects of these forces. Outside, the killings continue. Above the family, on top of the table, which would anyway be of little help in the event of a direct hit on the house, lies the corpse of the disputed father.

The saying of things previously unsaid does, however, despite its attendant pain, effect a kind of release. It is the dark, hidden aspects of Greta's past (and also of Helen's) that, along with their dying father, called them home. After this scene, having attended their father's funeral, and contacted the past they have tried to exclude, they return to England. Their two siblings remain behind. Manus, who in the middle of the dreadful family argument turned savagely upon the mother who used to beat him, chooses nevertheless to stay with her. At the end of the scene he takes his mother's hand, and leads her across the dimly-lit room to the lighted doorway. Aoife stays behind for a few moments, looking back at her father from the doorway. Then she follows the others, closing the door behind her.

The final two scenes of the play take place in England, scene seven on Westminster Bridge at five in the morning and scene eight in Greta's home, where she is reunited with her baby. Both in setting and action, scene seven is a bridging unit between her childhood home and the adult home that she will now remake. Greta and Helen have come to Westminster Bridge to scatter the remains of their father's ashes into the Thames. Greta climbs on to the bridge wall to do this and, at the same time, she quotes from, and comments on, Wordsworth's sonnet 'Upon Westminster Bridge', then adds, 'Words! So do I cast out all devils!' (ibid.: 72). But words, as the play has demonstrated, are potent agents, devils perhaps, but difficult to cast out. The punning message of her Wordsworth quotation is a question: what are words worth? The answer, as Greta stands on the wall, the boundary marker that will, if she jumps, take her beyond a barrier from which she will not be able to return, seems to be that words like 'father' and 'grief' are still cold and heavy as lead to her, while ones like 'children' and 'home' are burning cinders that scorch her with anguish. One solution to this dilemma would be to follow her father's ashes into the river.

Whether she would have jumped had she been alone remains uncertain because Helen grabs hold of her and hangs on until she climbs down from the wall. Like the man from Mayo, the Hindu boy and dancing Melda, like Manus, too, who resembles Greta in his yearning for home, Helen replays aspects of Greta. Though more muted in expression than Greta's, Helen's grief at her father's death is also fierce. She too, she tells Greta, has recently seen visions. It was the night after they returned from Ireland. She had to go out in the car and, because she was in a state of shock, too 'numb with grief' to be fully aware of where her body began and ended, she shut her thumb in the car door. She spent the night with her thumb in a bag of ice, but she slept badly because of the pain. Around five in the morning, she opened her eyes and saw 'Wings and eyes of light were falling through the room. Swirling and falling and gathering, passing through the roof and walls' (ibid.: 74). In three ways Helen's vision replicates Greta's earlier experiences. It reveals the permeability of boundaries (the wings and eyes of light pass *through* the roof and walls). The 'Swirling and falling and gathering' of the light take the patterned form of a dance, and so recall dancing Melda, and the event takes place, as did Greta's Pentecostal experience, at five in the morning. The fact that scene seven also takes place also at five o'clock adds to the importance of this Pentecostal connection. Michael Flynn died on Easter Saturday. It is now after Easter, moving, in the Christian calendar, towards Pentecost when there appeared to the apostles 'what seemed to be tongues of fire, which parted and came to rest on each of them'. Filled 'with the Holy Spirit', they 'began to speak in strange languages, as the Spirit gave utterance to each' (*The Acts of the Apostles*, 2, 3–5). Near the end of scene seven, Greta hears a voice in her ear, not a spirit voice, but the voice of a baby – laughing. Like the wail of the banshee in scene two, though totally dissimilar to this sound in what it promises, the baby's laughter calls her home.

In the final scene Greta is at home, 'rocking a baby, telling it a story'. 'After Easter', she begins, 'we came to the place. It was snowing in the forest and very cold into the fifth month' (Devlin 1994: 75). She was with her mother, and they were hunting, but their bodies were numbed by the cold and they were hungry because they could find nothing to eat. They sat down by a stream and, looking up, Greta saw a huge, black stag upon the skyline. It 'was from the cold north' and, as she watched, it leapt from the ridge on which it was standing, 'leapt through hundreds of years, to reach [them]. And arrived gigantic in the stream' (ibid.). Greta's mother was frightened of the stag but Greta realised that it was simply hungry and, taking some berries from her bag, she fed it from the palm of her hand. The stag wanted to kiss her but she knew that she mustn't let it because its face was frozen, and if she touched it she would die of cold. But gradually, as it ate, its face was transformed and it began to take on human features. And then the snow began to melt and the sound of rushing water filled her ears 'with a tremendous sound' (ibid.). Greta got up on the stag's back and together they flew to the summit of the world – the source of all the world's rivers and her child's and her own place of origin. With her 'After Easter' story Greta finds the voice she has been seeking. The final words of her narrative, 'and this is my own story' (ibid.), are also the last words of the play.

The voice in which Greta finally speaks, her own Pentecostal 'tongue of fire', is at once personal, maternal and narrative. A storyteller throughout the play, she tells finally a story of origins. In place of the biblical tale of Genesis, she presents a frozen world to which the expected spring has failed to come. She and her mother hunt – for solutions to their dilemma – but their feelings are too numbed by the cold for them to be able to help themselves. The stag, black against the white snow, huge, potent, free-moving in the frozen landscape, is a representation of difference. Other than Greta and her mother, it offers also, through its pagan connotations, an alternative to the cultural perspective that holds the women in its icy grip. Despite the stag's Otherness, Greta recognises its loving connection to herself. Her feeding of the berries to it is, in a sense, a reclamation of Eve's taking of the apple (instead of stealing fruit, Greta gives it as a form of nurturance), and also a revisioning of the Eucharist. In an act of communion with the stag, she gives it the reminder she carries with her of the rebirth that may await the dead earth, the sowing and harvesting that would follow the thawing of the ice of winter. The fact that she has the berries in her bag reveals the stag, and the solution it offers, to be really aspects of Greta. It (she) *is* her past, the ancient past that is the source of all life, as well as her more recent national, familial and religious past, and she carries with her also a means of coming to terms with that past. She has re-entered the pain of the past, but then moved onwards. Though she stood poised for a few moments on the wall of Westminster Bridge, she did not follow her father's ashes into the water. The stag *does* leap down from its point of eminence, but its journey, as Greta's in a slower, more stumbling way has been, is into life. Perched on the stag's back, Greta hears the sweet rushing of the rivers and knows that spring has come at last. The story of origins is also a birth narrative. It tells of Greta's rebirth into life. Additionally, it relates the baby's birth journey, its movement from the past, which will always be its point of becoming, into the present: 'And he [the stag] took me', Greta tells the baby, to 'the place where the rivers . . . where you come from' (ibid.).

Through the telling of her final story, Greta enters the 'inner room' she has sought for so long. What entering this room reveals itself to be is *having room*, room to move freely, space, above all, within which to breathe. As the world thaws, and its rivers run freely, so, too, breath fills her lungs. It is a sense of ease and freedom similar to that which her other-worldly birth experience gave her. Then, the old priest, the dead hand of the past, tried to smother her, but when she obeyed the kind, warm voice and turned around, she found that she could breathe after all. In her origins story, Greta remoulds the past into the figure of

RETROSPECTIVE

Greta's quest for 'home', voice and her 'inner room' involves geographical and spiritual journeys. A voyager within, and also beyond, place and time, she seeks 'the place of the heart', and time to relax within this space. All her journeys occur within the paradoxically freeing constraints of theatre. The pliability of stage space and time map the possibilities available to her. My aim in this book has been also an attempt at cartography, a mapping of the journeys characters take in a range of contemporary plays by women. Though the journeys are distinctive to the individual plays, they also overlap. The characters' needs are particular yet related. Within performance time, the audience experiences the journeys as simultaneously linear and focused intensely within the 'now', but when the performance is over, what remain within the mind's eye are snapshots. Precise, yet haunting, in their evocation of something beyond themselves, they resemble the moments Hannah Snell celebrates at the end of *Warrior*.

Like Hannah, I thread a chain of moments, in my case from the plays I have discussed in these pages. First, a chain that follows (almost) the book's sequence: a chain of doors, and the rooms beyond them. The first bead of my chain is Nora, closing the door of a diminutive house behind her. Then a door opens onto the claustrophobic, dark-red room from which a woman, Janet (Rutherford's daughter), later stumbles, a shawl draped over her head. The door in *Granite* is heavy and firmly closed. Poppy from *Vows* stands at the door of her doll's-house cupboard surrounded by toy plates and dishes. In *Real Estate* Gwen collects the few mementoes she wishes to retain from her past, then closes the door of that past behind her. Goneril and Regan

201

leave Lear's tower-castle and Cordelia watches their figures, etched upon the skyline. Mary Traverse closes the door of her father's house and enters the public street that is the world of men. Christina and Greta re-enter rooms, exploring what these may still have to offer them.

At the end of this chain I have cheated slightly with regard to the order of the beads: my analysis of *Queen Christina*, in chapter five, precedes that of *The Grace of Mary Traverse*. I have also left out a fair number of related, yet slightly differently-shaped, beads: Augustine, for example, exiting through a 'window of light', the future room in which Eleanor of Aquitaine will be imprisoned, and the 'bounded room' that Mary Traverse inadvertently entered. Other, yet again subtly different, beads form a chain of thresholds: Pandora in *Vows*, poised at the top of her staircase created from a chest of drawers; Jo, also poised, and waiting, at the end of *Piper's Cave*; and four, further threshold endings: Maria del Amor on the edge of meeting her girlfriend; Agathe about to imprint her feet in the snow in *The Taking of Liberty*; Hannah Snell sailing off in her boat towards an (hopefully) alternative future; and *Frankenstein's Mothers*' 'man unman' in quest of a map of self.

The man unman brings me to two further chains, the first of hands, the second of dolls. In *Frankenstein's Mothers* Mary (at this point also the Creature) stretches her hands through the bars of a 'cage', trying to reach her mother (Frankenstein – the creator). In their attempt to make contact with her dead mother, Mary's hands suggest others that are also death-linked: those of Elise, smoothing the sheets on the bed of Mary's dying child in *Blood and Ice*, and Greta's father's hand coming up out of the coffin in *After Easter*. Hands in *Rutherford and Son* are signs of both hatred and sacrifice, Janet untying her father's boots whilst she averts her face epitomising the former, Mary's hands sewing in the firelight, while all around her lie the dark imprisoning fells, the latter. In *My Mother Said I Never Should* hands similarly represent anger and love. In the penultimate wasteground scene, hands glint in the darkness as Jackie concocts a spell with which to kill her mother, but in the final wasteground scene, Margaret (her mother) lovingly holds out her hand to Jackie. Another mother's and daughter's hands, those of Vera and Louise in *Variations*, almost meet, but, at the last minute, reconciliation proves impossible. Enid and Del hold each other, however, at the end of *Leave Taking*, as do the two young women in *Pax*, and, near the end of this play, the two older women also enact an embrace of a kind, the Domesticated Woman holding in her hand a brush with which she gently strokes the Keeper's hair.

The doll chain is suggested by the man unman through its connection with the reversible doll and the monster doll that Elise sews in *Blood and Ice*. Further, perturbing doll-beads are the dolls that act as exemplars for Mary Traverse of the ideal, 'dead' woman into which she is trying to transform herself at the beginning of the play. Dolls can however suggest valuable ways of reclaiming, and building on, childhood experiences, as in *Vows, Variations* and *Queen Christina*; and in *The Love of the Nightingale* Philomele articulates through her doll self what she cannot otherwise express. Ursula in *Byrthrite* also uses a doll (dummy) – though of the witchfinder, not of herself – to tell her story and to demonstrate her rejection of the role of victim.

Through her doll-double, Philomele also becomes part of the chain of Otherness that begins with Janet's intuition of further possibilities in the moorland outside Rutherford's house besides its wintry barrenness. In *Granite*, Judith is unable to find alternative ways of interpreting the wind and the sea, and, though she envies their restless power, she remains a prisoner. Otherness in *Blood and Ice* gives birth to a nightmarish sequence of mirrored images, as it does also in *Variations* and *Chiaroscuro*, but, gradually, all the characters in these plays move to a new relationship with the ghosts that haunt them. Little Cog, in *Ironmistress*, also rescues Shanny Pinns from Martha's relegation of her to nothing more than a 'ghost on a hill', while in *Two Marias* Maria del Amor helps her dead namesake to find peace. Josie and Lily in *The Skriker* and Greta in *After Easter* are haunted by worlds Other than, yet correspondent with, the world of surface reality. In *Warrior*, a similar haunting leads Hannah Snell to undertake a mission on behalf of the future, with – the play suggests – some possibility of success. Churchill's view in *The Skriker* is uncompromisingly bleak. Lily's entry into the Underworld cannot redeem the future. Society at large must take responsibility for what has been disowned, and there appears to be no sign that this is likely to happen. A different, woman-related aspect of the Underworld is, however, seen as capable of being reimagined in *Pinchdice and Co.*, and in *After*

Easter Greta's acceptance of the double nature of experience leads to her apprehension of the necessary interrelation of dark and light.

Light, dark, chiaroscuro, create a pattern of beads that cannot be strung in a linear fashion. These, the dancing beads, are Nora's spinning tarantella, Judith's abortive dance in *Granite*, Augustine's anarchic 'upside-down' sabbath, Cordelia spinning 'for Daddy', Louise dancing for her own pleasure in *Variations*, and the play of possibilities suggested by pregnant Melda in *After Easter* dancing to the tune of 'The Harvest Home'. Their shimmering movement leads me, finally, away from visual images, towards a polyphony of voices. So many women speak out in the plays telling their stories and claiming spaces as their own, that, in this case, a representative few must suffice. With eyes closed therefore, listening in darkness, I hear – and ask the reader who has come with me this far to hear – once again snatches of sound: from *The Taking of Liberty*, *Byrthrite*, *Bondagers*, *Chiaroscuro*, and *After Easter*. 'While you've a voice you can speak / You can make yourself heard', Agathe affirms (Robson 1991: 268). Jane promises that, if Rose's buried play is never unearthed, another woman will one day rewrite and remake it. Tottie's stories of the ghostly ploughman and of future fields, empty of folk, meld with the voices of Yomi, Beth, Aisha and Opal retracing the lives of their foremothers. Greta achieves her journey's goal: the telling of her story.

End Lines

Upon the opened book, a stage.
A door awaits.
Beyond: a garden, street, wasteground, a hill.
Past terrains form, new lands arise.
Paths shape, reshape.

The moment stills.
Within a room a source-tale weaves.
Voices enfold.
Words cluster, jostle, urge and soar.
Lights fade to black as pages close.

BIBLIOGRAPHY

PLAYS BY WOMEN

Churchill, C. (1994) *The Skriker*, London: Nick Hern Books.

Dane, C. (1949) *Granite*, London: Samuel French.

Daniels, S. (1991) *Byrthrite*, in *Plays: One*, London: Methuen.

De Angelis, A. (1990) *Ironmistress*, in *Plays by Women: Eight*, selected and introduced by M. Remnant, London: Methuen.

Devlin, A. (1994) *After Easter*, London: Faber and Faber.

Furse, A. (1996) *Augustine (Big Hysteria)*, The Netherlands: Harwood Academic Publishers.

Gee, S. (1991) *Warrior*, London: Samuel French.

Gems, P. *Queen Christina* (1986) in *Plays by Women: Volume Five*, selected and introduced by M. Remnant London: Methuen.

Glover, S. (1993) *Bondagers, Theatre Scotland*, 2, 6: 29–44.

Kay, J. *Chiaroscuro* (1987), in *Lesbian Plays*, selected and introduced by J. Davis, London: Methuen.

Keatley, C. (1990b) *My Mother Said I Never Should*, London: Methuen.

Kilcoyne, C., Ben-Tovim, R., Dowse, J., Harrison, L. and Pendlebury, S. (1994) *Frankenstein's Mothers*, unpublished.

Lavery, B. (1991) *Her Aching Heart, Two Marias, Wicked*, London: Methuen.

Levy, D. (1987) *Pax*, in *Plays by Women: Volume Six*, selected and introduced by M. Remnant, London: Methuen.

Lochhead, L. (1985) *Blood and Ice*, in *Plays by Women: Volume Four*, selected and introduced by M. Wandor, London: Methuen.

Munro, R. (1986) *Piper's Cave*, in *Plays by Women: Volume Five*, selected and introduced by M. Remnant, London: Methuen.

Page, L. (1990) *Real Estate*, in *Plays: One*, London: Methuen.

Pinnock, W. (1989) *Leave Taking*, in *First Run*, selected and introduced by K. Harwood, London: Nick Hern Books.

Robson, C. (1991) *The Taking of Liberty*, in Robson, C. (ed.) *Female Voices Fighting Lives: Seven Plays by Women*, London: Aurora Metro Publications.

Sowerby, G. (1991) *Rutherford and Son*, in Fitzsimmons, L. and Gardner, V. (eds) *New Woman Plays*, London: Methuen.

Warren, L. (1991) *Vows*, unpublished.
Wertenbaker, T. (1989) *The Love of the Nightingale and The Grace of Mary Traverse*, London: Faber and Faber.
Wilkinson, J. (1991) *Pinchdice and Co.*, in Griffin, G. and Aston, E. (eds) *Herstory: Volume One*, Sheffield, UK: Sheffield Academic Press.
Women's Theatre Group and Elaine Feinstein (1991) *Lear's Daughters*, in Griffin, G. and Aston, E. (eds) *Herstory: Volume One*, Sheffield, UK: Sheffield Academic Press.
Yeger, S. (1991) *Variations on a Theme by Clara Schumann*, in *Plays by Women: Nine*, selected and introduced by A. Castledine, London: Methuen.

SECONDARY TEXTS

Adelman, J. (1992) *Suffocating Mothers: Fantasies of Maternal Origin in Shakespeare's Plays, Hamlet to The Tempest*, London: Routledge.
Anderson, B.S. and Zinsser, J.P. (1990) *A History of Their Own: Women in Europe from Prehistory to the Present: Volume One*, Harmondsworth, UK: Penguin.
Boose, L.E. and Flowers, B.S. (eds) (1989) *Daughters and Fathers*, Baltimore and London: John Hopkins University Press.
Brecht, B. (1962) *Mother Courage and Her Children*, trans. E. Bentley, London: Methuen.
Briggs, K.M. (1967) *The Fairies in Tradition and Literature*, London: Routledge and Kegan Paul.
Carlson, S. (1993) 'Issues of Identity, Nationality and Performance: The Reception of Two Plays by Timberlake Wertenbaker', *New Theatre Quarterly*, 9, 35: 267–89.
Cixous, H. and Clément, C. (1986) *The Newly Born Woman*, trans. B. Wing, Manchester, UK: Manchester University Press.
Furse, A. (1991) 'Big Hysteria', *Plays and Players* 450: 16–17.
—— (1992) *Augustine (Big Hysteria): Writing the Body*, London: Paines Plough Occasional Papers.
Gilbert, S.M. and Gubar, S. (1979) *The Madwoman in the Attic: The Woman Writer and the Nineteenth-Century Literary Imagination*, New Haven and London: Yale University Press.
Griffin, G. and Aston, E. (1991) Introduction to *Herstory: Volume One*, Sheffield, UK: Sheffield Academic Press.
Huggan, G. (1990) 'Philomela's Retold Story: Silence, Music and the Post-Colonial Text', *Journal of Commonwealth Literature*, 25, 1: 12–23.
Ibsen, H. (1980) *Plays: Two*, trans. M. Meyer, London: Methuen.
Keatley, C. (1990a) 'Art Form or Platform? On Women and Playwriting', interview with Lizbeth Goodman, *New Theatre Quarterly*, 6, 22: 128–40.
Marder, E. (1992) 'Disarticulated Voices: Feminism and Philomela', *Hypatia* 7, 2: 148–66.
Mellor, A.K. (1989) *Mary Shelley: Her Life, Her Fiction, Her Monsters*, London: Routledge.

Moi, T. (1988) *Sexual/Textual Politics: Feminist Literary Theory*, London, Routledge.

Page, L. (1990) 'Emotion is a Theatrical Weapon', interview with Elizabeth Sakellaridou, *New Theatre Quarterly*, 6, 22: 174–87.

Shelley, M. (1947) *Mary Shelley's Journal*, ed. F.L. Jones, Norman: University of Oklahoma Press.

—— (1985) *Frankenstein*, Harmondsworth, UK: Penguin.

Showalter, E. (1987) *The Female Malady: Women, Madness and English Culture, 1830–1980*, London: Virago.

Stowell, S. (1992) *A Stage of Their Own: Feminist Playwrights of the Suffrage Era*, Manchester, UK: Manchester University Press.

Turner, E. (1994) 'Louise Page', in K.A. Berney (ed.) *Contemporary British Dramatists*, London: St James Press.

Walkowitz, J.R. (1992) *City of Dreadful Delight: Narratives of Sexual Danger in Late-Victorian London*, London: Virago.

Warner, M. (1976) *Alone of All Her Sex: The Myth and the Cult of the Virgin Mary*, London, Weidenfeld and Nicolson.

—— (1994) *Managing Monsters: Six Myths of Our Time*, London: Vintage.

Woolf, V. (1966) *Collected Essays: Volume Two*, London: Hogarth Press.

INDEX